Slow and Steady
Get Me Ready
for Kindergarten

Slow and Steady
Get Me Ready
for Kindergarten

A Parent's Handbook
For Children from Birth to Age 5

By June R. Oberlander
and
Hannah J. Oberlander Knecht, M. Ed.

Photography by
Jessi Mach and Amanda Reise
Limericks by Allie Jansen Harshner

Updated Edition

XULON PRESS

Slow and Steady Get Me Ready For Kindergarten
A Parent's Handbook For Children from Birth to Age 5
by June R. Oberlander and Hannah J. Oberlander Knecht, M. Ed.

Printed in the United States of America

ISBN 9781591602361

www.xulonpress.com

Acknowledgements

I cannot express enough thanks to my grandparents, Clyde and June Oberlander, for entrusting to me the responsibility of updating this book for the generation of parents in the 21ˢᵗ century. Thirty years ago, my grandmother embarked on the journey of writing *Slow and Steady Get Me Ready* with the hope that it would reach thousands of parents who wanted to provide enriching activities that would develop the skills a young child needed to be successful when he or she began school. I am so grateful to both of them for taking the risk to self-publish in faith that one day this book would have a lasting impact. It is because of their dedication and perseverance that *Slow and Steady Get Me Ready* is known around the world. I am thankful for their generosity and confidence in me to launch the updated edition.

Thank you to the Mach family, Reise family, and Conners family for generously welcoming me into their homes to work with their children so that photographs could be added to each activity for this updated edition.

The completion of this project could not have been accomplished without the support of my parents, Steve and Shelley Oberlander. Thank you for showing me that parents have a crucial impact on their children's education and development. A special thank you to my mom, whose creativity and love of learning inspired many of the activities in the Age Four section. Thank you, Mom, for faithfully reading aloud to us kids growing up and for all of your creative ideas that are peppered throughout this book. It truly made a difference. Thank you to my family, especially my brother Noah, for the encouragement to keep going for ten years until this project was completed.

Finally, to my caring, loving, and supportive husband, Damian: my deepest gratitude. Your reassurance when the times got rough meant so much. It was a comfort and relief to know that you were by my side, encouraging me through the long hours of revising and editing. My heartfelt thanks.

Dedicated to my Granny, who always believed in me and entrusted me with the gift of updating her ideas for the next generation of parents, and to Amanda, a beloved Pre-K teacher who touched the lives of many children as they embarked on their learning journeys.

Dear Educator,

This book is most definitely for you! The activities in this book can be easily adapted for the classroom, even though they were originally designed for parents to do with their children in the home. Know that I had you, the educator, in mind when I updated this edition of *Slow and Steady Get Me Ready for Kindergarten*. My grandmother, a proud former public school teacher, would be thrilled to know that this book is used as a resource for both educators and parents alike!

The lessons, activities, and suggestions are just as much for you as for the parent of a young child. Whether you are a preschool teacher, day-care facilitator, or work with young children in any capacity, the activities in this book can be set up in stations around a classroom for individual students or for small groups of three to four children. Depending on the students' abilities, children can work at the activities independently, with a peer, or with the guidance of a teacher.

Lessons in the Age 4 section that highlight specific picture books can be used in Pre-K and kindergarten classrooms. Teachers can adjust the activities presented for each picture book into whole-class lessons that meet state requirements and national standards of learning.

Although the activities are grouped by age for each of the five sections, they can be modified by teachers to fit the specific needs of their students at whatever age they are. Kindergarten teachers and early elementary school teachers can use the lessons that focus on letter recognition, phonemic awareness, and pre-reading from the Age 3 and Age 4 sections.

Physically handicapped students will benefit greatly from the activities that center around fine and gross motor skills. Occupational therapists who teach students with significant delays will find those activities for developing sensory and fine motor skills applicable whether they work with pre-school or even high school students. Autistic students will benefit from the activities in all five sections—no matter their age—depending on their learning and communication needs.

Students with learning disabilities will need more repetition when completing the activities that require critical thinking and problem solving so that they can build confidence and stamina in these areas. Chunking the activities into short, manageable parts will enable students with difficulties to achieve small goals that will in turn motivate them in the long run. Teachers can reference the development boxes at the bottom of each page to guide them in choosing activities that will meet their students' needs.

I am elated to provide the education community with a resource that provides enriching activities for teachers to use in their classrooms. As a teacher myself, I am aware of the learning gap so many children have between home and school. Through this book, I hope to bridge that gap by enlightening parents to the fact that they are teachers too and by empowering them with the tools to prepare their young children for our classrooms at school and for their roles as citizens in this beautiful world.

Thank you for your support!

Table of Contents: Age 0 Activities

Age 0 Activity 1	Tips About Beginning Movement	3
Age 0 Activity 2	Response to Light	4
Age 0 Activity 3	Moving an Object	5
Age 0 Activity 4	Cradle Gym	6
Age 0 Activity 5	Mirror and Pendulum	7
Age 0 Activity 6	The Sock Ball	8
Age 0 Activity 7	Response to a Noise Maker	9
Age 0 Activity 8	Colored Mobile	10
Age 0 Activity 9	Large Muscle Activities	11
Age 0 Activity 10	Eye-Hand Coordination	12
Age 0 Activity 11	Observing Different Faces	13
Age 0 Activity 12	Peek-A-Boo	14
Age 0 Activity 13	Spool Worm	15
Age 0 Activity 14	Listen to the Sounds	16
Age 0 Activity 15	Jingle Rolling Container	17
Age 0 Activity 16	Coffee Can Drum	18
Age 0 Activity 17	Nursery Rhymes	19
Age 0 Activity 18	Where is Thumbkin?	20
Age 0 Activity 19	Pat-A-Cake	21
Age 0 Activity 20	This Little Piggy	22
Age 0 Activity 21	Wiggle to Reach	23
Age 0 Activity 22	Down and Drop	24
Age 0 Activity 23	Make Some Noise	25
Age 0 Activity 24	Sock Ball Throw	26
Age 0 Activity 25	Jingle Bell Feet	27
Age 0 Activity 26	Toss Up and Down	28
Age 0 Activity 27	Stack and Fall	29
Age 0 Activity 28	Paper Noise	30
Age 0 Activity 29	Shake, Listen, and Find	31
Age 0 Activity 30	Watch the Ball	32
Age 0 Activity 31	Bowl and Ball Roll	33
Age 0 Activity 32	Sizes	34
Age 0 Activity 33	Blowing Bubbles and Water Splash	35
Age 0 Activity 34	Shoe Box House	36
Age 0 Activity 35	I Spy	37
Age 0 Activity 36	Face Recognition	38
Age 0 Activity 37	Feely Squares	39
Age 0 Activity 38	Poke to Feel Rough and Soft	40
Age 0 Activity 39	Drop It In a Container	41
Age 0 Activity 40	Pull and Let Go	42
Age 0 Activity 41	Name and Find It	43
Age 0 Activity 42	Which Hand?	44
Age 0 Activity 43	Listen and Do More	45
Age 0 Activity 44	Command and Do	46
Age 0 Activity 45	Where Does It Belong?	47
Age 0 Activity 46	Point to It	48
Age 0 Activity 47	Stick and Unstick	49
Age 0 Activity 48	Turn It Over	50
Age 0 Activity 49	In and Out of the Box	51
Age 0 Activity 50	Home Sounds	52
Age 0 Activity 51	Face and Head Game	53
Age 0 Activity 52	Spool Stack	54

Table of Contents: Age 1 Activities

Age 1 Activity 1	Pick Up	58
Age 1 Activity 2	Lids and Containers	59
Age 1 Activity 3	Let's Play Ball	60
Age 1 Activity 4	Let's Go Walking	61
Age 1 Activity 5	Look at Me	62
Age 1 Activity 6	What Made That Sound?	63
Age 1 Activity 7	What's Outside?	64
Age 1 Activity 8	What is Moving?	66
Age 1 Activity 9	What Can I Smell?	67
Age 1 Activity 10	Clothespin Fishing	68
Age 1 Activity 11	Can I Dress Myself?	69
Age 1 Activity 12	Exploring With Dirt, Sand, or Rice	70
Age 1 Activity 13	Cardboard Box House	71
Age 1 Activity 14	Rhythm Band Music	72
Age 1 Activity 15	Exploring With Water	73
Age 1 Activity 16	Through the Hole	74
Age 1 Activity 17	Finger Paint Bag	75
Age 1 Activity 18	Paint With a Brush	76
Age 1 Activity 19	Inside and Outside	77
Age 1 Activity 20	Upstairs and Downstairs	78
Age 1 Activity 21	Explore With Play Dough Part 1	79
Age 1 Activity 22	Cardboard Puzzles	80
Age 1 Activity 23	Drop Into the Bottle	81
Age 1 Activity 24	I Can Carry a Tray	82
Age 1 Activity 25	Envelope Boat With Fish	83
Age 1 Activity 26	Where Is the Room?	84
Age 1 Activity 27	Big and Little	85
Age 1 Activity 28	Stepping Stones	86
Age 1 Activity 29	Stencil Up and Down	87
Age 1 Activity 30	Veggie Stamps	88
Age 1 Activity 31	This Side, That Side	89
Age 1 Activity 32	On and Off Rubber Bands	90
Age 1 Activity 33	Straw and Spool Stack	91
Age 1 Activity 34	Stuff It In the Box	92
Age 1 Activity 35	Clothespin Snap	93
Age 1 Activity 36	Shake and Find	94
Age 1 Activity 37	Basket of Flowers	95
Age 1 Activity 38	Dip and Dab Paint Activity	96
Age 1 Activity 39	Collect and Return	97
Age 1 Activity 40	Rip It	98
Age 1 Activity 41	Pots and Lids	99
Age 1 Activity 42	Funnel Fun With Colored Rice	100
Age 1 Activity 43	The Big Button	101
Age 1 Activity 44	Fold It	102
Age 1 Activity 45	Where Is It?	103
Age 1 Activity 46	Squeeze the Dropper to Move the Water	104
Age 1 Activity 47	Button, Zip, Snap, Velcro	105
Age 1 Activity 48	Listen and Draw	106
Age 1 Activity 49	Open and Close	107
Age 1 Activity 50	Hide and Seek	108
Age 1 Activity 51	Humpty Dumpty	109
Age 1 Activity 52	Jack in the Box	110

Table of Contents: Age 2 Activities

Age 2 Activity 1	Top and Bottom	114
Age 2 Activity 2	Play Dough Fun Part 2	115
Age 2 Activity 3	Scrunch and Toss Into the Bag	116
Age 2 Activity 4	Make a Necklace	117
Age 2 Activity 5	Box Skating	118
Age 2 Activity 6	My Name	119
Age 2 Activity 7	Learning Colors	120
Age 2 Activity 8	Finger Paint Bag	121
Age 2 Activity 9	Jump and Hop	122
Age 2 Activity 10	My Family	123
Age 2 Activity 11	I Can Paint	124
Age 2 Activity 12	Farm Animals	125
Age 2 Activity 13	Put It In a Line	126
Age 2 Activity 14	Jack Be Nimble	127
Age 2 Activity 15	Feely Bag Fun	128
Age 2 Activity 16	The Three Bears	129
Age 2 Activity 17	Sock Match	130
Age 2 Activity 18	Outline the Shape	131
Age 2 Activity 19	Up, Down, and the "Simon Says" Game	132
Age 2 Activity 20	What Belongs in the Drawer?	133
Age 2 Activity 21	Rub-A-Dub-Dub	134
Age 2 Activity 22	I Spy Red, I Spy Blue	135
Age 2 Activity 23	Slide and Roll	136
Age 2 Activity 24	I Can Dress Myself	137
Age 2 Activity 25	Clapping Hands	138
Age 2 Activity 26	Car Roll	139
Age 2 Activity 27	Coat Hanger Hoop	140
Age 2 Activity 28	Eggs in the Carton 1-2-3	141
Age 2 Activity 29	Fruits to See, Feel, Smell, and Taste	142
Age 2 Activity 30	Ladder Walk	143
Age 2 Activity 31	Is It Hot or Cold?	144
Age 2 Activity 32	Tall and Short, Big and Small	145
Age 2 Activity 33	Through the Tunnel	146
Age 2 Activity 34	Bowling	147
Age 2 Activity 35	Paper Plate Pull	148
Age 2 Activity 36	Little Boy Blue	149
Age 2 Activity 37	Leaf Matching	150
Age 2 Activity 38	On or Under	151
Age 2 Activity 39	How Far Can You Throw?	152
Age 2 Activity 40	My Color Booklet	153
Age 2 Activity 41	Belongings	154
Age 2 Activity 42	What Is Its Use?	155
Age 2 Activity 43	Food and Numbers	156
Age 2 Activity 44	Foot Pushing	157
Age 2 Activity 45	Comic Strip Sequence Fun	158
Age 2 Activity 46	Tiptoe	159
Age 2 Activity 47	Colored Fish Sort	160
Age 2 Activity 48	Ball Bounce	161
Age 2 Activity 49	Early Skipping Fun	162
Age 2 Activity 50	Animal Moves	163
Age 2 Activity 51	Matching Pictures	164
Age 2 Activity 52	Colorful Fishing	165

Table of Contents: Age 3 Activities

Age 3 Activity 1	Spooning, Scooping, and Pouring	168
Age 3 Activity 2	Obstacle Line	169
Age 3 Activity 3	Day and Night	170
Age 3 Activity 4	Scissors	171
Age 3 Activity 5	Shape Stencils	172
Age 3 Activity 6	Hit or Miss	173
Age 3 Activity 7	Hole Punch Row	174
Age 3 Activity 8	Name the Sound	175
Age 3 Activity 9	Listen and Draw Book	176
Age 3 Activity 10	Guess It! Riddles	177
Age 3 Activity 11	Create a Picture	178
Age 3 Activity 12	Where Does It Belong?	179
Age 3 Activity 13	Sponge Painted Turtle	180
Age 3 Activity 14	Penny and a Nickel	181
Age 3 Activity 15	Two Parts Make a Whole	182
Age 3 Activity 16	Box House and Brown Bag Activity	183
Age 3 Activity 17	Tearing Strips	184
Age 3 Activity 18	Three Triangles	185
Age 3 Activity 19	Footprint Shapes	186
Age 3 Activity 20	How Does It Taste?	187
Age 3 Activity 21	Set the Table	188
Age 3 Activity 22	Sink or Float	189
Age 3 Activity 23	The Alphabet Song	190
Age 3 Activity 24	Fabric Match	191
Age 3 Activity 25	Shadow Fun	192
Age 3 Activity 26	Gallop Fun	193
Age 3 Activity 27	Trace the Shapes	194
Age 3 Activity 28	Learn to Tie Your Shoes	195
Age 3 Activity 29	Fold It and Discover Symmetry	196
Age 3 Activity 30	Magnet Fun	197
Age 3 Activity 31	True or False	198
Age 3 Activity 32	Clothespin Toss and Count	199
Age 3 Activity 33	Listen and Move	200
Age 3 Activity 34	What is Missing?	201
Age 3 Activity 35	Tell Me How To Make It	202
Age 3 Activity 36	Family Groups	203
Age 3 Activity 37	Hopscotch Fun	204
Age 3 Activity 38	Finish It	205
Age 3 Activity 39	Shape Play	206
Age 3 Activity 40	Junk Box	208
Age 3 Activity 41	Mail a Letter	209
Age 3 Activity 42	Spaghetti Letters	211
Age 3 Activity 43	Sewing Fun	213
Age 3 Activity 44	Telephone	214
Age 3 Activity 45	Head, Shoulders, Knees, and Toes	216
Age 3 Activity 46	Letter Aa Fun	218
Age 3 Activity 47	Bouncing Bb	220
Age 3 Activity 48	Cc is for Cake	222
Age 3 Activity 49	Dig In the Dirt for Dd	224
Age 3 Activity 50	Eggs in the Basket	226
Age 3 Activity 51	Let's Go Fishing	228
Age 3 Activity 52	Gg is For Green Grass Grow	230

Table of Contents: Age 4 Activities

Age 4 Activity 1	The Hh Hat Game	235
Age 4 Activity 2	Ii For Inchworm	237
Age 4 Activity 3	Jj For Jack-in-the-Box	239
Age 4 Activity 4	Kk For Kite	241
Age 4 Activity 5	Ll is For Lollipop	243
Age 4 Activity 6	Mm For My Mittens	245
Age 4 Activity 7	Nn is For Night Time	247
Age 4 Activity 8	Oo is For Octopus	249
Age 4 Activity 9	Pp is For Pickle	251
Age 4 Activity 10	Qq is For Quilt	253
Age 4 Activity 11	Rr is For Rocket	254
Age 4 Activity 12	Ss is for Snake	256
Age 4 Activity 13	Tt is for Treetops	258
Age 4 Activity 14	Uu is for Umbrella	260
Age 4 Activity 15	Vv is for Vase	262
Age 4 Activity 16	Ww is For Wagon	264
Age 4 Activity 17	The Musical Xylophone	266
Age 4 Activity 18	Wind the Yarn	268
Age 4 Activity 19	Zero	270
Age 4 Activity 20	Labeling	272
Age 4 Activity 21	Ball Activities	273
Age 4 Activity 22	Rope Jumping	274
Age 4 Activity 23	Feel and Tell	276
Age 4 Activity 24	Healthy Foods	278
Age 4 Activity 25	Jumping A Distance	280
Age 4 Activity 26	Number Stairs and Counting	281
Age 4 Activity 27	The Clock	282
Age 4 Activity 28	Patterns	284
Age 4 Activity 29	My Name	285
Age 4 Activity 30	Bear Loves Weather	286
Age 4 Activity 31	If You Give A Mouse A Cookie	287
Age 4 Activity 32	The Little Red Hen	289
Age 4 Activity 33	Curious George	291
Age 4 Activity 34	The Story of Ferdinand	293
Age 4 Activity 35	Are You My Mother?	295
Age 4 Activity 36	The Colorful Mouse	297
Age 4 Activity 37	Mike Mulligan and His Steam Shovel	299
Age 4 Activity 38	Corduroy	300
Age 4 Activity 39	The Little House	302
Age 4 Activity 40	City Mouse, Country Mouse	304
Age 4 Activity 41	Richard Scarry's Please and Thank You Book	306
Age 4 Activity 42	Madeline	308
Age 4 Activity 43	Blueberries For Sal	309
Age 4 Activity 44	The Tale of Peter Rabbit	311
Age 4 Activity 45	Billy and Blaze: A Boy and His Pony	313
Age 4 Activity 46	The Giving Tree	315
Age 4 Activity 47	Make Way For Ducklings	317
Age 4 Activity 48	The Story About Ping	319
Age 4 Activity 49	Ox Cart Man	321
Age 4 Activity 50	Alexander and the Terrible, Horrible, No Good, Very Bad Day	323
Age 4 Activity 51	Wemberly Worried	325
Age 4 Activity 52	Look Out Kindergarten, Here I Come!	327

Age Zero: From Birth to One Year

Welcome to the joy of being a parent! From the moment your child came into this world, your role transformed into the caretaker and nurturer of your sweet little one. Children are not only a huge responsibility but are also a bountiful blessing! With patience and persistence that is saturated in parental love, each baby has the potential to grow into a healthy, active young person ready for the world he or she was born into.

So Many Changes

You will notice so many changes in the development of your baby during Age Zero. That is why the activities you will find in this section will grow as your child does throughout the weeks and months that bring about so many rapid changes. In the early Age Zero activities, the goal is to prompt your baby to respond to the stimulation of his or her five senses.

Development at Different Rates

Keep in mind that babies develop at different rates and not necessarily in the same areas at the same age. Your baby may not be ready for some of the activities suggested and that is perfectly normal! The activities in this book are not labeled by particular weeks of your baby's life on purpose! When your baby appears unresponsive to an activity presented, try again at a later time. That might mean later in the day, the next day, or the next week. I encourage you not to give up but to keep trying!

Repetition With Patience

Introducing your baby to something new takes patience on your part. When he or she is responsive to the skill activities, repeat them often with your baby. The more a baby repeats an activity, the more secure and responsive he or she will be. The foundation for learning is the introduction of a skill and then its repeated practice. Since an infant's thinking, reasoning, and association processes are very immature, repetition is essential to your baby's development and success.

Just the Right Time

The developmental skill activities in this section are designed to help develop thinking, reasoning, and association. The key to a baby's learning is introducing and developing skills at the right time. Thus, going too far ahead in introducing more advanced activities may not be the best thing for your baby. Then again, you are the best judge of what your baby is capable of. A gap in the learning and development of an infant is what researchers and educators believe causes many learning and behavior problems at home and school. So observe what your child is ready for and facilitate the activities that are right for your child at the given moment. Use the Table of Contents for each age as a guide. You may want to skip ahead every so often to complete activities with your child that he or she appears ready for. Then revisit those activities that were skipped or repeat those that were most interesting for your baby at this stage.

Don't Be the "Comparative Critic"

Too many parents are hyper-focused on comparing their child's development to other children's development in the fear that their own child is falling behind. Take a deep breath and relax! Your child is in his or her own race, and you will benefit from working with your child on the skills he or she is ready for. This book is meant to be used as one tool in your parenting toolbox. There are a myriad of other resources to help guide and coach you through the parenting process. Don't get bogged down being the "comparative critic" and instead cheer your baby on, praising him or her for what he of she is capable of doing now.

Positive Attitude

Even though routine and consistency will benefit your baby, keep in mind that a set time to complete the activities in this book with your child is too regimented and may cause anxiety for both you as the caretaker and your baby. Talk to your baby and use good voice inflection with praise, consistency without pressure, gentleness, and love. As your baby embarks on the new adventure ahead, encourage your child as he or she grows to impart a positive attitude toward himself or herself and his or her environment.

Siblings

You may have picked up this book for the first time already having parented other children through the ages of zero to five! Your baby's siblings are an essential part of your child's development in the family unit. Invite the baby's siblings to join in the activities with you as you model and work with your young one. Older children may find a sense of responsibility and ownership as they learn how to care and play with their baby sibling in constructive and meaningful ways.

Sign Language

Early communication with your baby is possible through sign language. Teach your infant simple signs to reduce the frustration between parent and baby. Equip your baby with the tools to communicate what he or she needs to set the foundation for learning early on. Even though your baby cannot talk yet, he or she will respond to sign language and begin using it when you repeatedly offer it as a communication option on a daily basis. First signs should include: eat, milk, more, mom and dad. These words are meaningful to your baby, and there will be motivation to learn those signs before others. Sign language has the potential to reduce crying and whining, which are your baby's ways of getting your attention when he or she needs or wants something. There are many helpful books and websites (with simple teaching videos) that can help you get started: just Google "baby sign language," and you will be amazed with what you discover!

Note

The author and publisher are not liable for any injury or death incurred due to the misuse of the suggested materials and directions. As with all child-related activities, materials should be selected with careful attention to child safety; adult supervision is essential.

Age 0 - Activity 1 – Tips About Beginning Movement

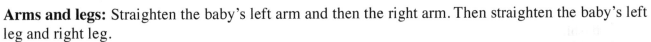

Head: Support the baby's head, because it is wobbly.

- To help the baby become aware of both sides of his or her head, gently turn the baby's head while he or she is laying down.

Hands: Let the baby grasp your finger.

- The grasp is a prenatal reflex and will weaken as the baby's eye-hand coordination develops.
- Put the baby's palms together, helping to develop a feeling and awareness of both sides of his or her body.

Arms and legs: Straighten the baby's left arm and then the right arm. Then straighten the baby's left leg and right leg.

- As you exercise your baby's body parts throughout the first few weeks, you will notice that the baby will stretch his or her arms and legs as he or she adjusts to his or her new environment.

Feet: Touch and hold the baby's left foot then right foot.

- Beginning with the left and then the right begins making the baby aware of the left to right movement familiar in our world.

Talk and wrap up: Your baby will learn to recognize and respond to his or her mother's voice at a very early age.

- Sing or hum to your baby. Playing soft lullabies for your baby will begin encouraging his or her sense of hearing.
- Wrap your baby up securely in a blanket for the first few weeks of life.
- For the past nine months, the baby has felt secure curled up. The blanket provides a cocoon-like feel for the baby.

This activity develops:
- Beginning movement of the baby's body parts
- Sense of touch and hearing
- Adjustment to new environment

Age 0 - Activity 2 – Response to Light

Background:
- At birth, a baby is sensitive to light, shiny, and moving objects and will usually respond by turning his or her head to follow the light.
- The baby's eyes may appear to be out of focus. *However, there is no need for concern.*

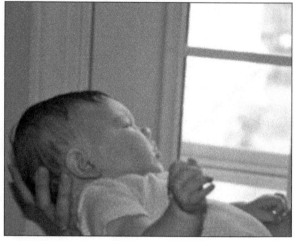

Light response activity:
- Open the blinds, shades, or curtains so the sunlight shines into the room from a window. Does your baby turn his or her head to the light?
- Close the blinds or shades and turn on a lamp on the other side of the room or use a flashlight.
- Avoid shining the light in the baby's eyes.
- Allow the light to shine on the wall.

Repeat activities:
- Babies learn best at this age by repetitive learning.
- Being consistent with your interaction with your baby may help to prevent a learning lag.

This activity develops:
- Light awareness
- Movement of head from side to side for a purpose

Age 0 - Activity 3 – Moving an Object

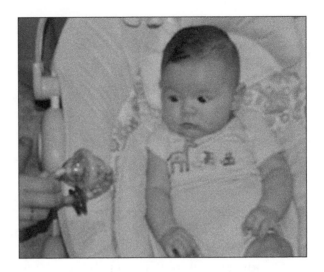

You will need:
- Baby rattle or a toy for your baby to hold

Questions to ask:
- Does your baby fix his or her eyes on you?
- When you hold a rattle or object in front of the baby's line of vision, does he or she look at it?

Move the rattle from left to right:
- Do the baby's eyes follow from left to right?
- This is the beginning of left to right eye movement training, which is a prerequisite for reading.

What if my baby's eyes do not react to the rattle or its movement?
- Do not be concerned! Infants do not develop at the same rate in all areas.
- Repeat and practice this activity as well as the previous activities several times throughout the days and weeks to come and observe the baby's reactions.

Reminders:
- Continue to move the baby's entire body from left to right at various times to reinforce laterality.
- Talk, sing, hum, or play music to keep the baby's senses keen.
- During the first month of life, a baby is adjusting to his or her new environment, so their senses of touch, sight, and sound need much stimulation.
- Periodically, move your baby from his or her stomach position onto his or her back.

This activity develops:
- Listening awareness
- Visual stimulation

Age 0 - Activity 4 – Cradle Gym

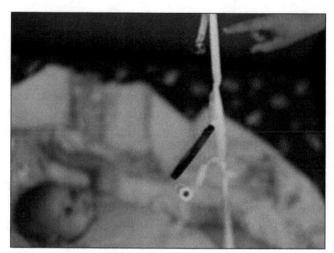

You will need:
- 4 pieces of elastic
- Colored spool, bell, plastic lid
- Shiny aluminum foil

Set up:
1. Tie a piece of elastic across the width of the crib.
2. Tie 3 pieces of shorter elastic 3 or 4 inches apart to the longer piece.
3. On the end of each elastic, tie an object each day in progression to the end of the dangling piece. A little bell can be added low enough so that the baby will be able to reach it when ready.

Introduce with the spool:
- Interest the baby by moving the spool back and forth and talk to him or her while you interact with your baby.
- Observe the baby's eyes. Does he or she watch the moving spool or try to grasp it?

Add a shiny lid:
- Observe the baby's reactions.
- Move both the spool and the lid back and forth.

Add a jingle bell:
- Move the bell to make a sound.
- Does your baby attempt to touch the object that makes sound?

Observation questions:
- Have your baby's arms and legs straightened out?
- Does the baby turn his or her head more easily?
- Does the baby lift his or her head slightly?
- Does the baby follow a moving object?
- Does the baby tend to turn his or her head when you move throughout the room?
- Does the baby's whole body seem to lean in the direction that you move, the direction of light or sound?

Age 0 - Activity 5 – Mirror and Pendulum

You will need:
- Mirror (non-breakable)
- Paper plate with a funny face drawn
- String or elastic

Mirror activity:
- Hold the baby close enough to the mirror to look at himself or herself in it.
- Does the baby reach out for the image in the mirror or talk to the image?
- Talk to the baby in an expressive voice and call him or her by name as you look at the baby in the mirror.

Pendulum set up:
- Prop the baby up in an infant seat. Be sure to support the baby's head with a rolled-up blanket to take stress off the neck.
- Hang a funny face drawn on a paper plate from a string or piece of elastic that is attached to the top of a door, doorway, ceiling fan, or something high in clear view of the baby's eyes.

Pendulum swing:
- Push the paper plate on the string so that it swings back and forth like a pendulum. Try to encourage the baby to watch it move back and forth.
- The pendulum can be added to the cradle gym and can serve to interest the baby for brief periods of time.

This activity develops:
- Awareness of his or her own image
- Beginning listening skills
- Interest in making sounds by watching
- Visual stimulation
- Awareness of movement initiating a response

Age 0 - Activity 6 – The Sock Ball

You will need:
- Old sock
- Bubble wrap, newspaper, rags, old stockings
- String

Make a sock ball:
1. Fill an old sock with bubble wrap, newspaper, rags, or old stockings.
2. Tie a piece of string around the top of it to close it.
3. Secure it to the rail of the crib or playpen with string.

Sock ball activity:
- With the baby lying on his or her back, move the attached sock ball back and forth from left to right and in clear view of the baby's eyes.
- Does the baby look at the ball and watch it move?
- Does he or she attempt to touch or move it?

Not interested? Try again later.
- If your baby is not interested in the sock ball, try again later.
- If the baby is interested, encourage the activity, but remember that a baby's attention span is brief.
- Be patient. Keep talking to your baby with good voice inflection as it stimulates his or her hearing.

Observation questions:
- Can your baby raise his or her head slightly when on his or her stomach?
- Is your baby's neck getting stronger?

This activity develops:
- Beginning steps in eye-hand coordination
- Awareness of the sock ball and movement
- Enhancement of the sense of touch
- Verbal stimulus to encourage eye-hand movement

Age 0 - Activity 7 – Response to a Noise Maker

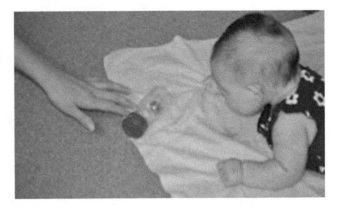

You will need:
- Rattle, bell, jingle bell inside of an empty spice container, or something that makes noise

Make a sound:
- With the noisy object, observe whether your baby turns his or head, eyes, or body toward the direction of the sound.
- Make the sound first on the left of the baby and observe.
- Then move to the right of the baby and make a sound.
- Let the baby touch the rattle or bell.
- Hold the rattle in front of the baby. Does he or she reach for it? If so, let your baby grasp the object.

Reach with arms:
- Lay the baby on his or her stomach on the floor. Roll the jingle bell in the spice container toward and away from the baby. Encourage the baby to reach for the object that is making noise.

What does it mean when my baby cries?

Babies develop different kinds of cries. You may start to learn how to distinguish between them.

A baby may cry, because:
- hungry
- stomachache or gas bubble
- wet or dirty diaper
- angry or wants attention
- bored

These cues should be your signal to interact with your baby. Try the activities when your baby seems like he or she is needing your attention. The activities do not need to be done at the same time everyday. Whatever cry your baby makes, respond to his or her needs with love, tenderness, and a soft, responsive voice.

Age 0 - Activity 8 – Colored Mobile

You will need:
- 3 plastic lids
- 3 elastic pieces
- orange, red, yellow, green, blue, and purple construction paper

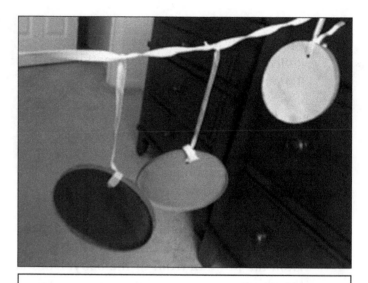

Make a colored mobile:
1. Cover three plastic lids with the construction paper.
2. Cut the pieces of paper the size of the three lids.
3. Glue the pieces to the front and back of each lid, so that every side is a different color.
4. Punch a hole in the top of each lid and string them to each side of the crib or playpen with elastic pieces.

Lid 1:
- Front → orange
- Back → red

Lid 2:
- Front → yellow
- Back → green

Lid 3:
- Front → blue
- Back → purple

Dangle and move:
- Allow the lids to dangle so that the baby can focus on the objects, watch the movement of the lids, and begin to distinguish color.
- Allow the baby to bat at the lids to make them move on his or her own.
- If your baby does not respond to the dangling lids, try again at another time.

This activity develops:
- Awareness of moving objects
- Stimulus to initiate a response to moving objects
- Awareness of colors
- Desire to grasp a moving object

Age 0 - Activity 9 – Large Muscle Activities

You will need:
- Stuffed animals
- Blanket to lay your baby on

What are gross motor activities?
These are activities that develop your baby's large muscles for movement and sense of touch.

Muscle awareness activities:
- Place the baby face down on a blanket that has been spread out on the floor.
- Gently straighten the baby's left arm and observe the baby's response. Then the right arm.
- Do the same with the left and right legs.
- Does your baby lift his or her head and focus on his or her left and right arms when you move them?

Add stuffed animal:
- When the baby shows some sign of response to the movement of the arms and legs, place a stuffed animal in front of the baby.
- Does the baby attempt to reach for it or does he or she show no interest?
- Do not expect the baby to grab it. Your baby is still developing the gross motor skills to do this successfully but opportunities to practice always help!

This activity develops:
- Awareness of his or her body and body parts
- More of an awareness of left and right laterality
- Vague awareness of hand grasping

Age 0 - Activity 10 – Eye-Hand Coordination

You will need:

- Sock ball from Activity 6

Sock ball activities:

- Lay your baby on his or her back. Put the sockball on the baby's stomach.
- Roll it along the baby's body across the chest and up to the baby's neck.
- Watch the baby's eyes and hands.
- Does the baby attempt to reach for the sock ball, or do his or her eyes watch the movement?
- Be patient; he or she will respond when ready.

This activity develops:
- Tactile sensation that stimulates the baby to grasp a moving object
- Skill in focusing on a moving object
- Skill in listening to sounds when you talk to him or her
- Developing eye-hand coordination

Age 0 - Activity 11 – Observing Different Faces

You will need:
- Wall mirror
- Paper plate

Mirror activity:
- Show the baby his or her face in a large wall mirror.
- Call the baby by name and say, "I see (baby's name)."
- With the baby still looking in the mirror, use a paper plate and block the baby's view.
- Gradually slide the plate from left to right, so that the baby's face comes into view.
- As you do this say, "Peek-a-boo, I see (baby's name)."
- Try this activity with your face in the mirror too.

Facial Recognition: Babies recognize and distinguish human faces, especially exaggerated facial expressions.

Learning to play a game:
- Your baby looks, listens, and responds.
- Through this game, your baby is becoming more aware of his or her name.

Repeat:
- Repeat this and other activities, especially those that the baby did not readily respond to.
- Repetition is very important for sequential learning, confidence, and the mastery of basic concepts.

This activity develops:
- Awareness of his or her face
- Purpose for looking and listening
- Interest in interacting with another person

Age 0 - Activity 12 – Peek-A-Boo

You will need:
- Paper plate with a funny face drawn on it

Front and back activity:
- Show the baby the face on the lid.
- Turn it over and show the baby the blank side.
- Turn it back over (from left to right) and say, "Peek-a-boo" as the face gradually comes into view.

Your baby is learning:
- To be aware of the front and back of an object.
- To follow the movement of the face, thus visually training them from left to right.

Use your hands to play:
- Extend this activity by using your hands to hide your face and play peek-a-boo with the baby.
- Your baby may surprise you one day and hide his or her face to play the game with you.

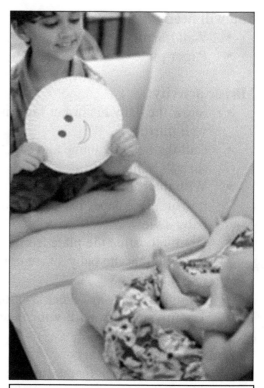

Keep in mind: These activities are great opportunities for older siblings to interact with their younger sisters or brothers.

This activity develops:
- Awareness of a face
- Awareness of the concepts, *front* and *back*
- Early motivation by initiating a purpose for observing

Age 0 - Activity 13 – Spool Worm

You will need:
- 4 large spools
- Piece of elastic

Make a spool worm:
1. String 4 spools together with a piece of elastic.
2. Tie knots on either end of the spool worm.
3. Draw a face with a sharpie on one end of the spool worm to create the "head."

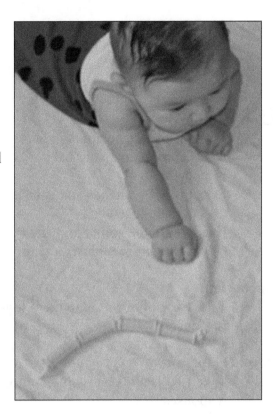

Wiggle the spool worm on the floor:
- Place the baby face down on a blanket and allow the baby to stretch his or her arms and legs to squirm.
- Roll the spool worm in front of the baby, encouraging him or her to watch as you roll it.
- If the baby attempts to reach for the spool worm, move it slightly away so as to encourage the baby to wiggle forward.
- These are the beginning steps of crawling.

Tap the spool worm:
- Pull the two end spools apart, and tap the spools together to make a tapping sound.
- Do this several times to interest the baby and motivate him or her to grasp the spool worm as this skill continues to develop.

> This activity develops:
> - Baby's body muscles by using a stimulus to initiate stretching and squirming in an attempt to grasp
> - Awareness of movement through the sense of touch
> - Motivation to move forward

Age 0 - Activity 14 – Listen to the Sounds

You will need:
- 2 spools
- 2 jar lids
- 2 spoons

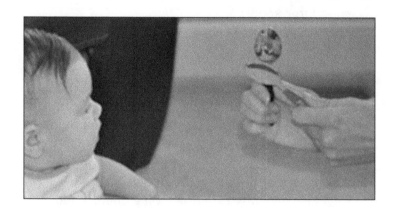

Clap your hands:
- Make a sound by clapping your hands and observe your baby's responses.
- Take the baby's hands and attempt to clap them together.
- Exaggerate the sound and say, "clap," each time that you clap.

Spool clap:
- Take two spools and tap them together to make a sound and observe your baby's responses.

Jar lid clap:
- Take two jar lids and tap them together to make a sound and observe your baby's responses.

Spoon tap with rhythm:
- Tap two spoons or something else that is safe to use and make a sound.
- Repeat the tapping with a rhythm of 1-2, 1-2. Talk to the baby and try to encourage him or her to listen.

Rhythm:
- Try tapping other objects together to the rhythm of 1-2, 1-2.
- Clap your hands to this rhythm when you are holding or playing with your baby.

> This activity develops:
> - Awareness of different sounds
> - Awareness of the origin of different sounds
> - Listening skills
> - Awareness of the rhythm 1-2

Age 0 - Activity 15 – Jingle Rolling Container

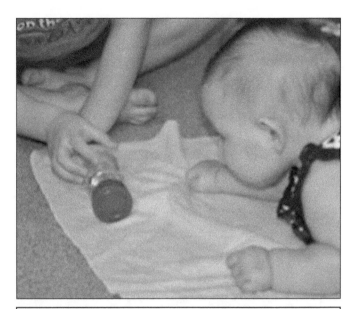

You will need:
- Empty spice container
- Jingle bell

Roll on the baby:
- Place the baby on his or her back and roll the container down and back up to the chest for tactile sensation.
- Repeat if the baby is responsive.

Roll toward the baby:
- Lay the plastic container on its side and roll it toward the baby.
- Make sure that the container is clearly visible to the baby.
- Allow the baby to stretch his or her arms to squirm.

Older sibling? Encourage an older brother or sister to gently roll the jingle bell spice container to entertain your baby.

Activity extension:
- A jingle bell may be placed inside the container before rolling it to the baby for further awareness and stimulation.

Talk to encourage:
- Talk to your baby with a positive voice inflection, encouraging your baby to watch and grasp the rolling container.

This activity develops:
- Awareness of a rolling object
- Skill in watching a moving object
- Basic skill in attempting to grasp
- Listening skill as you talk; this aids in vocabulary development

Age 0 - Activity 16 – Coffee Can Drum

You will need:
- Empty coffee can with lid

Tap the top to make a sound:
- Prop your baby into a sitting position.
- Model with your hand tapping on the plastic lid of the coffee can to make a sound.
- Allow your baby to tap on the top of the plastic lid.
- If he or she needs assistance, gently take your baby's hand and tap it for him or her until your baby recognizes to do it on his or her own.

Drum a beat:
- Tap the patterned rhythm of 1-2, 1-2 on the coffee can lid.
- Talk to your baby and encourage him or her to listen as you tap and say, "1-2, 1-2."
- Do not expect the baby to tap out a pattern on his or her own.

Repeat and practice with time:
- Over time if you repeat this activity often, your baby may be able to make the pattern as he or she gets older.

> This activity develops:
> - Awareness of sound
> - Awareness of a rhythmical pattern
> - Listening skills
> - Sense of touch

Age 0 - Activity 17 – Nursery Rhymes

You will need:
- Nursery rhyme book from the library

Read, recite, repeat:
- Choose some of your favorite rhymes and read, recite, or sing these rhymes for your baby to hear.
- Repeat each one several times.
- The nonsensical words of these "catchy" rhymes will entertain the baby as he or she listens.

Show pictures:
- Show the baby the picture that corresponds to the rhyme. The brief glance at the pictures will serve to develop beginning associations of pictures and words.

Rhymes:
- Rhymes have rhythms that are useful in developing early listening skills.
- Repeat the recitations of the nursery rhymes whenever it is possible as the baby learns to listen.
- As he or she begins to talk later on, he or she will recite parts of his or her favorite rhymes spontaneously.

Nursery rhyme books like *Mother Goose* can be read and recited aloud for any age group! Starting early is a fantastic way to introduce your child to repetition and rhythm!

This activity develops:
- Language enrichment
- Listening skills
- Interest in repetition
- Interest in rhythm

Age 0 - Activity 18 – Where is Thumbkin?

Touch and say:
- Thumb → Thumbkin
- Forefinger → Pointer
- Middle → Middleman
- Ring finger → Ringman
- Little finger → Pinky

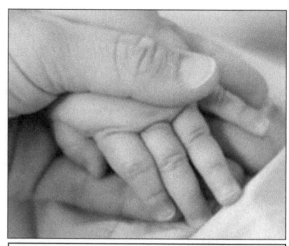

Pretend conversation:
- Use both hands to carry on a pretend conversation with the left and right fingers as you say or sing the song below to the tune of "*Frère Jacques*" also known as "Are You Sleeping?"
- Each finger (L for left and R for right) should appear and disappear to correspond to the words.

> **Where is Thumbkin? Where is Thumbkin?**
> (L) *Here I am. (R) Here I am.*
> (L) *How are you today, sir?*
> (R) *Very well, I thank you.*
> (L) *Run away.*
> (R) *Run away.*

Repeat with the other fingers:
- Substitute the correct finger for the word, *Thumbkin*. For example, "Where is *Pointer*?"

Hide-and-seek with fingers:
- Hide your fingers behind your back and sing the words as you move the correct fingers forward to correspond to the song lyrics.

This activity develops:
- Listening and observational skills
- Awareness of associating finger movement with the words of the finger play song
- Further awareness of left and right

Age 0 - Activity 19 – Pat-A-Cake

Model:
- Hold the baby in your lap and model placing your hands together and then apart.
- Repeat several times so that the baby is aware of what you are doing and say the Pat-a-cake rhyme.

> *Pat-a-cake, pat-a-cake, baker's man.*
> *Bake me a cake as fast as you can.*
> *Roll it and pat it and mark it with a B,*
> *And put it in the oven for baby and me.*

Baby's turn:
- If your baby is interested, encourage him or her to put his or her hands together and apart as you say the rhyme.
- If your baby is not interested, encourage the baby to copy the pat-a-cake movement as you model again and gently hold your baby's wrists and help him or her.

Substitute and repeat:
- If you substitute the initial letter of the baby's name and use the baby's name in the rhyme, he or she may listen more attentively.
- Remember that babies enjoy and need much repetition.

> This activity develops:
> - More awareness of hands
> - Listening skills
> - Awareness of rhythm and rhyme
> - Observational skills

Age 0 - Activity 20 – This Little Piggy

This little piggy went to the market. (big toe)
This little piggy stayed home. (second toe)
This little piggy had roast beef.
(third toe)
This little piggy had none.
(fourth toe)
And this little piggy cried,
"Wee, wee, wee" all the way home.
(little toe)

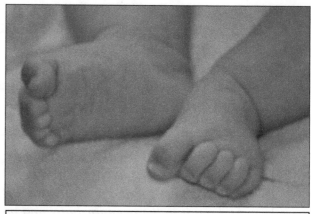

Repeat the rhyme many times in the future. The baby will soon begin to play with his or her hands, feet, fingers, and toes.

Barefoot toe names:
- Touch each toe and use good voice inflection while saying the following rhyme, starting with the big toe.

Tactile learning:
- The tactile sense of touching each of the body parts will help the baby match the body movement with the body parts.
- The baby will soon realize that he or she can initiate and control the movement of the hands, feet, fingers, and toes.

This activity develops:
- More awareness of the feet and toes
- Listening skills
- Enhancement of the sense of touch

Age 0 - Activity 21 – Wiggle to Reach

You will need:
- Strip of wide ribbon about 12 inches long
- Spool or empty spice container

Wiggle ribbon strip:
- Prop the baby up in a sitting position on the floor.
- Move the strip of ribbon in a wiggly fashion and try to interest the baby to reach for it.

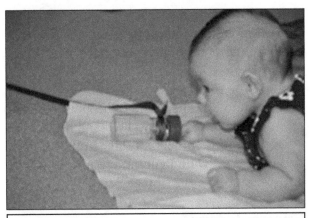

Body contact with the floor and the struggle to move toward an object should create an interest in the basics of crawling.

Baby's turn:
- Allow the baby to touch and hold the strip on his or her own.
- Gently withdraw the strip and lay it down in front of the baby.
- Give the baby an opportunity to reach for the strip.
- Go back to wiggling the strip, if the baby does not try to reach for it.

Attach an object to make it a game!
- Tie a spool or small spice container to one end of the wide ribbon strip.
- Gradually pull the strip away and encourage your baby to wiggle forward to reach or grasp the object.
- Place the baby's hand on the object and slowly pull the strip away.

Reminder: Do not leave the baby alone to play with the ribbon strip.

No interest? Try at another time.
- This activity is designed to stimulate the baby to want to move forward.
- Eventually the baby will discover that he or she can move forward and obtain an object with very little effort.

This activity develops:
- Eye-hand coordination
- Eye contact and control on a moving object
- Interest in reaching and moving forward

Age 0 - Activity 22 – Down and Drop

You will need:
- Spoon or clothespin
- Other safe objects the baby can drop

Model how to drop:
- Show the spoon or clothespin to the baby and allow him or her to hold and feel it.
- Hold the object slightly higher than the baby's eye view and encourage him or her to watch as you drop the object.

New word: do*wn*
- Does the baby attempt to reach for the object?
- Call the object by name *clothespin* or *spoon*.
- Hold it up and let it fall. Then say the word *down* as you drop the object.
- Repeat and emphasize the new words.

Baby's turn to drop:
- Hand the object to the baby.
- Does he or she attempt to drop or throw it?
- Retrieve the object for the baby to drop or throw it again and again until the baby loses interest.
- Try other safe objects for your baby to hold and drop.

This activity develops:
- Eye-hand coordination
- Awareness of the concept *down*
- Sense of touch
- Listening for the different sounds that objects make when they fall

Age 0 - Activity 23 – Make Some Noise

You will need:
- Coffee can
- Wooden spoon
- Shoe box
- Paper bag stuffed with scrunched up newspaper
- A piece of wood
- Various objects safe for your baby to tap on and listen for the different sounds.

Rhythm practice:
- Allow your baby to tap on the top of a coffee can with a wooden spoon to make a noise. Your baby may need your help holding the wooden spoon.
- Model tapping out the 1-2 rhythm on the can and then let your baby practice on his or her own.

Line up objects in a row to tap on:
- Place the following objects in a row: coffee can, shoe box, paper bag stuffed with scrunched up newspaper, and a piece of wood.
- With your help, the baby can hold the wooden spoon and tap on the objects in the row.

Short attention span:
- The different sounds will serve to interest and entertain the baby briefly.
- This activity is great to repeat on a regular basis.

This activity develops:
- Feeling sense of sound vibrations when produced when tapping various objects
- Eye-hand coordination
- Awareness of different sounds
- Free exploration

Age 0 - Activity 24 – Sock Ball Throw

You will need:
- Old sock filled with scrunched up newspaper or cotton balls

Hold and model throw:
- Allow the baby to hold and feel the sock ball.
- Take the sock ball gently from the baby and throw it a short distance. Make sure that it is within the baby's eye view.

Baby's turn:
- Give the sock ball to the baby and encourage him or her to throw it.
- Help him or her to try to aim and throw the ball.

Toss game:
- At another time, sit on the floor facing the baby and toss the sock ball gently to him or her.
- Encourage him or her to pick up the ball and toss it back.
- Try to avoid negative comments if your baby wants to hold the sock ball instead of tossing it back or puts it down.

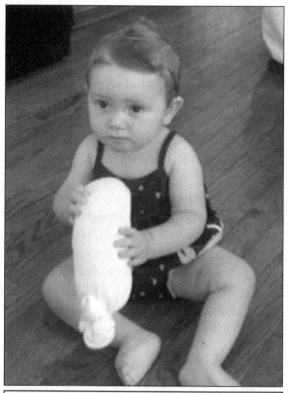

Praise the baby for any positive attempts that he or she makes to throw the sock ball!

Repeat and practice over time:
- With practice, the baby will learn to coordinate and be able to toss the ball.
- Do not expect your baby to have the ability to aim accurately. This will come later.

This activity develops:
- Awareness of throwing and tossing an object for a purpose
- Eye control in focusing on a moving object
- Enhancement of the sense of touch
- Further development of eye-hand coordination

Age 0 - Activity 25 – Jingle Bell Feet

You will need:
- Jingle bell attached with safety pin to baby's sock or shoe

Jingle bell feet activity:
1. Lay the baby on his or her back and bring his or her left leg up so that he or she can grasp his or her foot. Jingle the bell attached to this foot, so the baby can hear it.
2. Place his or her left leg back down and lift the right leg, so that the baby can grasp his or her right foot. Jingle the bell attached to this foot so the baby can hear it.
3. Repeat and let your baby play with his or her feet with the sound of the jingle bells interesting him or her.

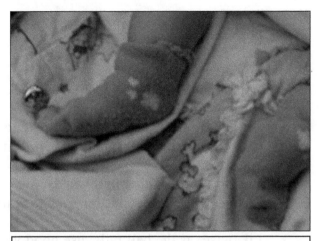

Tip: Note which leg the baby moves first. He or she may be showing a right or left sided preference at an early age.

Questions to ask:
- Does the baby repeat this activity independently?
- Which leg does he or she attempt to move first?
- Does he or she move the same leg first every time?

Why left before right?
- It's best to continue to move the left leg (or arm) first when you initiate this and other activities. This is suggested mainly to develop the concept of left and right through the sense of touch.
- The jingle bells enhance the awareness of left and right through the use of sound.

> This activity develops:
> - Further awareness of left and right
> - Further awareness of feet
> - Free exploration
> - Grasping coordination
> - Enhancement of the sense of touch

Age 0 - Activity 26 – Toss Up and Down

You will need:
- Sock ball

Model tossing *up*:
- With both hands, model tossing the sock ball up in eye view of the baby.
- Talk to the baby as you do this and encourage the baby to look up and watch the ball as it goes up.

Voice inflection for learning new words:
- Change your voice inflection each time the ball goes up as you say the word *up*.
- Likewise, as the ball falls, use good voice inflection for the word *down*.

Baby's turn:
- Give the ball to the baby and encourage him or her to use both hands and toss the ball up.
- Be sure to praise him or her for his or her efforts.

Up and down: Use the word *up* as you say, "Watch the ball go *up*!" Use the word *down* as you say, "Watch the ball go *down*!"

Don't forget repeating previous activities! Just because you and your child have participated in the activity once does not mean that your child will not enjoy or benefit from the activity by doing it again.

A reminder about the order of activities: The activities in this first section of Age 0 may be attempted in any order. Some of the activities may be better suited for your child's needs later or earlier. You know your child's abilities best as you are with your child each and every day and are observing his or her developmental progress.

This activity develops:
- Eye-hand coordination
- Understanding of up and down
- Eye contact with a moving object
- Confidence through praise and encouragement

Age 0 - Activity 27 – Stack and Fall

You will need:
- 4 large plastic laundry detergent caps or blocks
- Other objects that can be stacked
- 3 squares or rectangles cut from Styrofoam meat trays large enough to support 2 or 3 detergent caps

Why only 3? At this age, too many objects to stack may cause excessive stimulation and overwhelm your child.

Stacking activity:
1. Model stacking three objects and knock them down while the baby is watching.
2. Repeat this several times. If the baby wants to help, encourage him or her to do so.
3. Then, both of you knock them down. Use the word *down* as the objects fall.
4. Encourage the baby to stack the three objects without your help.
5. Praise your baby with positive feedback for any effort he or she shows.
6. Throughout the week, find other objects that the baby can stack.

Enrichment activity ideas:
- Add a fourth detergent cap for your baby to stack with.
- Model how to stack the detergent caps on top of one another by placing a Styrofoam square between the caps for extra support to balance and stabilize them for assembling a higher stack.

This activity develops:
- Eye-hand coordination
- Interest in copying or following directions
- Further understanding of the concept "down"
- Enhancement of the sense of touch

Age 0 - Activity 28 – Paper Noise

You will need:
- Paper sheets that can be balled up
- Shoe box
- Stuffed animal or toy that can fit inside of the shoe box

Ball up paper to make noise activity:
1. Take one of the sheets of paper and ball it up in your hands and make as much crumpling noise as you possibly can.
2. Give the baby a piece of paper and encourage the baby to ball it up.
3. Repeat this activity as long as the baby remains interested. If there is no interest, try again later.

Trash can game:
- Put the balls of scrunched paper in the trashcan.
- Make a game of it by taking turns putting the paper balls in the trashcan.

This activity develops:
- Small hand muscles
- Enhances listening
- Encourages the baby to copy or attempt a task independently
- Awareness of the concept "inside"

Do It Together! Ball up a sheet of paper at the same time as the baby to make sure that he or she understands what you want him or her to do.

Age 0 - Activity 29 – Shake, Listen, and Find

You will need:
- Empty oatmeal cylinder can, coffee can, or shoebox with lid
- Small toy

Shake, listen, and find activity:
1. Place a small toy inside the chosen container and close the lid.
2. Shake the container to make a sound.
3. Ask the baby what is inside, and stress the word *inside*.
4. Open the container and let the baby peek inside.
5. Take the object out of the container and let the baby feel it and look at it.
6. Name the object and tell the baby to put it back in the container.
7. Replace the lid and shake the container to repeat this activity.

This activity can grow with your child! As he or she gets older, place objects inside the coffee can and have your child shake it on his or her own before discovering what is inside.

Extension: Change the object that is placed in the container to add interest and assist the baby in learning the names and sounds of different objects that are chosen to hide in the container.

Hide-and-seek toy game:
1. Show the baby the toy that you plan to hide in the shoebox.
2. Place the toy inside a shoebox that has been stuffed with crushed paper.
3. Shake the closed shoebox and listen to the noise.
4. Close the box and encourage the baby to open it and find the hidden toy "inside" the shoebox. Stress the new word *inside*.
5. Repeat this activity and allow the baby to attempt to find the hidden toy independently.

> This activity develops:
> - Listening
> - Understanding of the concept "inside"
> - Eye-hand coordination
> - Association skills

Age 0 - Activity 30 – Watch the Ball

You will need:
- Ziploc bag
- Small ball and other small objects that can be placed in the bag

Model the activity:
1. Allow your baby to hold and feel a small ball.
2. Then place the ball in a zip-lock bag and fasten it securely.
3. Use your finger and push the ball around inside the bag.
4. Tell the baby that the ball is inside the bag, and stress the word *inside*.

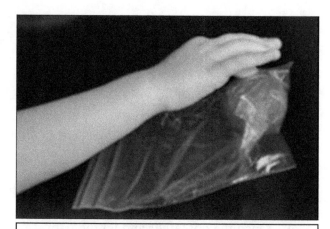

This new experience will serve to entertain the baby briefly, briefly, but never leave your child with the bag alone.

Baby's turn:
- Allow the baby to feel the ball and push it around independently.
- Encourage the baby to watch the ball as it moves around inside the bag.
- Show the baby how you can stop the ball with your hand, release it, and move the ball again.
- Other objects can be placed inside the bag individually, so that the baby can push and explore the movement of different objects.

This activity develops:
- Sense of touch
- Eye-hand coordination
- Free exploration
- Skill in keeping the eye on a moving target

Age 0 - Activity 31 – Bowl and Ball Roll

You will need:
- Large plastic Tupperware or flat pie or cake tin
- Small ball

Model activity:
1. Push the ball around the edge with your finger.
2. Allow it to roll freely but keep it in motion.
3. Encourage the baby to watch as the ball moves around.

> **Does the baby try to stop the ball?** If so, you know that the baby is paying attention!

Baby's turn: Help the baby get the ball in motion and give him or her as much independence as possible with continuing the ball's movement around the edge of the container.

> **Repeat:** If this activity is repeated enough, the baby will become aware of the restrictive movement of the ball in a boundary of a circle.

Enrichment: Tilt activity
- Tilt the container and move it, so that the ball moves around the edge of the container in a circular motion, keeping the ball inside the rim of the container as it moves.
- Repeat this activity several times so that the baby can watch the ball move.
- Help the baby hold the container to repeat.

> This activity develops:
> - Enhancement of the sense of touch
> - Awareness of a circle
> - Skill in keeping the eye on a moving target
> - Beginning independence and confidence
> - Eye-hand coordination

Age 0 - Activity 32 - Sizes

You will need:
- Unbreakable mixing bowls
- Set of measuring cups

Model activity:
1. Place the mixing cups in clear view of the baby's reach.
2. Arrange in order of size with the smallest one on the left.
3. Stack the smallest cup inside the next smallest and so on.
4. Use the words *large* and *small* as you stack and unstack the cups.

Baby's turn:
- Give the baby an opportunity to do the stacking and un-stacking.
- Help the baby order them if he or she needs assistance.

Awareness: Through this activity, your baby will become aware of different sizes and the round shape of the objects!

Stack by size: Other stackable objects like mixing bowls and Tupperware containers would work well for this activity too. Enable your child to discover through seeing, feeling and doing.

This activity develops:
- Awareness of size
- More of an awareness of circular shape
- Sense of touch
- More of an awareness of left and right
- Independence

Age 0 - Activity 33 – Blowing Bubbles and Water Splash

You will need:
- Bubble blowing solution or liquid detergent
- Bubble wand
- Wash cloth
- Sponge
- Plastic measuring cups

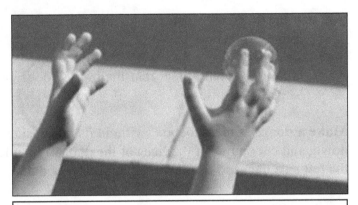

Repeating the sounds that the baby makes encourages him or her to practice and motivates him or her to want to communicate verbally.

Play with bubbles:
- Blow bubbles for your baby to watch and play with
- The bubbles are round and colorful, and the baby may watch and even try to catch and pop them.
- When a bubble pops say, "The bubble popped."

During bath time:
- Make a splashing sound with the water.
- Exaggerating it will capture the baby's attention.
- As you talk to the baby say, "Splish, splash" or something similar.

Wring out a wet washcloth:
- Listen to the sound a washcloth being wrung out makes.
- Give the baby a small sponge and encourage him or her to listen for the water sounds.

Babies enjoy interesting sounds and are more attentive when good voice inflection is used!

- Plastic measuring cups can also be used in the bathtub to make interesting sounds with pouring the water.

This activity develops:
- Skill in watching a moving object (bubble)
- Awareness of the round shape of bubbles
- Listening for different sounds
- Enhancement of the sense of touch

Age 0 - Activity 34 – Shoe Box House

You will need:
- Empty shoe box
- Scissors
- Spool or small object that fits in the "doorway" of shoe box house

Make a door: Turn a shoebox (without its lid) upside down, and cut on two of the lines of the doorway but leave the left side uncut so that the door can be opened and closed.

Open and close: Open the door and place the spool or small object inside the house. Emphasize the word *open*, as you open the door. Then close the door of the shoebox house, emphasizing the word *close*, as you close the door.

Baby free play: Allow the baby to hold and examine the spool or small object that you placed inside the shoebox house.

Learning new words: Be sure to review the words *inside* and *outside* as you move the spool or toy accordingly.

- Does the baby attempt to put the spool inside the house or does he or she show little or no interest? If there is no interest, try again later.

This activity develops:
- Awareness of the concepts *inside* and *outside*
- Eye-hand coordination
- Beginning steps in following directions
- Independence
- Awareness of *open* and *close*

Age 0 - Activity 35 – I Spy

You will need:
- Cardboard or poster board
- Scissors

Make a mirror:
1. Draw an outline of a mirror by placing a small round plate on top of the cardboard and trace the circular outline. Then include a handle at one end.
2. Cut a round hole where the glass mirror would ordinarily be in the frame.

"I Spy" game:
- Look at the baby and say, "I see (call the baby by name)."
- If other members of the family are present, pretend to see them in the "magic" mirror and call them by name.
- Use the mirror and name objects in the room that are in clear view of the baby. For example, " I see a table."
- Touch the object identified to reinforce the idea that all objects have names associated with them.

I Spy as I grow: As the child gets older, describe objects and have him or her identify them based on the description.

This activity develops:
- Interest in playing a pretend game
- Listening skills
- Visual skills
- Association of the name and object of different things

Age 0 - Activity 36 – Face Recognition

You will need:
- Picture of your baby's face

Face recognition exercise:
1. Place the picture of the baby face down on the floor.
2. Slowly turn the picture over and say, "Peek-a-boo."
3. Put the picture face down again and repeat the activity.

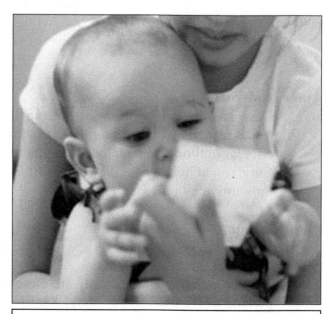

Change the voice inflection as you say the word *peek-a-boo* each time the picture is turned over.

Family names: This activity will help the baby learn to call the family members by name!

Family member's face recognition game:
- At another time, place a picture of a family member's face down on the floor and play the peek-a-boo game.
- As you slowly turn the picture over to reveal the face say, "Peek-a-boo, I see (use the family member's name)."

This activity develops:
- Interest in playing a game
- Skill in identifying family members
- Association skills
- Listening skills

Age 0 - Activity 37 – Feely Squares

You will need:
- Poster board
- At least 6 scraps of textured fabric or felt
- Fabric scissors
- Hot glue gun or stapler

Directions:
1. Cut the poster board into 12 square pieces about 5 x 5 inches.
2. Cut two matching fabric pieces into 5 x 5 inch squares until you have 6 sets.
3. Hot glue or staple the different fabric squares to the cut poster board pieces.

Feel each cloth square:
1. Place the squares side by side to resemble a patchwork quilt and allow the baby to explore.
2. Talk about colors and textures with your baby as he or she feels each square.

Matching activity extension:
- The baby may benefit from seeing and feeling two identical squares of matching cloth.
- When the baby is more familiar with the squares, he or she may show an interest in matching them.

Interesting fabrics to use:
- Silk
- Fake fur
- Suede
- Metallic
- Quilted material
- Other textured cloth

This activity develops:
- An awareness of different colors
- An awareness of different textures of cloth
- An awareness of like textures

Age 0 - Activity 38 – Poke to Feel Rough and Soft

You will need:
- 2 Styrofoam paper plates
- Bottle cap
- Piece of sandpaper
- Cotton balls

Directions:
1. Make 6 indentations on the paper plates by pressing the cap firmly on the plates.
2. Cut sandpaper the size of one plate and lay it inside one of the inverted plates so that the rough side faces the holes in that plate.
3. Pack loosely pulled cotton balls on top of the smooth side of the sandpaper sheet.
4. Place the other Styrofoam plate with the inverted side facing down on top of the other plate.
5. Staple or tape the two paper plates containing the sandpaper and cotton together.

Encouragement: The baby may be reluctant to poke his or her finger in the holes. He or she may need your encouragement to use his or her finger to poke in the holes of the paper plate.

Poking to feel:
- Poke your index finger in each of the holes on the "rough" sandpaper side.
- Turn the connected plates over and poke your index finger at random in the holes on the "soft," cotton side.
- Allow the baby to explore on his or her own.

This activity develops:
- Eye-hand coordination
- Free choice exploration
- Enhances the sense of touch
- Awareness of "rough" and "soft" textures
- Confidence

Age 0 - Activity 39 – Drop It In a Container

You will need:
- Coffee can or formula can
- Spool
- Scissors
- Masking tape

Directions:
- Take an empty coffee can with a plastic lid and remove the metal piece from the bottom end with a can opener.
- Place masking tape on any rough edges.
- Trace and then cut a hole in the plastic lid with a pair of scissors.
- The hole should be circular and a little larger than an empty sewing spool.

Model activity:
- Take a spool and drop it in the hole of the plastic lid.
- Lift the lid and find the spool.
- Repeat this activity several times.

Baby's turn: Give the baby a spool and encourage him or her to drop it in the hole of the plastic lid.

Encouragement and praise:
- This activity can be used later for the baby to do independently.
- Encourage and praise are necessary for motivation.

This activity develops:
- Eye-hand coordination
- Sense of touch
- Skill in following directions
- Independence

Age 0 - Activity 40 – Pull and Let Go

Activity assembly:

1. Use a large rubber band or a piece of elastic and fasten it securely to any small safe object such as a spool, rattle, a plastic lid, etc.
2. Tie this securely to a chair, table, playpen rail, or a doorknob so that the attached object will hang freely.

Model activity:

- Show the baby how you can pull the object and let it go.
- The baby will see that the object returns to its original position.
- Pull the attached object several more times while the baby watches you.
- Encourage the baby to help you pull or allow the baby to pull the object independently.
- Continue doing this until the baby loses interest.
- Be sure and praise the baby for any positive response that he or she makes.

Pulling and poking: Babies of this age enjoy pulling, poking and pushing objects around and will work independently if a few safe objects are made available to him or her.

This activity develops:
- Eye-hand coordination
- Sense of touch
- Skill in following directions
- Independence
- Confidence

Age 0 - Activity 41 – Name and Find It

Hold the book:
- Give the baby a book to hold and allow him or her to examine it.
- Tell the baby that he or she is holding a book.
- Ask the baby to give the book back to you.

Find the book:
- Tell the baby to watch as you hide the book under a pillow or magazine.
- Tell the baby to go and find the book.
- Retrieve the book if the baby does not seem to understand.

The word *book*. Repeat the word *book* as often as possible and eventually the baby will say the word *book*.

With other items. Choose different familiar toys like a stuffed animal to hide from the baby.
- However, hide only one object at a time.
- Call the object by name as you hide it.
- The baby will be more confident if you hide it in the same place. However, if the baby can readily find the hidden item, try another hiding place, such as under the sofa or a table. Try to hide it under something each time so that the baby will understand the spatial concept "under."
- Much praise and encouragement are needed for the motivation of this type of activity.

This activity develops:
- Following directions
- Listening
- Language development (names of objects)
- Visual perception in finding the correct objects
- Confidence
- Independence

Age 0 - Activity 42 – Which Hand?

You will need:
- A small object like a spool that will fit in the palm of your hand
- Other small objects

Directions:
- Show a small object to the baby as you identify the name of it.
- Close your hand to hide the object, and show the baby both closed fists.
- Then open your hands to reveal the hidden object. Repeat several times.

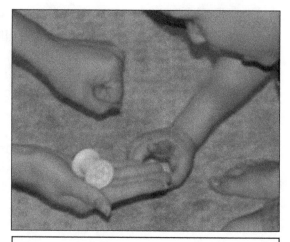

The goal is for the child to remember which hand he or she saw you hold the object in.

Alternate hands. After the baby is comfortable with this activity, feel free to alternate hands.

Hint: Changing hands behind you may tend to confuse and frustrate the baby.

This activity develops:
- Memory recall
- Association of object and the correct hand
- Interest in playing a game

Age 0 - Activity 43 – Listen and Do More

Three objects in a row. Place three objects(rattle, sock ball, stuffed animal, spoon, etc.) in a row in front of the baby.

Call them by name from left to right. Start on the left and name each object that has been placed in the row. Allow the baby to touch or hold the objects as you call them by name from left to right.

Ask for the baby to hand you each object. If the child does not understand, pick up the object and call it by name. Keep doing this until the baby understands and hands you the correct object. Be sure to praise the baby for any positive response that he or she makes.

Repeat to build confidence. If you repeat this activity often enough, the baby will gain more confidence and will welcome a change in the position of the three objects. Later the three objects may be exchanged for other items and used with the same procedure.

This activity develops:
- Following directions
- Listening
- Language development (names of objects)
- Visual perception in finding the correct objects
- Confidence
- Independence

Age 0 - Activity 44 – Command and Do

Assemble the following in a row:
- Teddy bear
- Coffee can
- Spool
- Medium-size ball

Hug the teddy bear. Model the action. Then, encourage the baby to do the activity on his or her own.

Drop the spool into the coffee can. Encourage the baby to drop the spool into the coffee can on his or her own.

Roll the ball. Model rolling the ball to the baby. Then, encourage the baby to roll the ball back to you on his or her own.
- Continue to do this until the baby understands how to go and get the ball even though it was not rolled directly to him or her.
- Try to avoid rolling the ball a long way, because it will be difficult for the baby to retrieve and roll the ball to you.

Left and right: Start each activity that corresponds with the objects from left to right.

This activity develops:
- Skill in following directions
- Listening skills
- Language development
- Eye-hand coordination
- An understanding of affection by hugging the teddy bear

Age 0 - Activity 45 – Where Does It Belong?

You will need:
- Mitten or oven mitt that is larger than the baby's hand
- Large bedroom slipper
- Hat that is easy to put on the baby's head

Mitten. Put the mitten on your hand and take it off.
- Encourage the baby to put the mitten on either one of his or her hands.
- Help the baby put the mitten on if it is necessary. Talk to the baby as you practice doing this.

Slipper. Put the slipper on your foot and take it off.
- Then encourage the baby to try it on his or her foot. Allow him or her to choose either foot.
- Help him or her if necessary. Practice this as long as the baby is interested.

Hat. Place the hat on your head and encourage the baby to take it off of your head.
- Does he or she put the hat on his or her head? If not, encourage him or her to do so.

Mitten, slipper, or hat? Place the mitten, slipper, and hat in a row. Tell the baby to put the mitten on. Does he or she put it on his or her hand or just watch you? Show him or her how, if he or she does not understand.

This activity develops:
- Listening to and following directions
- Language enrichment
- Association skills
- Confidence and independence

Age 0 - Activity 46 – Point to It

Picture of a baby's face. Cut a picture of a baby's face from a magazine or draw a face and show it to the baby.

Point to facial features and call by name. Point to the left eye on the picture of the face and say, "eye." Gently touch the baby's left eye and then touch your left eye and say the word *eye* again. Follow the same procedure for the other facial features. Repeat this activity several times or until the baby loses interest.

Touch the parts of the face and call by name. Throughout the week and whenever possible, stress the parts of the face. If the baby seems confused, spend several days on the eyes. Spend several days each on the nose, mouth, ears and hair.

Getting your baby's attention: Clap your hands and use good voice inflection to motivate the baby's interest and give him or her confidence.

Application: Point to pictures of faces in magazines and books whenever possible and allow the baby to point to the eyes, nose, mouth, ears, and hair of each face. This will enable the baby to associate the facial parts in pictures as well as those in real life.

This activity develops:
- Listening skills
- An awareness of the parts of the face
- Skill in associating different parts of the face

Age 0 - Activity 47 – Stick and Unstick

You will need:
- Masking tape or Velcro strips
- A baby toy(s)

Stick toys to the ground using masking tape or Velcro strips. Hard floors and linoleum will work best. You can also lay wax paper down on the carpet to create the "stick."

Model how to "unstick" the toy. Pretend that the toy is stuck. Then show your baby how to pull the toy off the floor.

Can you help me? Give your baby wait time after asking this question to see how he or she responds. Ask your baby to pull the toy from the floor with your help until he or she attempts to unstick the toy from the floor on his or her own.

Multiple objects: Spread out five toys, small cardboard books, or other handheld objects that the baby can "unstick" from the floor with Velcro strips or masking tape.

Frustration and safety reminders: If your baby gets frustrated, assist him or her with pulling the object from the floor so that he or she can gain success with the activity over time.

This activity develops:
- Problem solving
- Eye-hand coordination
- Memory
- Confidence and independence

Age 0 - Activity 48 – Turn It Over

Directions:
1. Select five simple, colorful pictures like a ball, house, bird, baby, and dog from a magazine or print them from the Internet.
2. Glue the pictures to one side of an index card or a plastic lid. Place them on a flat surface in a row with all of the pictures facing up.

Model turning over the cards and calling each picture by name.
- Begin on the left side and turn the first picture over.
- Say the word *over* and tell the baby the name of the picture that is on the card or lid.
- Do the same for the other four pictures keeping them in a row.

Baby's turn to find the pictures.
- Tell the baby that you have turned the card or lid over to find the picture.
- Encourage the baby to turn the second card over.
- Stress the word *over* and tell the baby the name of what is on that picture.

Helpful tips:
- Other pictures may be substituted for this activity. Choose simple, colorful pictures with little detail.
- Tell the baby the name of each picture before turning the pictures over.
- Use only a few pictures at a time to avoid confusing the baby. This will help to increase the baby's vocabulary, as well as teach him or her the spatial concept of "over."

This activity develops:
- An awareness of the concept "over"
- Eye-hand coordination
- Association skills
- Vocabulary enrichment
- Independence and confidence

Age 0 - Activity 49 – In and Out of the Box

You will need:
- Empty shoe box or empty Tupperware container
- Block
- Cup
- Stuffed animal
- Small toy
- Spoon

Model activity:
- Name the objects as you place each item inside the shoebox and emphasize the word *in* to the baby.
- Remove each item from the shoe box and place the items in front of the child outside of the shoe box. Emphasize the word *out*.

Baby's turn:
- Ask the baby to call the items you pick up by name.
- Then, instruct the baby to put the item inside of the shoebox like you modeled before.
- Encourage the baby to take one of the objects out of the box, name it, and then put it back in.
- Stress the words *in* and *out* and praise the baby for any positive response that he or she makes.

Hint:
- Give only one command at a time to avoid confusion.
- Remember to use only a few objects at a time. Too much clutter confuses babies.

This activity develops:
- Language development in naming objects
- Enhances the sense of touch
- Eye-hand coordination
- An awareness of the concepts *in* and *out*
- Independence
- Confidence

Age 0 - Activity 50 – Home Sounds

Home sound each day. Stress one familiar home sound each day throughout the week. Exaggerate the sound verbally.

Baby imitates the sound. Encourage the baby to imitate the sound that you make.

Home sounds. Listed below are some suggestions that you can use in making some home sounds. Many other sounds may be added to this list.

Appliance	Sound
Washing machine	"swish, swish"
Dryer	"mmmmmm"
Dishwasher	"squish, squish"
Telephone	"ring, ring, ring"
Vacuum cleaner	"zzzzzzzzz"
Person walking	"clip, clop"
Door bell	"ding, dong"
Car	"brm, brm"

This activity develops:
- Skill in associating home sounds with the correct object
- Verbal stimulation to imitate the sounds of home objects
- Listening for a purpose

Age 0 - Activity 51 – Face and Head Game

You will need:
- Large blank piece of paper or cardboard
- Markers
- Buttons, spools, felt, and other objects to be used for facial features

Trace the outline of your child's head with a marker on a blank piece of paper or cardboard and tell the child that you are drawing a picture of his or her head. As you draw the picture, point to each facial feature (left eye) that you draw, and point to your own and the baby's own facial feature (left eye) that matches.

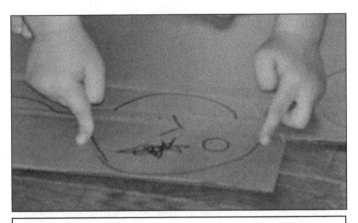

Draw: Your child may want to "draw" an eye or other facial feature with your assistance using the marker.

Baby's turn: Take his or her pointer finger and trace around the outline of the drawn head. Have the baby touch each of his or her facial features and the drawn facial features as you emphasize their names aloud.

Repeat and apply. In addition, point to the faces of the family, as well as those found in books and magazines to identify the parts of the head.

With markers. Use large buttons, spools, felt pieces, chipsof paper or anything that can be used for markers. The markers should be easy for the child to pick up and hold. Use the drawn picture of a face and instruct the child to put a marker on the facial feature that you name aloud.

> **Warning:** Do not leave the child alone with any markers that can be swallowed!

Make a puzzle. Paste a picture of a large face on cardboard or construction paper. Then cut the face in two pieces (left and right). Tell the child to put the face together.

> This activity develops:
> - Eye-hand coordination
> - Association skills
> - Listening and language development
> - Following directions and confidence
> - Awareness of left and right

Age 0 - Activity 52 – Spool Stack

You will need:
- Several spools of all shapes and sizes
- String, yarn, or a pipe cleaner
- Tape

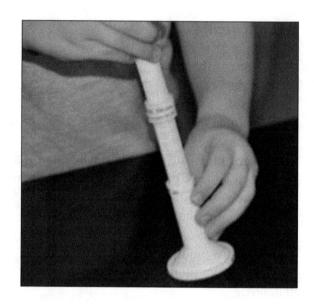

Free exploration. Allow the child to explore with thespools. If the child does not show an interest in them, encourage him or her to look at, feel, push, roll, tap, or stack and knock them down. You may need to show the child how, but be sure to allow the child to play and explore before introducing any further activity.

Roll the spools. You and your child can have fun rolling a spool back and forth to each other.

Rhythm 1-2. At another time, encourage the child to bring two spools together and tap out the rhythm of 1-2, 1-2. Sing the words, "one-two, one-two" as you clap your hands together. Stand and tap your feet on the floor to the rhythm of 1-2, 1-2.

Stack the spools. Show the child how to stack the spools into sets of two or more.

String the spools with yarn. The spools can be strung together with string or yarn. A pipe cleaner can be twisted to make a needle. Thread the string or yarn through the eye of the needle and secure the first spool for the child with a large knot or piece of tape. Show the child how to string the spools and encourage him or her to try it independently. Help him or her whenever it is necessary. Remember to give praise for any positive actions.

This activity develops:
- Free exploration
- Rhythm and awareness of the pattern 1-2
- Awareness of sets of two
- Eye-hand coordination
- Independence

Age One: From One-year-old to Two-years-old

From Curiosity to Confidence

Your curious one-year-old is beginning to display signs of independence, but he or she still needs much supervision and guidance in exploration and play. Life is a busy time for your one-year-old. Your child is more aware of himself or herself. At this age, he or she is curious and will readily explore his or her immediate environment by feeling, poking, digging, pulling, pushing, peeking, and banging. Be a proactive parent about this, by making sure that the discoveries your child is making are safe. The suggested activities in this section provide multiple ways to allow your child safe exploration with your careful guidance.

Discovering Communication

He or she will show more affection and will use gestures or point to convey wishes. Don't forget that sign language can be introduced at this age as well if you have not already tapped into its benefits before. Use an Internet Google search or your local library to investigate the many resources that are available

to teach your child sign language to reduce frustration in the communication gap between you and your one-year-old. Gradually over the coming year, your child will begin to communicate more with a limited verbal, vocabulary. Encourage your child to take the risks to talk and express himself or herself. The more you interact with your one-year-old by talking, reading, showing, and performing activities, the more comfortable your child will be in attempting to use words too!

The Importance of Wait Time

Praise your child for all efforts made to verbally communicate and validate what he or she is trying to say by giving "wait time." Wait time is the length of time you wait to listen for your child to respond. Teachers in the classroom are urged to use wait time between asking a question and having a student respond. In the same way, wait to respond for three whole seconds before finishing your child's statement or moving on. See if using wait time makes a difference in communicating with your young talker.

Building Trust and Affection

Listening to your child is just one way that you can begin to instill trust and security between you and your child, which in turn will motivate your child's learning. Hug your little one and say, "I love (child's name)." The more you model giving affection, the more your child will become aware of love and affection for others. Love and affection are necessary for a child's self image and confidence.

The Best Time to Learn Something New

Try to understand your child by observing his or her daily patterns and behaviors. Notice when your child seems to be looking for something to do. The suggested activities in this section can be introduced at a time when your child is eager to learn something new. But keep in mind that these activities are recommended to be recycled as review activities throughout the next twelve months.

Make the Activities Work for You

As a parent, watch for the right moment to interject the suggested activities into your child's day-to-day experiences. Skim the Table of Contents not only to determine which activities your child may be ready for but also to decide what activities will fit into your own schedule! For example, if you plan to spend a lot of your day in the kitchen, Activity 2 "Lids and Containers" or Activity 41 "Pots and Lids" may be just the trick to keep your child busy with a learning activity in the kitchen floor by your side. If you are planning to spend some time outside, consider the "Let's Go Walking" or "What's Outside?" activities. The order of these one-year-old activities is not regimented in this section, so make the activities work for you and your child. With this being said, recognize if your child is not quite ready or capable for an activity that you may introduce. Children develop their skills at various rates throughout these young years.

Modeling First

The key to effectively teaching your child to solve problems and to take risks is to model how to do it first. You will notice that the first step to most of the activities in this section is showing your child how to complete a task or engage in an activity successfully. Once your one-year-old sees how from you or an older sibling, he or she will be eager to join in or try on his or her own. Children between the ages of one and two watch their parents' and siblings' every move. If you have older children, remind them that their younger brother or sister is watching and will try to copy their good (or bad) behavior.

Short Attention Span

Since a one-year-old has a short attention span, look for just the right time to introduce an activity. If you begin an activity with your youngster and are not able to complete it, put it away for later, and pull it back out at another time! Planning an exact time each day to do the activities is not recommended, because young children are not time clocks even though they may be on a general schedule. Your child may sense regimentation and display negative behavior. This is not to say you should not encourage your child to stay with a task longer! But be reasonable with your one-year-old and don't push him or her too hard to stay with a task for longer than he or she can take. Learning new skills should be fun, so surround the introduction of meaningful activities with a positive attitude.

Chunking Activities into Parts

Recognizing that your one-year-old has a short attention span, chunk the activities in this section into short, manageable parts. You will notice that many of these activities have already been chunked for you. Use these parts as opportunities to "take a break," so that you can spread out one activity into three or four activities. For example, Activity 27 "Big and Little" can be broken up into three activities. Activity one can be showing your child big objects and sorting those. Activity two can be showing your child small objects and sorting those. And activity three can be sorting both big and little items into two different piles.

Read Books Aloud
Books with large, colorful pictures that have little detail appeal to children of this age group. Your little one will delight in hearing books read over and over, even though he or she may not sit still long enough for the books to be completed at a given time. Board books are recommended at this age as well as books with songs, rhymes, and rhythms. Several of these are given in the Age One activities, so feel free to repeat them often. Your child will soon be reciting his or her favorite ones from memory.

The Importance of Repetition
Going back to repeat activities in the Age Zero section of this book is highly recommended. Young children will grow in their confidence when they revisit activities that may have given them difficulty when first attempted. With time and practice these activities will be much easier for them now. Repeating is also part of the learning process. Just because you have covered an activity once does not mean that your child has completely grasped a concept or learned a skill. I encourage you to introduce an activity from this section to your child and then repeat it the next day, later in the week, and then come back to it again in a month. Hopefully, your child will begin to remember these activities and remind you of what he or she liked about them.

Activities that Grow with your Child
Keep in mind that the activities in the Age One section will grow with your child. Returning to these activities when he or she is older will continue to build confidence and self-esteem. You may notice that the children featured in the photos for this section are not all one-year-olds. Two, three, and four-year-olds will also enjoy these activities!

Note
The author and publisher are not liable for any injury or death incurred due to the misuse of the suggested materials and directions. As with all child-related activities, materials should be selected with careful attention to child safety; adult supervision is essential.

Age 1 - Activity 1 – Pick Up

Big objects you will need:
- Large paper bag
- Cup
- Block
- Spool(s)
- Clothespin
- Spoon

Little objects you will need:
- Small container
- Raisin
- Button
- Piece of yarn
- Paper clip
- Key

Put the big objects in a row. Instruct the child to put each item in the bag as you name it aloud. Tell the child to empty the bag and repeat the process. Then have the child pull the items out of the bag as you name them aloud and line them in a row.

> **Straight-line help:** If your child is having trouble putting the objects in a straight row, use a piece of masking tape to help him or her. Your child can place the objects on the masking tape line to form a straight row.

Find the objects around the room. Name one of the objects and ask the child to find it around the room and place it in a bag. Help the child if necessary.

Pick up little objects from the row. After placing the little objects in a row, have the child pick up the objects you name and place them in a small container.

Hint: *Repeat this activity only with close supervision to prevent the child from swallowing or choking on these small items.*

> This activity develops:
> - Fine motor skills
> - Listening
> - Following directions
> - Language enrichment
> - Awareness of *in* and *out*, such as *in* the bag or container

Age 1 - Activity 2 – Lids and Containers

Pans with lids. Collect a coffee can and lid, a pan with a matching lid, a Tupperware container with a lid, and several other things with matching lids.

Put the lids on the pans. Once the materials are assembled, show three of these containers to the child and allow him or her to remove and replace the lids. The child may need some help putting the correct lids on the containers, but be sure and allow the child the privilege of trial and error.

Change the type of containers throughout the week and try to let the child work independently whenever possible. Use a maximum of three containers at a time. Too many containers will confuse the child. Use the words *on* and *off* as the lids are put on and taken off.

Take on and off: Make certain that the lids will be easy for the child to take on and off. If the task is too difficult, the child will become frustrated and lose interest.

Other things with lids. Throughout the week, call the child's attention to other things that have lids. It may be in the bedroom, kitchen, bathroom, or other places. This will serve to expand your child's awareness of things in his or her immediate environment.

This activity develops:
- Problem solving through free exploration
- Awareness of *on* and *off*
- Awareness of matching lids
- Enhancement of the sense of touch

Age 1 - Activity 3 – Let's Play Ball

You will need:
- A ball for the child to grab and control
- Cardboard box to roll the ball in
- Plastic bottle

Roll the ball activity: Sit with the child and roll the ball a short distance to the child. Talk to the child and encourage him or her to catch the ball as it is rolled to him or her. Continue to do this until the child loses interest.

Repeat this activity often to develop skill in watching and receiving a ball. Praise the child whenever he or she responds positively.

Roll it straight. Once the child is comfortable in watching and receiving a ball, ask the child to roll the ball back to you. To encourage rolling the ball straight, place books on each side of the ball's path or use long blocks, a broom, or a mop for boundaries. At first, encourage the child to use both hands to roll the ball. Gradually, the child will develop skill and will be able to roll a ball successfully with one hand.

Make a tunnel to roll the ball through: A tunnel can be made with a cardboard box by cutting an opening on opposite sides of the box. A table, chair or building block tunnel may also be used for the child to roll the ball under.

This activity develops:
- Eye-hand coordination
- Tactile sensation (feel of the ball)
- Following directions
- Associating different uses for one object, the ball
- Language development by listening to words used during the activity

Age 1 - Activity 4 – Let's Go Walking

You will need:
- Strip of masking tape 5 feet long

Model walking on the straight line.
Pretend that the line is a bridge over water. Encourage the child to stay on the bridge and not accidentally fall and get wet!

Not walking yet? Remember all children develop at different rates. If your child has not begun walking yet, hold his or her hands while standing and encourage him or her to put one foot in front of the other while using your support for balance.

Child's turn. Instruct the child to put one foot in front of the other so that the heel of one foot touches the toe of the other foot. Also suggest that the child hold both arms out straight to help him or her maintain balance. Praise the child even if he or she seems to find this activity difficult.

Repeat this activity often throughout the week. The child will soon become confident in crossing the pretend bridge. You may even observe the child doing this activity independently!

Walking backwards. Once your child has mastered walking forward on the straight line, show the child how to walk backwards on the straight line. Remind your child to keep his or her eyes on the line when walking backwards. Keep trying later if at first your child shows difficulty.

This activity develops:
- Leg, foot and eye coordination
- Language interaction
- Concentration
- Following direction
- Independence

Age 1 - Activity 5 – Look at Me

You will need:
- Large sheet of blank paper or cardboard
- Crayons or markers

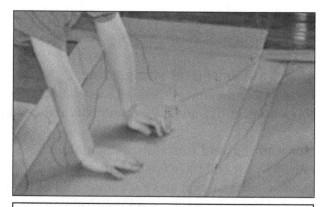

Trace the child's outline. Lay the child down on a large sheet of paper or cardboard. Trace the outline of the child's body. Tell the child to get up and look at the shape of his or her body on the paper.

Draw facial features. Ask the child what facial features to draw before you draw them. Point to the position where the particular feature should be, and ask the child what should be drawn there. Praise the child if he or she responds correctly. If not, identify the facial feature as you draw them in place. *If your child is not yet talking, this is a great way to ask where certain features are located on the cardboard body and have your child point.*

Use the outline to associate body parts. Name the neck, arms, hands, chest, stomach (tummy), legs, feet, and toes.

Colors in clothing. Look at the child's clothing and name the main color that the child is wearing. Ask the child to find that one color among the crayons that you have been using. If the child needs help, repeat the question and direct the child to look more closely. Introduce only one color at a time, and delay adding another color until the child is very comfortable in identifying a specific color.

Model coloring. Sketch in the clothing with a crayon on the outline. Show the child how to hold a crayon or marker.

The scribbling stage of writing or drawing will take place during this activity. The arms, legs and body on the paper will probably all be scribbled on. Note that most of the scribbling is up and down or round and round.

Holding a crayon: The child should be allowed to hold the crayon the way he or she feels most comfortable, even though you may have shown him or her the correct way. A child at this age may switch hands to color. It is best to allow free movement of the crayon regardless of the line boundaries of the clothing.

This activity develops:
- An awareness of the body shape
- Skill in associating the outline with himself or herself
- Awareness of a specific color and its name
- More awareness of the body parts and matching a specific color
- Language enrichment and eye-hand coordination

Age 1 - Activity 6 – What Made That Sound?

You will need:
- Timer
- Bell
- Marble in a container
- Water in a container

Say the name and hear the sound. Ring the bell or timer and say its name. Roll the marble around in the container and say its name. Swish the water around in the closed plastic container and say *water*. Do this several times and encourage the child to repeat the words too.

Hide and guess by listening. Put the containers behind something that will hide them. The hiding place must be where the child can easily go and retrieve one of the three things.
- Choose one object and make a noise with it.
- Ask the child to find the one that made the sound.

Hint: If the child makes a mistake, keep working with the same noise maker until the child successfully finds the correct one.

Other items that make sounds. Choose three other different things and tell the child to close his or her eyes or turn around while you make a sound with one of the materials. The child can then be instructed to point to the correct one. Continue to make the child aware of specific sounds throughout the house and outside.

> This activity develops:
> - Listening skills
> - Association skills
> - Following directions
> - Vocabulary enrichment
> - Confidence

Age 1 - Activity 7 – What's Outside?

Read a book and go outside. Borrow several books from the early childhood section of the library that have pictures of trees, flowers, birds, and houses. Read and talk about the pictures and tell the child some things that are found outside. Take your child outside after reading the book and point out some things that are found outside that you read about in the book.

Trees and the color green. Walk near a tree. Touch the tree and talk about how tall and big it is. If possible, let the child feel a green leaf. Emphasize that the leaf is the color green.

Flowers to touch and smell. Show the child some flowers if they are in bloom and let the child touch and smell them. Remind the child that he or she should not pick flowers without permission. Make the child aware that trees, grass, and flowers all have green leaves.

Dig in the soil and pick up a rock. Go to a place outside where some soil is visible. Take a stick and dig a little to loosen it. Let the child dig too. Encourage the child to feel the soil and tell the child that trees, grass, and flowers live in the soil. Explain that even though soil helps living things grow, soil itself is not a living thing. Pick up a rock and tell the child that a rock is NOT a living thing either. Beginning the conversation with your child about living and nonliving things early will make him or her aware and familiar with these concepts.

Roots of plants. Show the child the roots of some weeds if possible. Let the child feel the roots and observe the root hairs. Explain that roots soak up water and minerals for the trees, grass, and flowers to help them grow, and that roots also hold the plants in the ground. Make the child aware that trees, grass, and flowers are *living things*.

> *Do not expect the child to understand all of this. You are making the child aware of his or her environment. This should motivate the child to think. You can break up this activity into several parts and talk about one new thing outside every day.*

Read a book and recall. At another time during the week, read and look at a book about trees, grass, and flowers. Can your child recall anything that you saw, felt, or talked about outside? Does the child recognize the color green?

Birds. Look for birds outside. Talk to your child about where birds live and describe their nests, eggs, and how they move. Talk about how birds are different colors, because their feathers are different colors.

Yellow sun, blue sky, white clouds. Continue to discuss the colors and names of different natural surroundings. Caution the child about looking directly at the sun. He or she should know that this can damage the eyes.

Stars and Moon at night. Show the child the sky at night and point out the moon and the stars. Your discussion will depend on the child's interest. At this age, it is for awareness, and children are curious about their natural surroundings.

This activity develops:
- An awareness of the outside world
- An awareness of the colors green, yellow, blue, and white
- Vocabulary enrichment
- Enhancement of the sense of touch
- Skill in associating what is found outside and in a book

Age 1 - Activity 8 – What is Moving?

You will need:
- Stuffed animal
- Plastic cup
- Ball
- Yarn or elastic
- Blanket

Set up: Tie a piece of yarn around each object leaving 12 inches free for the child to pull. Then cover them with a blanket, but leave the three strings visible from the cover.

Model activity: Pull the string that is attached to the stuffed animal and instruct the child to watch. Be sure that you do not expose the objects that are covered. Ask the child to name the object that is moving. Tell the child to look at the shape of the covered moving object. If the child has difficulty naming the object, retrieve it for the child and identify it again. Cover the stuffed animal again and repeat the process. Do this until the child is secure in naming the moving stuffed animal.

Child's turn to pull the hidden objects with the string: Encourage the child to work independently by covering the objects and pulling the strings one at a time. The child will enjoy watching the objects move. He or she will realize that he or she is causing the motion and will find it challenging to cover the objects completely. This will encourage him or her to solve the problem when accomplishing this task.

Repeat activities. Remember to repeat some of the activities from the previous weeks, especially those that seemed difficult for the child at that time. Children enjoy and need the repetition.

This activity develops:
- Language interaction
- Visual discrimination
- Eye-hand coordination
- Independence
- Problem solving

Age 1 - Activity 9 – What Can I Smell?

Activity 1:
- Cotton balls
- Vanilla
- Apple juice
- Cold coffee

Activity 2:
- Orange juice
- Tomato juice
- Vinegar

Activity 3:
- Cinnamon
- Lotion
- Perfume
- Soap
- Other smells

Set up: Pour a little of each on cotton balls. Show the child the original container for each liquid. Have the child sniff and smell each of the liquids. Name them but do not expect the child to recall their names.

Directions: Allow the child to smell the vanilla and ask him or her to point to the correct container. If the child fails, allow him or her to smell each liquid again and identify each container again.

Warning: Tell the child that some things can hurt us if we smell them too closely. *Emphasize that he or she should never smell from any bottle or container without permission, because it could be dangerous.*

Other smells. As you work in the kitchen, encourage your child to smell the different foods that you cook. With supervision, make the child aware of the common smells of the baking of bread, cake, and cookies. Some children are curious about the different smells of spices, especially cinnamon.

Purpose of the nose. Make the child aware that some things smell good and others do not. Talk about the nose and its location. Explain to the child that the nose is used for breathing and smelling.

This activity develops:
- An awareness of the sense of smell
- Skill in matching and associating different smells
- Free exploration of safe smells

Age 1 - Activity 10 – Clothespin Fishing

You will need:
- Coffee can with plastic lid
- 12 in. string
- Clothespin

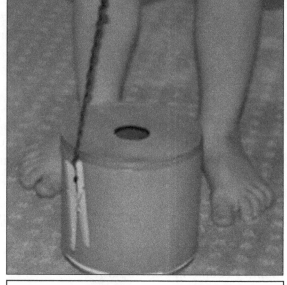

This activity will grow with your child!
So use it again when he or she gets older too!

Set up: Cut a hole in the plastic lid, a little larger than a clothespin. Place the lid on the can. Lower the attached clothespin through the hole in the plastic lid and hold on to the string.

Child's turn: Hand the child the string with the attached clothespin and tell the child to pull the string and lift the clothespin up through the hole. Allow the child to solve the problem. If the child has difficulty, assist him or her in lifting the clothespin through the hole. Be sure to praise the child for trying.

Different objects. Different objects of similar size may be substituted and put through the hole in the same manner. A different lid may be used if some of the objects are too large for the present hole. The child should be encouraged to work independently.

Fish the clothespin through the hole: For more of a challenge, reverse the activity and dangle the clothespin above the hole, lowering it slowly into the can. Give your child a turn to try.

This activity develops:
- Eye-hand coordination
- Skill in problem solving
- An awareness of the different materials used for "fish"

Age 1 - Activity 11 – Can I Dress Myself?

You will need:
- Large cardboard box
- Scissors
- Crayon
- Old shirt
- Other pieces of clothing to dress the figure with

Set up: Find a box at the grocery store that is taller than your child. Cut one long side loose from the box, and lay it flat. Trace around the child's outline with a crayon and cut it out. Together, you and your child can draw in the eyes, nose, and mouth. The child will get the feeling of the movement in drawing. Praise the child for helping. Invite the child to name the parts of the face.

Dress and undress. Use an old shirt and help the child put it on the cardboard figure. Then assist the child in removing the shirt. Allow the child to attempt to dress and undress the figure independently. However, be available to help the child to avoid frustration.

Keep in mind: This activity may be a work in progress. If it is too difficult to "dress" the cardboard, another option is to lay the clothing items in the right place on the cardboard.

Add other clothing. Give the child a pair of big socks, mittens, and a hat. Explain to the child where each piece of clothing is worn and the purpose of each. The body parts can also be reviewed at this time.

This activity develops:
- Awareness of the shape of the body
- Awareness of the body parts
- Language interaction
- Problem solving in dressing and undressing the figure
- Awareness of the purpose of clothing

Age 1 - Activity 12 – Exploring With Dirt, Sand, or Rice

You will need:
- Dishpan
- Dirt, sand, or rice
- Old shower curtain
- Wooden
- Mixing bowl
- Assorted sizes of measuring cups
- Large beans

Take it outside: This activity can be controlled inside, but can be done more easily outside.

Set up: Fill a dishpan half full of dirt, sand, or rice. Place an old shower curtain or blanket underneath the dishpan to catch any spills.

Free exploration. Allow the child to freely explore the dirt, sand, or rice, but make certain that the child does not eat or throw it.

Ask the child to tell how the dirt, sand, or rice feels. If there is no response, talk to the child about the feel of whichever one of the three you are using.

Fill containers. Later, show the child how to fill the containers by using his or her hands, the spoon, or shovel. Model how to empty the container out and start over again. Make the child aware that it takes several handfuls, spoonfuls, or shovelfuls to fill a container.

Remind your child not to put the dirt, sand, or rice in his or her mouth as it is not for eating.

Try beans! Large beans may also be used for this activity. The child can pour the beans or pick them up in handfuls. This is also a good activity for older preschoolers, so refer back to it as your child gets older.

This activity develops:
- Enhancement of the sense of touch
- Eye-hand coordination
- An awareness of different sizes of containers, especially large and small
- Free exploration
- Skill in associating what can be used to fill the containers
- Language interaction

Age 1 - Activity 13 – Cardboard Box House

You will need:
- Large cardboard box from a furniture or appliance store
- Sharp knife or scissors
- Spool for doorknob
- Masking tape
- Markers

Make a house:
1. With a large cardboard box, draw and cut out a door large enough for the child to go in and out of easily.
2. Leave the left side of the drawn door intact, so the door can open and close. Use masking tape to tape over any rough edges.
3. Draw and cut out two more windows, and encourage the child to help you decorate the outside of the house with markers.

Playtime: Invite the child to move into his or her new house. Once the child becomes familiar with the house, he or she will enjoy going in and out of the house, carrying toys back and forth to his or her new home, or taking a nap in the cardboard house.

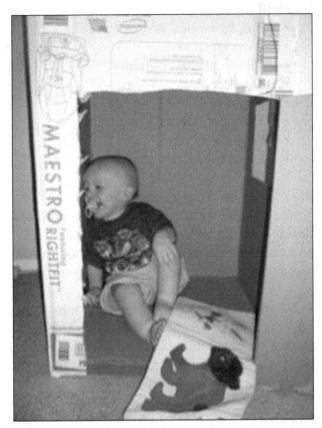

This activity develops:
- Language interaction
- Fine and gross motor coordination
- An awareness of "outside" and "inside" the cardboard house
- Security or a feeling of possessing something of his or her own

Age 1 - Activity 14 – Rhythm Band Music

You will need:
- Empty oatmeal box or coffee can
- Wooden spoon
- Closed plastic container
- Small pebbles
- 2 spoons
- 2 wooden blocks
- Keys on a ring
- Dried beans in a closed container

Make a drum. Find an empty oatmeal box or coffee can and replace the lid to make a pretend drum. Give the child a wooden spoon and encourage him or her to tap on the drum. Allow him or her to do this until he or she loses interest.

1-2-3 rhythm. Sing or chant, "Rum, tum, tum, beat the drum," which is a 1-2-3, 1-2-3 rhythm. Repeat the chant until the child attempts to repeat what you say. Then use the pretend drum and tap on it to the rhythm. Give the child a try to tap the rhythm out.

Rock shaker with 1-2-3 rhythm. Put a few small pebbles inside a closed plastic container. Let the child shake and rattle the container and listen to the new sound. While the child shakes the pebbles in the container, you can tap out the 1-2-3 rhythm with the pretend drum.

Other music makers. Two spoons can be tapped together, and two wooden blocks can be tapped or rubbed together to produce different sounds. A bunch of keys on a ring make a jingle when they are shaken. Also, dried beans in a tightly closed container will make sounds too. All of these materials can be used to emphasize the rhythmical pattern of 1-2 and 1-2-3.

This activity develops:
- Auditory discrimination
- An awareness of different rhythmical patterns
- Eye-hand coordination
- Independence
- Free exploration

Age 1 - Activity 15 – Exploring With Water

You will need:
- Sponge
- Wash cloth
- Cotton ball
- Paper towel
- A piece of celery
- Any other material that absorbs water
- Dishpan or plastic tub
- Water
- Transparent container
- Food coloring

Sponge play: Dip the edge of the sponge in the water and let the sponge absorb some water until it is completely wet. Let the child hold the sponge. The child will become aware of the change in the feel and weight of the sponge. Wring out the sponge and let the child play with the sponge and dabble with his or hands in the water.

Bath time. Give the child a dry wash cloth and tell him or her to put it in the water. Ask the child how the washcloth feels. If there is no response, discuss the wetness of the water and explain that the washcloth soaked up all the water that it could hold, making it heavier. Hold the washcloth up and allow the child to observe the water as it drips down from it.

Cotton ball color change. In a container filled with water, add a few drops of food coloring. Identify the chosen color by name. Take a dry, white cotton ball and put it into the colored water. The child will enjoy seeing the white cotton ball change color. Repeat this activity with a paper towel, but encourage the child to choose a different color of food coloring.

Celery color change. Give the child a stalk of celery at another time and encourage him or her to smell, feel, and taste it. Place the celery stalk in a container of water and add red or blue food coloring to the water while the child is watching. Place the stalk of celery in the colored water. From time to time, let the child observe how it absorbs water and changes color over the next day.

This activity develops:
- Further awareness of the sense of touch
- Eye-hand coordination
- Free exploration
- Observational skills

Age 1 - Activity 16 – Through the Hole

You will need:
- 5 keys about the same size
- Plastic container or coffee can
- Circles cut from Styrofoam meat trays
- Buttons
- Pennies
- Plastic bread tabs

Set up: Cut a slit from a plastic container or coffee can lid. The slit should be large enough so that the keys can be pushed through the hole. Place the lid on the container.

Push through the hole and into the container. Encourage the child to pick up a key and push it through the slit in the lid of the container. Allow the child to continue until all of the keys have been pushed through the slit. Remove the lid, empty out the keys, and repeat the process.

Add on: Once the child has mastered this activity with keys, try the other objects listed above. These materials will not only add variation, but they will enhance the experiences for the child.

The activity develops:
- Fine motor control
- Problem solving
- Following directions
- Eye-hand coordination
- Independence and confidence
- Enhances the sense of touch

Age 1 - Activity 17 – Finger Paint Bag

You will need:
- Finger paint
- Wax paper
- Old shirt for a smock
- Ziploc bag
- Packing tape

Set up: Use a spoon and place a blob of finger paint on a large sheet of wax paper taped to a table.

Model: Show the child how to move and slide the fingers and hands across the wax paper. Use the word *slippery* and *wet* in your conversation with the child.

Child's turn: Encourage the child to move his or her hands up and down, back and forth, and around. Use the pointer finger to make some dots across the paper and allow the child to explore.

Use a paint bag instead! If your child is prone to putting fingers in his or her mouth, the paint bag option allows you to eliminate this potential problem!

How to save finger paint art: Press a piece of computer paper firmly over the picture. Carefully lift the top edge of the paper and pull it away from the wax paper. You will then have the picture printed on the paper. When the picture is *dry*, allow the child to feel it. Talk about how the paint feels different now that the water has evaporated.

Less mess? Make a paint bag!
1. Fill a Ziploc bag with a little bit of paint.
2. Seal the bag shut. Add packing tape to secure.
3. Set on the table and let the child make shapes with his or her fingers on the paint bag.

This activity develops:
- Free exploration
- Creativity
- Fine motor control
- More awareness of wet, dry, and slippery
- Independence and confidence

Age 1 - Activity 18 – Paint With a Brush

You will need:
- Large sheet of old newspaper
- Tape
- Food coloring
- Water in a pan
- Paintbrush

Set up: Tape an old newspaper to a table top. Mix a few drops of food coloring with water and place the paintbrush in the colored water. Model how to brush over the newspaper gently while your child is watching.

Child's painting exploration: Allow the child to explore with the paintbrush and colored water. Assist the child only when it seems necessary and praise the child for trying.

Different color every day: Daily painting with a new color might motivate your child. With practice, the child will make progress in handling the paintbrush and painting.

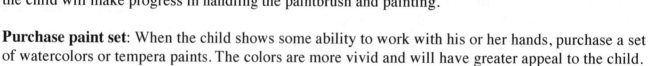

Purchase paint set: When the child shows some ability to work with his or her hands, purchase a set of watercolors or tempera paints. The colors are more vivid and will have greater appeal to the child.

> The activity develops:
> - Eye-hand coordination
> - Free exploration and creativity
> - More awareness of different colors

Age 1 - Activity 19 – Inside and Outside

You will need:
- Cardboard or paper plates
- Scissors
- Markers
- Hoola hoop
- Bean bag

Set up: Cut two circles from the cardboard or paper plates. One circle should be bigger than the other. Color the circles with markers.

Put the smaller circle inside of the larger circle. Show the child how the *smaller* circle fits inside of the *larger* one. As you do this, tell the child about what you are doing. Emphasize the word *inside*. Then take the smaller circle and place it on the left of the larger circle and tell the child that you took the smaller circle outside of the larger circle. Emphasize the word *outside*.

Hoola hoop and beanbag toss activity. Lay a hoola hoop down on the floor and encourage the child to jump inside and outside of the circle. The hoola hoop may also be used for the child to throw a beanbag inside of the boundary. The spatial concepts of *inside* and *outside* should be emphasized through conversation so that the child will understand.

The activity develops:
- An awareness of *inside* and *outside*
- An awareness of *large* and *small*
- Gross motor coordination
- Eye-hand coordination
- Following directions

Age 1 - Activity 20 – Upstairs and Downstairs

You will need:
- 3 stairs or
- 3 boxes that are weighted inside for stability for temporary stairs

Set up: If you do not have stairs in your home, place the imitation stairs against a wall to give the illusion of real stairs.

Emphasize the words *up* and *down*. Encourage the child to go up and down the stairs with the following jingle:

> (Child's name) goes up, up, up.
> (Child's name) comes down, down, down.

Practice. With much practice, the child will soon gain enough confidence to go higher up the stairs. For safety reasons, three stairs should be enough for a child of this age without supervision.

Talk about safety. The child should be made aware of the consequences if he or she is not careful when climbing and descending the stairs. The child should also be told not to leave toys on the stairs, because they may cause someone to fall.

> The activity develops:
> - An awareness of *up* and *down*
> - Self-confidence
> - Independence
> - Gross motor coordination
> - Listening

Age 1 - Activity 21 – Explore With Play Dough Part 1

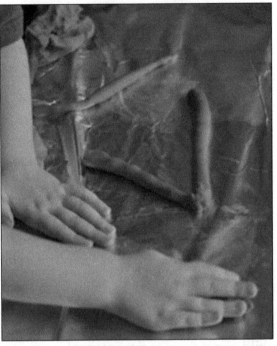

Play Dough Recipe

1 cup flour
1 tablespoon oil
1 cup water
½ cup salt
2 teaspoons cream tartar
food coloring

Mix ingredients. Cook over medium heat until the mixture forms a ball. Knead until smooth. Keep in a plastic bag or sealed container.

Set up: Tape wax paper to the table top for easy cleanup.

Play: Give the child a piece of play dough that can be held comfortably in his or her hands. Show the child how to squeeze, roll, and pat the clay. Encourage the child to poke, pull, roll, and break the clay into pieces. Let the child play under your guided supervision.

Reminder: Explain to your child that the play dough is not for eating. No ingredients are toxic if he or she accidentally eats some of it. Once your child has tasted the play dough, he or she probably won't want to eat the play dough as it is very salty.

Play dough shapes: Roll the play dough into a long roll and join the two ends together to make a circle and other shapes. Talk to the child about each shape that you make.

The activity develops:
- Fine motor coordination
- Enhancement of the sense of touch
- Free exploration
- Language enrichment through conversation
- Creativity
- Independence

Age 1 - Activity 22 – Cardboard Puzzles

You will need:
- 3 large pictures with bright colors and little detail printed from the internet
- Glue
- Cardboard
- Scissors

Before: Show the child each picture and identify it by name (house, truck, or tree).

Set up: Glue each of the pictures to a piece of cardboard and allow them to dry. Then cut each picture in half from top to bottom, so each picture has a total of two puzzle pieces that fit together in the middle.

Puzzle activity: Mix the pieces of one puzzle and place them on the floor. Encourage the child to put them together to make a picture. If your child is confused, model first and then let your child try. Help the child if he or she does not seem to understand and talk about each picture.

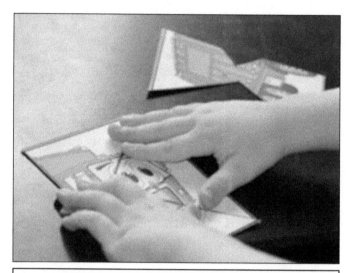

Only three puzzle pieces: It is advisable to use only three puzzles at a time, because too many pieces will confuse young children.

Independent play: These puzzles can be used over and over. The child will become more confident at putting the pictures together on his or her own.

More puzzle pictures: Three other pictures with more detail may be cut from a magazine or newspaper and be used in the same manner. These pictures may be cut into either two or three pieces. The child will be more successful if the picture images are large, colorful, and have little detail.

Enrichment: As your child gets older, he or she may need more of a challenge. You may want to combine the puzzle pieces of all three pictures for your child to unscramble and then put together once he or she is confident with just one.

This activity develops:
- An awareness that two or more parts make a whole
- More awareness of color
- Language enrichment through conversation
- Eye-hand coordination

Age 1 - Activity 23 – Drop Into the Bottle

You will need:
- Large plastic, non-breakable bottle with narrow opening
- Popsicle stick
- Pencil with no point
- Clothespin
- Other safe objects that will easily go through the small opening

Drop small objects into the bottle. Encourage the child to choose an object and drop it into the narrow opening of the bottle. Assist the child if necessary.

Listen for the sound. Exaggerate the sound as you imitate it in some manner. Words like *ping* and *plop* will serve to make the child listen more closely as each object is dropped into the bottle.

Turn the bottle upside down to get the objects out. Allow the child to use both hands and shake the objects out. Repeat this activity and encourage the child to work independently. Assist the child only when he or she appears to need help.

This activity develops:
- Eye-hand coordination
- Problem solving
- Listening for a purpose
- Self-confidence
- Following directions
- Language interaction

Age 1 - Activity 24 – I Can Carry a Tray

You will need:
- Meat tray
- Small block
- Spool(s)
- Clothespin
- Spoon
- Other lightweight, non-breakable objects
- Small plastic ball

Set up: Place the lightweight, non-breakable objects on a meat tray.

Carry the tray with everything on it. Encourage the child to balance the tray and carry it a short distance. Then instruct the child to bring the tray back without dropping any of the items. If one falls off the tray, tell the child to pick up the object that fell and place it back on the tray. If the child has any difficulty, be ready to assist but allow the child to do as much independently as possible.

Balance a ball on the tray. At another time, place a small plastic ball on the tray. Instruct the child to walk carefully with the tray and to watch the ball. With patience and guidance, your child will succeed. Observe the way that the child balances the tray and make positive suggestions for the child to keep the ball on the tray. If the ball falls off, tell the child to get the ball and to try again. Remind the child to walk slowly, carefully, and to watch the ball. With patience and guidance your child will succeed.

This activity develops:
- Skill with the sense of balance
- Coordination using both hands
- An awareness of *light* and *heavy*
- Skill in manipulation and observation of different objects on the tray
- An awareness of stationary objects and the effect that the moving ball has on balance

---

Age 1 - Activity 25 – Envelope Boat With Fish

You will need:
- 4 cut out fish from different colored index cards using a simple stencil
- Large business envelope for a boat
- Markers to decorate boat and fish

Fish in the boat. Encourage the child to pick up a fish and put it in the boat. This will require the child to separate the two flaps of the envelope and slip the fish inside. Call the fish by color when the child picks up the fish in the boat. After all the fish have been "caught" and are in the boat, you can take the fish out and start again.

Count the fish. Write a number on each of the fish from one to four. Teach your child the first four numbers and what they look like. Count the fish several times to make sure that the child understands counting one to four before going any further.

Find the fish with the number. Begin teaching your child what numbers look like. Use the numbered fish and instruct the child to find the fish with a specific number on it to put in the envelope.

At this age, your child will most likely only listen to you count aloud. But with repetition, he or she will begin to join in.

This activity develops:
- Skill in picking up a flat object
- Eye-hand coordination
- Problem solving
- Confidence
- Independence
- Language interaction

Age 1 - Activity 26 – Where Is the Room?

Rooms of the house.
1. Take the child by the hand and together walk to his or her room. Explain where you are headed.
2. Walk with the child to your room and have a conversation about where you are going together.
3. Then walk to the bathroom and identify it. Make sure that the child knows the names of these three rooms.

Child shows the rooms of the house. Ask the child to show you his or her room. If the child seems confused, show him or her again to remind him or her where it is located. Repeat this until the child can show you the correct room asked for.

Repeat to gain confidence. Continue this activity with your room and the bathroom. If the child still seems to be confused, try again at another time.
However, if the child is successful and appears to be enjoying this activity, choose other rooms of the house and repeat the process.

Be patient. It may take several days for the child to go to the correct room when requested, but praise and encouragement are keys to motivation and success.

> This activity develops:
> • An awareness of rooms and their positions
> • Following directions
> • Language interaction
> • Confidence

Age 1 - Activity 27 – Big and Little

You will need:
- Big spoon and little spoon
- Big lid and little lid
- Empty toilet paper roll and paper towel roll
- Big shoe and little shoe
- Other big and little objects

Show the difference between big and little. Pick up the big spoon and explain that it is bigger than the other spoon. Identify them as *big* and *little* several times as you continue to show the child the big and little objects of each kind. Place the big and little items of the same set together, preferably in a row.

Sort what is big. From the pile of big and little objects, ask the child to find all of the *big* items. As the child works, praise him or her when the right objects are chosen. If the child picks up an incorrect item, tell the child what it is, identify the size, and tell the child to put it back in place.

> **Tips:**
> - Continue working only with the concept of *big* until the child is confident in choosing the bigger item correctly.
> - Avoid using the word *large*.
> - Interchanging words at this age may confuse the child.

Identify what is little. Introduce the *little* concept when the child is secure in choosing the bigger object. Changing the commands for the child to choose between *big* and *little* during one sitting of this activity may be too difficult and confusing for him or her.

Caution: It is better for your child to be confident in doing an activity than to be confused and frustrated with one that is too difficult. *This goes for all previous activities as well.*

> This activity develops:
> - An awareness of the concepts *big* and *little*
> - Vocabulary enrichment in naming the objects
> - Following directions
> - Skill in making a choice
> - An awareness of comparison
> - Eye-hand coordination

Age 1 - Activity 28 – Stepping Stones

You will need:
- Big carpet piece (or bath mat)
- Little carpet piece (or place mat)
- Small toy fish or crab

Set up: Lay the big and little carpet pieces in front of each other like a path with a small space between.

Step to the next carpet square activity:
Model and instruct the child to step on the big carpet piece first. Then to step forward on the little carpet piece. Instruct the child to turn around, pick up the big carpet piece and place it in front of the little carpet piece. The child can continue to step forward on the squares, placing the next square in front of the other as he or she takes a step forward.

Carpet size: Both carpet pieces should be small enough for the child to lift and move but big enough for the child to stand on.

An object such as a toy fish or crab may be placed at the end of the given point as an incentive for the child to move forward.

Stepping-stones across a river. The squares can be called stepping-stones for the child to use in crossing a pretend river. Remind the child to be careful, so that he or she does not lose his or her balance and fall into the river. Increasing the distance between the carpet squares each time will challenge him or her to try harder to be careful.

This activity develops:
- Better coordination of large and small muscles
- An increased awareness of *big* and *little*
- Independence
- Confidence
- An awareness of distance
- Following directions
- Enhancement of the sense of touch in moving the square pieces

Age 1 - Activity 29 – Stencil Up and Down

You will need:
- Stencil of a rectangle 2" x 6" out of cardboard
- Crayons of different colors
- Paper
- Tape

Set up: Tape the paper to the table top, and then tape the rectangle stencil on top of the paper.

Up and down stencil time. Move your finger up and down with your child, feeling the cut out area of the cardboard piece. Have the child choose a crayon. Name its color. Instruct the child to move the crayon up and down inside the cut out area. Tape the cardboard stencil to another place on the paper and allow the child to do it again.

Across from left to right. Follow the same procedure as before, except turn the cut out rectangle so that the longer sides are in a horizontal position. With a crayon, the child can move the crayon back and forth from side to side on the paper that is underneath the cardboard stencil.

Up and down. Up and down.
I am drawing, up and down.

Back and forth and across you go.
Left to right and now I know.

This activity develops:
- An awareness of vertical and horizontal direction
- An awareness of boundaries
- Eye-hand coordination
- Freedom of choice
- An awareness of different colors
- Language interaction with the jingles

Age 1 - Activity 30 – Veggie Stamps

You will need:
- Tempera paint
- Blank paper
- Old shirt for smock
- Paper plate

Vegetables for stamping:
- Carrot
- Celery
- Mushroom head
- Broccoli floweret

Set up: Cut off one end of a carrot. Tape the paper to a flat work area. Pour a little paint onto a paper plate.

Stamp the vegetables activity: Dip the cut end of the carrot in the paint and press it on the paper like a stamp. Allow the child to hold the carrot and take a turn stamping. Assist your child in pressing firmly to print the shape on the paper. Then allow him or her to stamp the vegetables while you supervise.

Tips:
- Remind the child of vegetables' colors.
- Make only two or three vegetables available at one time to prevent overwhelming the child.

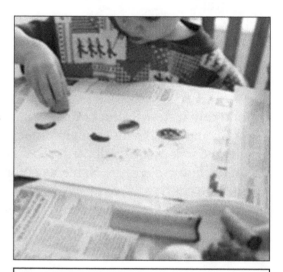

Vegetables: The child can make interesting pictures with a combination of different vegetables and colors.

This activity develops:
- Creativity
- An appreciation of the beauty of color and shape
- Eye-hand coordination
- Free exploration when stamping
- More of an awareness of different colors
- A new sensation with the sense of touch in stamping with different vegetables

Age 1 – Activity 31 – This Side, That Side

You will need:
- Piece of yarn
- Tape for boundary line

Ten small objects like:

Rubber ducky	Clothespin
Key	Block
Button	Paperclip
Crayon	Spoon
Cup	Cotton ball

Right and left: Use the words *right* and *left* to get your child used to recognizing these key words.

This Side = Left
That Side = Right

Set up: Use masking tape to make a straight line down the middle of a tabletop, dividing it into two halves.

This side, that side. Pick up an object and say "This side," as you place that object on the *left* side of the boundary formed by the yarn. Pick up another object and say, "That side," as you place the second object on the *right* side of the boundary. Have the child alternate placing an object left and then right in a pattern.

Using words. Encourage the child to say, "this side" when the child places an object on the left side of the boundary. Encourage the child to say, "that side" when the child places an object on the right side.

This activity develops:
- Listening skills
- Eye-hand coordination
- Further awareness of left and right
- Enhancement of the sense of touch of the different objects
- Verbal skills
- Confidence

Age 1 - Activity 32 – On and Off Rubber Bands

You will need:
- 10 rubber bands of various sizes
- Doorknob
- Small plastic container to keep rubber bands in

Put rubber bands on the doorknob: Show the child how to put a stretchable band on a doorknob. Then allow the child to try to put one on the doorknob. If the child is successful, allow him or her to put the rest of the rubber bands on the door independently. This activity may be easier with a round doorknob. Depending on what kind of doorknobs you have in your house, you may want to wait on this activity until your child has better fine motor skills.

Take rubber bands off the doorknob. When all of the rubber bands are on the doorknob, show the child how to take them off and place them in a container. Encourage the child to repeat this activity until he or she loses interest.

Independence: Completing activities on his or her own at this age is exciting for your child. Modeling shows the child how but enables him or her to do it by himself or herself even if he or she struggles a little.

Enrichment. The child can place a rubber band on every doorknob in the house. Then you can instruct the child to remove all of the rubber bands from the doorknobs and place them in the container.

This activity develops:
- Following directions
- An awareness of stretchable materials
- An awareness of *on* and *off*
- Problem solving
- Independence
- Eye-hand coordination
- Fine motor skills

Age 1 - Activity 33 – Straw and Spool Stack

You will need:
- Several long straws
- 10 sewing spools

Spools are easily found at a local craft or fabric store by asking a sewing machine instructor or distributor for any leftover or discarded spools from a class or demonstration!

Stack and knock down: Stack the spools on top of each other. Gently knock the stack of spools down.

Stack with a straw in the center. This time place a straw in the center of the stack while stacking. Attempt to knock the stack down as you did before. What happens?

Compare the two stacks: Ask the child to knock the two stacks down. The child will realize that the one stack will stay in place, while the other stack can be readily knocked down.

Stack the spools high: Encourage your child to stack the spools as high as he or she can. Next, the child can carefully put a straw in the center of the stacked spools. If the stack is high enough, two straws may be needed. The child may just enjoy exploring with the spools instead of stacking.

Encourage his or her discovery:
- Roll the spools back and forth.
- Stack the spools with straws for support.
- Knock the spools that are stacked down and watch them fall.

This activity develops:
- Eye-hand coordination
- An awareness of different size spools
- Visual skills through observation of the spools
- An awareness of more than one
- An awareness of support to prevent the spools from falling

Age 1 - Activity 34 – Stuff It In the Box

You will need:
- Strips of cloth knotted together to form a long chain
- Shoe box or upside down tissue box with a hole in the lid about an inch wide

Set up: Stuff the cloth chain through the hole in the lid. Continue until almost all of the chain is inside of the shoe box and only a small piece of it is sticking out of the hole in the box.

Pull the cloth chain out. Model pulling the cloth chain out of the box through the hole. Allow the child to have a turn pulling the cloth chain knot by knot out of the box. Emphasize the word *out* as the child pulls the chain out of the box.

Stuff it back in the box. Once the cloth chain has been completely pulled out of the box's hole, take one end of the chain and model stuffing it back inside of the box through the hole. Allow the child to continue pushing the cloth chain back into the box. Emphasize the word *in* while your child is doing this.

This activity develops:
- More awareness of *in* and *out*
- Skill in manipulating the strip
- Tactile enhancement
- Skill in visual observation

Age 1 - Activity 35 – Clothespin Snap

You will need:
- Shoebox without a lid
- 12 clothespins
- Red dot stickers

Set up: Put sticker dots around the top edge of the box about 3 inches apart.

Put the clothespin on a dot.
- Use an upside down clothespin to place on one of the sticker dots at the top edge of the box.
- Encourage the child to try to put the clothespin on the next red dot.
- Continue with this activity until all of the clothespins are used.
- Help the child if needed during the activity.
- Show your child how to take the clothespins off.
- Emphasize the words *on* and *off*.
- Count the clothespins with the child for number awareness.

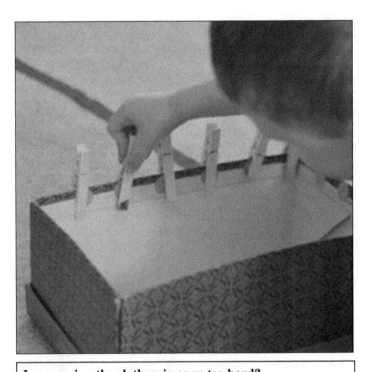

Is squeezing the clothespin open too hard?
Don't worry! Use the upside down "open" side of the clothespin to begin. As your child's fine motor skills and hand strength develops, squeezing the clothespin open will be his or her next challenge to conquer.

Enrichment. This activity may be repeated many times and will be more interesting with colored or painted clothespins and a decorated shoebox. As the child progresses, stickers, shapes, numbers, or letters may be used instead of red dots.

This activity develops:
- Eye-hand coordination
- An awareness of *on* and *off*
- Tactile enhancement
- Matching one to one
- Skill in visual observation

Age 1 - Activity 36 – Shake and Find

You will need:
- 3-5 spice containers covered with construction paper
- Jingle bell
- Paper clip
- Button
- Marble
- Teaspoon of rice or beans

Set up: Put one of the objects inside a spice container and cap it. Leave all the rest of the containers empty and place them in a row.

Shake and listen. Shake each container and encourage the child to listen for a sound from one of the containers. By listening, the child should be able to choose the container that has the object inside.

Play a game. Change the object out for another item. Use only one item in a container at a time to compare with the other empty containers until the child is confident. Then two containers can be used with the objects inside. The child can later sort the ones that make a sound and play the game "This Side, That Side" as in Activity 31 through this listening activity.

This activity develops:
- Skill in auditory discrimination
- Listening for a purpose
- Skill in making a logical choice
- Memory recall

Age 1 - Activity 37 – Basket of Flowers

You will need:
- Piece of Styrofoam
- Plastic cup, grocery berry basket, or other container
- 5 flowers (made from tissue paper and pipe cleaner)

How to Make Tissue Paper Flowers:

1. Cut about eight circles from tissue paper.
2. Stack the circles on top of each other.
3. To attach, poke the end of a pipe cleaner through the center of the circles.
4. Fold over the top of the pipe cleaner to hold the petals in place.
5. Scrunch up the paper and fluff out the petals to make them look like a flower.

Set up: Wedge the piece of Styrofoam into the container. Punch 5 holes in the Styrofoam and dot each hole with a red marker, so that your child will be able to clearly see the holes.

Model how to place the flower stem in the hole. Talk to the child about the parts of the flower including the stem and the petals.

Child's turn: Encourage the child to place a flower stem in each of the five holes of the Styrofoam. Direct the child to remove the flowers and then place them back in the holes several times.

Real plants outside: Take the child outside and show him or her a stem of a real plant (flower). Pull up a weed and show the child the root of the plant. Allow the child to feel and examine the root of the weed. Roots are connected to the stem and hold the plant in the ground. Instruct the child not to pick flowers without permission.

This activity develops:
- Skill in looking for detail (the holes in the Styrofoam)
- Matching one to one (flower to hole in the Styrofoam)
- An awareness of flowers, stems, and roots
- Language interaction

Age 1 - Activity 38 – Dip and Dab Paint Activity

You will need:
- Large Styrofoam meat tray
- Tempera paint
- Paint brush
- Paper
- Blunt pencil

Set up: Show your child how to hold the pencil and poke holes in the Styrofoam tray. Encourage the child to be gentle and press firmly to make good indentations in the tray. If this is too difficult for your child, feel free to make the holes yourself but be sure to give your child an opportunity to try.

Paint activity:
1. Model how to dip the paintbrush in the paint and then take the point of the paintbrush and stick it into one of the holes in the tray.
2. Fill the hole with several dabs of paint.
3. Begin filling another hole with paint.
4. When all of the holes have been filled with paint, lift the tray up off the paper to see the paint design made by hole imprints.

Poke activity: Allow the child to poke indentations on another Styrofoam tray for free exploration.

Questions to ask: If the child chooses to paint independently observe the movement of his or her painting strokes.

- Are they up and down?
- Are the strokes from left to right?
- Are they in a circular motion?

All of these arm movements are developmental. Through practice, your child's arm movements through drawing and painting will soon create basic forms of objects that will have meaning to the child.

This activity develops:
- Free exploration
- Eye-hand coordination
- More of an awareness of color
- Creativity
- Confidence and independence

Age 1 - Activity 39 – Collect and Return

You will need:
- Tote bag with handle for carrying
- 3 rooms for the child to visit
- 3 safe objects like a baby shoe, spool, and bell

Directions:
1. Place one safe object in each of the rooms the child will visit in the house.
2. Give the child a bag and go with him or her to the first room, instructing him or her to put the safe object in the bag.
3. Name the object and tell your child to put it in the bag.
4. Have the child go to the second and third rooms to collect the named objects.

Explain: Once the child has the three objects in the bag, ask the child to name each object. If he or she needs help, repeat the names of the objects. Talk about each of the objects and instruct the child to return each object to the room he or she found it in. Go with the child and assist if necessary.

Variation: This activity can be used with other rooms of the house and different objects. The child should be learning to identify each room by name and whose room it belongs to. This activity can be repeated outside using trees, sidewalks, light poles, and other stationary objects for boundaries.

This activity develops:
- Skill in memory recall
- Association of positions in space
- Following directions
- Language interaction
- Skill in observation and different objects
- Confidence and independence

Age 1 - Activity 40 – Rip It

You will need:
- Old magazine or paper that is no longer needed
- Large paper bag

Model: Give the child the magazine or paper and show him or her how to rip out the pages and tear them in half.

Remind the child that not all magazines are for ripping and that he or she may only rip old magazines with permission.

Crumple it up instead of ripping? Encourage your child to make scrunched balls with the paper if he or she is more interested in doing this instead.

Child's turn: Encourage the child to rip out a page from the magazine and put it in the opened paper bag. Allow the child to continue to rip and put the pages in the bag to "clean up." Emphasize the sound the paper makes when the pages are ripped.

Lay torn strips in a pile. To add on to this activity, show your child how to make a pile with the ripped strips of paper.

What to do if my child is tempted to eat the paper? It is a natural instinct for your child to want to put objects in his or her mouth during the early stages of development. If the child is more focused on eating the paper rather than ripping it or crumpling it, gently take the paper out of your child's hand and revisit this activity at another time.

Revisit previous activities: Previously completed activities from the Age 1 and Age 0 sections can be repeated. Not only will they be beneficial, but your child will also derive many new skills by repeating them.

This activity develops:
- An awareness that paper can be changed by ripping or crumpling
- Listening for a purpose (paper ripping)
- An awareness of how to clean up a mess (putting paper in the bag)
- Confidence and independence

Age 1 - Activity 41 – Pots and Lids

You will need:
- 3 pots with matching lids
- 3 small objects to put in the pots
- Masking tape or string for a line

Mix lids, explore, and watch: Mix the lids and the pots to allow the child to explore with the pots. Observe the child.
- Does he or she match the lids correctly with the pots?
- Does he or she just bang them to make noise?

Model: After some free playtime, show your child how each lid matches with the same-sized pot. Give your child a turn and help him or her if needed.

Put an object in the pot: Be sure the child knows the names of the three objects and place one object in each pot. After your child puts the lids on the pots, instruct the child to find a specific object in one of them. Continue with this activity until all three objects have been found successfully.

Explore or model first? Notice in this activity, the modeling of matching lids to pots was suggested after some free play. Sometimes giving your child exploration time on his or her own (with supervision), enables your child to figure out how things fit or match independently. This encourages problem solving.

Metal pot lid cymbals: Metal pot lids make excellent play cymbals. Your child can use them to clash together to make a cymbal noise!

This activity develops:
- Free exploration
- Problem solving
- Matching
- Sorting
- Independence and confidence

Age 1 - Activity 42 – Funnel Fun With Colored Rice

You will need:
- Funnel
- Different sized plastic bottles
- Big bowl
- Water, sand, or rice to fill the bottles
- Food coloring
- Rubbing alcohol

Model: Show the child how to use the funnel to pour into a large bowl and then pour and fill the plastic bottles using the funnel.

Child's turn: After a brief instruction, allow the child to work independently while you supervise. Dump the rice from the bottles back into a large bowl and repeat this activity as long as there is interest. Encourage your child to feel each material while he or she is working with it.

Make this an outside activity! In order to eliminate the stress of mess and clean up, throw a blanket out on the grass and have your child complete this activity outside!

Change the color of the rice: At another time, fill a bottle ¾ full with white rice. Then add a few drops of food coloring and two tablespoons of rubbing alcohol. Cover and shake well. Use the color change as a topic of conversation with your child. Reinforce the color's name and explain how the rice changed color from white to _____. Allowing your child to choose the color to change the rice will help him or her take more ownership of the activity!

This activity develops:
- An awareness of how to pour and fill a container
- An awareness of *empty* through free exploration
- Eye-hand coordination
- Tangible enhancement

Age 1 - Activity 43 – The Big Button

You will need:
- Plastic lid
- Scissors
- Piece of cloth
- Single hole punch
- Yarn 24 in. long
- Twisty bag tie
- Shirt or coat with large buttons

Set up:
1. Glue a piece of cloth to the top of a plastic lid.
2. Cut a slit in the cloth a little larger than the plastic lid.
3. Punch 4 holes in the plastic lid to resemble a button. You may need to use scissors to better puncture the lid if the lid's plastic is thick.
4. Tie a piece of yarn to a twisty bag tie. Twist the bag tie several times to make a "needle."

Developmental skills: This activity increases the fine motor skill and eye-hand coordination of poking the "needle" through the hole and dragging the string through it.

Sewing: Show the child how to use the needle to go in and out of the holes of the imitation button. Encourage the child to follow your directions, but if he or she insists, allow him or her to go in and out of the holes at random.

Button and unbutton: A shirt or coat with large buttons can be given to the child to practice buttoning and unbuttoning. Buttoning will most likely be easier than unbuttoning for the child at first. When the child shows enough skill, a shirt with smaller buttons may be introduced.

This activity develops:
- Problem solving
- Eye-hand coordination
- Tactile enhancement
- Following directions

Age 1 - Activity 44 – Fold It

You will need:
- Old magazine with colorful pages
- Old newspaper or paper

Model folding: Show the child how to fold the pages in half while the pages are still intact to the magazine.

Child's turn: Allow the child to fold the pages until he or she loses interest. Use the word *half* in talking with the child at various times throughout the week to emphasize the concept.

Triangle fold: At another time, use a magazine page to show the child how to fold the top right edge of the page down. A new shape (triangle) will be formed in the fold. Use the word *top* in your conversation with the child. If your child is interested in helping you make a triangle fold, give him or her a corner to fold. Use the words *top* and *bottom* with the child whenever possible to ensure that the child has a working knowledge of these concepts.

Interested only for a moment? Remember that the period of interest at this age is very brief. Don't force your child to stay with an activity if he or she is ready to move on to something else.

Make a hat:
1. Fold an old newspaper's top edges down diagonally to form two triangles.
2. Then fold each half of the opened bottom up to form a paper hat brim.

This activity develops:
- Feeling and folding paper
- Eye-hand coordination
- An awareness of *half* and *whole*
- An awareness of *top* and *bottom*
- An awareness that paper has more than one use
- Confidence and independence in folding

Age 1 - Activity 45 — Where Is It?

You will need:
- Sock ball or bean bag

Follow directions: Tell the child to find one of the following body parts at a time and touch it with a sock ball or bean bag.

- head	- arm
- eye	- hand
- nose	- leg
- ear	- foot
- mouth	- stomach (tummy)

Review body parts: If the child has difficulty, review the body parts and repeat the game. The more this activity is repeated, the more confident the child will become.

Point or touch? Instead of touching, the child may wish to point. Touching and pointing are two different concepts. The child should be encouraged to do one or the other when you are doing this activity with him or her. Holding an object and using it to touch something is more advanced than just pointing.

This is a three-step activity in which the child must (1) listen, (2) locate, and then (3) touch a specific body part.

Say its name: This is an activity that can grow with your child. As he or she begins talking, he or she can call out the name of the body part that he or she is pointing to.

This activity develops:
- Following directions
- Further enhancement of the sense of touch
- An awareness of the commands: *point* and *touch*
- Hand coordination
- Further awareness of body parts

Age 1 - Activity 46 – Squeeze the Dropper to Move the Water

You will need:
- Medicine dropper
- 2 clear containers
- Water
- Food coloring
- Meat baster

Set up: Place a drop or two of food coloring in one of the containers that has been filled with water. Show and tell the child that one of the containers is *empty* and the other one is *full*.

Squeeze up the water from the full container and then squeeze out the colored water into the empty container to begin filling it up. Model and explain the process first to your child, and then give him or her an opportunity to begin doing it with you.

Color Choice: Allow your child to choose the color of food coloring to change the color of the water! This will give your child a sense of ownership in the activity.

Meat baster: To speed up the process, you may show the child how to use the same process with a large meat baster, preferably transparent so the child can see the liquid. Once the child has the hang of what is expected, allow him or her to work independently.

This activity develops:
- Observational skills
- Following directions
- An awareness of *empty* and *full*
- Eye-hand coordination
- Freedom of choice (choosing food coloring)
- An awareness of air and air bubbles
- Confidence and independence

This is another great activity to do outside!

Age 1 - Activity 47 – Button, Zip, Snap, Velcro

You will need:
- Coat with large buttons
- Jacket with a zipper
- Tennis shoe with Velcro fastener
- Baby clothes with snaps

Button: Model how to button and unbutton the coat. Then allow the child to do this. With practice, your child will be able to button more successfully each time.

Zip: Model how to zip a jacket with a zipper. Talk him or her through how to zip up the zipper and zip down the zipper to unzip. Allow the child to try zipping and emphasize the sound that the zipper makes when the child moves the tab up and down.

Snap: Set a baby outfit with snaps in front of the child and model how to snap together the snaps and unsnap the snaps. Allow the child a chance to snap after you have modeled. He or she may need assistance with unsnapping the snaps as these may require more strength. Emphasize the sound that the snaps make when the two pieces snap together.

Velcro: Use a tennis shoe with a Velcro fastener or attach by sewing or gluing your own Velcro pieces onto a folded piece of cloth. Allow the child to open and fasten with the Velcro. Encourage him or her to listen for the sound that is made when the two pieces of Velcro are separated.

Velcro sneakers: This may be an ideal opportunity to introduce Velcro sneakers to your child. As he or she is practicing this skill, he or she may be encouraged to put on and take off his or her Velcro sneakers with less assistance.

Purpose: Talk to your child about the purpose of these materials from the activity. Try to make the child aware of the many things that are used for fastening materials together.

This activity develops:
- An awareness of different materials used for fastening clothing
- Problem solving
- Listening for the different sounds of the fasteners
- Confidence and independence
- Eye-hand coordination

Age 1 - Activity 48 – Listen and Draw

You will need:
- Several sheets of blank paper
- Crayons
- Kid-friendly songs

Set up a place for the child to color and draw while listening to music. Allow the child to choose a color from the crayon selection.
- Call the chosen color by name and ask the child to repeat the color's name.

Color to music: As the child listens, determine the beat and count and clap out the beats. Encourage the child to draw on the paper with the timing of the music.

Tips:
- Avoid correcting the child's movements.
- This activity is meant to infuse confidence in your child to use a crayon to draw — not to hold it correctly and write. There will be other activities in the future to introduce that!
- Continue to count and clap out the beat of the music to motivate the child to continue to move the crayon.
- When the music stops, praise the child for making such a beautiful "musical" picture.

Guiding: It may be necessary for you to guide the child's hand to give him or her the idea. Once he or she seems to understand, allow him or her to move the crayon freely around on the paper.

This activity develops:
- Free expression
- An awareness of rhythm
- Listening skills
- Large and small muscles of the arm and hand
- An appreciation of creative art
- Independence and confidence

Age 1 - Activity 49 – Open and Close

You will need:
- Door with a doorknob

Model and practice: Model opening a closed door by turning the doorknob. With the door still open, allow the child to practice turning the doorknob, because he or she may find it difficult once the door is closed securely.

Words *open* and *close*: Use the words *open* and *close* to teach the child about open doors and closed doors. Show your child other doors in your house that may or may not have a knob to reinforce the idea of open and closed. Examples are sliding doors, swinging doors, and types of cabinet doors. The child can practice opening and closing different kinds of doors whenever possible.

Safety: Talk about safety in the kitchen when opening and closing doors of the cabinets. Emphasize that the child should not open and close these cabinet doors without permission. As your child's curiosity and ability grows, placing child safety locks on cabinet doors and drawers is a vital part of keeping your house safe.

What does it mean to ask permission? Explain what the word *permission* means. Tell him or her that some of the cabinets contain materials that a child should not get into. Encourage your child to ask permission before opening a cabinet.

What is inside? Open each cabinet and allow him or her to peer inside, so that he or she will not be curious about the contents of each.

This activity develops:
- An awareness of the concepts *open* and *close*
- Free exploration
- Skill in turning knobs to open and close a door
- Independence and confidence
- Eye-hand coordination
- Language enrichment with discussing knobs, doors, and safety

Age 1 - Activity 50 – Hide and Seek

You will need:
- A room with plenty of places to safely hide

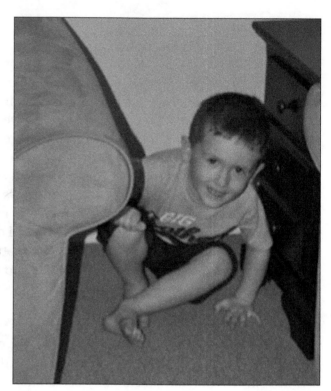

Model how to hide: Show your child how to hide behind a door or a piece of furniture. Encourage the child to cover his or her eyes with his or her hands. When you are hidden, ask the child to find you. Hopefully, the child will be listening and can find you.

Repeat for confidence: Do this several times and hide in the same place. When you think the child is secure with the game, hide in a different place that is close to the first hiding place. Continue to do this until the child loses interest.

Hide and seek: Encourage the child to hide on his or her own. Does the child hide in one of the places where you previously hid or does he or she find a new hiding place?

Finding new places to hide: Finding a new hiding place indicates that the child understands the game. If the child hides in the same place, he or she may need encouragement to find a different place to hide. *This is a game that very young children can play together with the guidance of an adult or older siblings.*

This activity develops:
- Listening for a purpose ("find me")
- Skill in tracing the sound of a person's voice
- An awareness of "out of sight" and "in sight"
- More of an awareness of a position in space
- Independence and confidence

Age 1 - Activity 51 – Humpty Dumpty

You will need:
- Cardstock paper
- Sharpie
- Markers
- Scissors
- Glue
- Velcro pieces

Read the rhyme:
Humpty Dumpty sat on a wall
Humpty Dumpty had a great fall
All the king's horses and all the king's men
Couldn't put Humpty together again.

Directions to Make Humpty Dumpty:

1. Cut 2 ovals out of cardstock paper.
2. Draw a line across the middle of each oval with a black marker.
3. Draw eyes, nose, and a mouth on the "Humpty" front oval and the lower half with a bright color (with your child's help).
4. Zig-zag cut the front oval in half from top to bottom like a broken egg.
5. Cut 4 small pieces of Velcro and glue these pieces on the top and bottom of the back (reverse) side of the piece that is cut.
6. Two pieces should be on the left and two on the right side.
7. Glue the matching Velcro pieces to the backside of the other piece, so that when the front and the back are matched together evenly they will be fastened with the Velcro.
8. Paper strips may be added for arms and legs.

Putting Humpty Dumpty together: Show the child how to take Humpty Dumpty apart. Then model how to put Humpty Dumpty back together. Encourage the child to say the rhyme with you and let the child break Humpty apart and put him back together while the lines of the rhyme are being said aloud.

Act out the rhyme: Let the child pretend to be Humpty Dumpty. The child can sit on a pillow to represent the wall. As the rhyme is being recited, the child can pretend to fall off the wall at the moment that the words are said in the rhyme.

This activity develops:
- An awareness of words that rhyme and dramatization
- An awareness that when something breaks it can be repaired

Age 1 - Activity 52 – Jack in the Box

You will need:
- Box or plastic Tupperware container that is large enough for the child to get inside

Model Jack-in-the-box rhyme: Squat down and tell the child to pretend that he or she is in a box with the lid closed like Jack.

> *Jack in the box all shut up tight*
> *Not a breath of air, not a ray of light.*
> *How dark it must be, you cannot see.*
> *Open the lid and out "pops" he!*

Act out the rhyme: Encourage the child to climb into the box. Tell the child that you are going to close the lid so that it will be dark inside until he or she opens the lid. Remind the child to listen and jump up when you say the word, "pops."

"Pop Goes the Weasel": Introduce this song and invite the child to walk around something that can be used as the "mulberry bush." As you and the child walk around the pretend bush, sing the action rhyme. On the word *pop*, clap your hands.

Enrichment: Show the child a picture of a monkey and a weasel. Tell the child that they are animals with fur and other facts that may be of interest to the child.

An activity that grows with your child! Your child may enjoy this activity until he or she grows too big to fit inside the box!

> *Round and round the mulberry bush,*
> *The monkey chased the weasel.*
> *The monkey thought 'twas all in fun.*
> *"Pop" goes the weasel!*

This activity develops:
- Listening for a specific word and then reacting
- More awareness of *open* and *close*
- Listening for sequence in the action rhymes
- Memory recall of the rhymes
- Gross motor skills
- Independence and confidence

Age Two: From Two-years-old to Three-years-old

Terrible Twos or a Terrific Time to Teach?
How can a parent transform the dreaded "Terrible Twos" into a terrific time to teach? As my grandmother would say, "The child of two needs much to do!" This section of *Slow and Steady Get Me Ready for Kindergarten* keeps your active child productive with short activities and games. Shift your child away from the drone of the TV and tablet by offering these hands-on activities instead. Keep in mind that your positive attitude about these activities will encourage your child to get excited about trying something new!

Meaningful Environment
Your two-year-old is more aware of his or her environment. Talk to your child about what he or she sees around your house, car, neighborhood, etc. Use short conversations about size, color, and shapes to connect what he or she already knows with what is unfamiliar to enrich your child's experiences.

Increased Vocabulary
Two-year-olds are verbal and may be interested in reciting short poems, nursery rhymes, and songs. That is why several of the activities in this section incorporate rhymes with activities to engage your child even more. Keep in mind that some children may tend to stutter at this age, because they think faster than they can speak. Be patient, listen, and use wait time to give your child the security necessary if he or she is struggling to express himself or herself. Encourage your child to speak for himself or herself rather than speaking for him or her. Talking can sometimes be a challenge to youngsters. Rather than enabling them to remain silent by offering them the words and communicating through "yes" and "no" head nods, ask your child to tell you with words what he or she wants. Then look your child in the eyes and give wait time until he or she responds.

Scribbling
Many of the activities in this section give your child opportunities to scribble in up and down strokes. Whenever a pencil, crayon, or marker is available for your child to use safely, let your child scribble. These up and down strokes soon develop into back and forth and circular strokes. Do not try to teach your child how to "hold the pencil" correctly at this age as it may deter him or her from attempting to scribble with confidence.

Praise Your Child

At age two, your child's creative art expression may be emerging. Praise your child and encourage him or her consistently. This will motivate your two-year-old to express his or her "view" of immediate surroundings. Creativity does not necessarily have "right" or "wrong" answers, so give your child this freedom. Negative criticism at this young age can have detrimental effects on the child's creativity and self esteem.

Read To Your Child

Throughout this section, board books and picture books are suggested that connect with the activities or ideas being investigated by your child. Even though your child will continue to have a short attention span, don't give up reading aloud to your child. Ask your child questions about pictures on the page that you are about to read to keep him or her interested. Enable your child to turn the pages for you and ask him or her to point to things on the pages that your child may recognize. Reading at age two can become an even more meaningful experience. With consistent repetition, your child will become accustomed to sitting still for lengthier amounts of time. It may take several sittings to complete a picture book, but keep at it! This is the start of literacy development.

Activities are Mini Lessons

Each activity presented in this section is a mini lesson for your child. Recognize that it often takes multiple attempts and repeated practice for your child to grasp a new concept. Sometimes you may start to teach your child something and an interruption or distraction prevents you from completing the activity or lesson. Pick it back up at a later time and be patient with both yourself and your child.

Large Muscle Activities

Most two-year-olds are excited to run, jump, kick, dance, pedal, push, pull, and throw. All of these large muscle activities enable your child to develop his or her gross motor skills. Giving your child a safe environment to participate in these large muscle games is just what he or she needs from you so that he or she can develop better coordination! Toddler proof a room(s) in your home and take your child outside to play so he or she can energetically engage in these large muscle activities without the fear or threat of breaking something of value to you.

Responsibility even at Two

Two-year-olds are active and busy, so how about get them busy doing something helpful around the house? Give your child simple chores to do daily that enable your little one to recognize that he or she has responsibility even at a young age. Chores can include picking up toys, putting dirty clothes in the hamper, wiping up messes, dusting with socks, carrying and putting away groceries, helping set the table, and making the bed.

The Value of Work: It's Not Too Early

Keep in mind, it will take longer for your child to do the chore than for you to do it on your own, but that is not the purpose of your child doing the chore. Responsibility and the value of contributing in house work as part of the family unit is a much more important life lesson than getting house chores done quickly. Too many parents do everything for their children, because it takes too long to wait for them to do it. This unintentionally creates a sense of entitlement that becomes a habitual expectation without parents realizing how damaging its effects are. Parents are in the business of making their children self-sufficient and able-bodied citizens, so start early by giving your child simple tasks that he or she is responsible for.

Your Child's Identity

Size differences are apparent to a two-year-old. He or she can identify the members of your family and that some are larger than he or she is. Two-year-olds are becoming much more aware of themselves. Your child may even know his or her name, age, and gender. Encourage your child to feel confident about who he or she is by asking your child to tell you and others these facts about himself or herself.

Imitation

Two-year-old children are watching everything that you and others around them are doing. They will listen to what you say and how you interact with others on a daily basis. Be aware that you are being watched and heard! Many words and sounds that your two-year-old hears are often imitated.

Playing Pretend

Real and fantasy stories are of interest to the child of this age, especially animal stories. He or she may pretend to be in his or her own world of fantasy while playing. This is very much a part of a child's need to sort out his or her feelings as he or she adjusts properly to the real world.

Note

The author and publisher are not liable for any injury or death incurred due to the misuse of the suggested materials and directions. As with all child-related activities, materials should be selected with careful attention to child safety; adult supervision is essential.

Age 2 - Activity 1 – Top and Bottom

You will need:
- Shoe box
- 2 small familiar items (toy, rattle, spool, block)

Review top and bottom: Show the child the top and the bottom of the shoe box. The long sides will represent top and bottom shelves.

Follow directions: Tell the child to put one of the items on the "top" shelf. Instruct the child to take the same item and place it on the "bottom" shelf. Repeat this activity using another item.

Three steps:
1. Listen for the item's name.
2. Listen for the place to put the item.
3. Place the item on the shelf.

Reminder: Too many objects may tend to confuse and frustrate the child. Stick with alternating between two objects for a while until your child shows confidence with this.

Optional: Index cards with the words *top* and *bottom* can begin making your child aware of the association of ideas with written words. Do not expect for your child to recognize these words at this time.

Apply to the real world: From time to time, show the child *top* and *bottom* shelves throughout the house. Ask the child an immediate follow-up question to reinforce the concept. Which shelf is the *top*? Which shelf is the *bottom*? If your child does not answer correctly, do not be discouraged. New ideas need to be repeated for your child to understand and retain the information.

This activity develops:
- An awareness of *top* and *bottom*
- Eye-hand coordination
- Tactile sensitivity in handling various items
- Listening skills

Age 2 - Activity 2 – Play Dough Fun Part 2

You will need:
- Play dough recipe from Age 1, Activity 21
- Tape
- Wax paper

Prepare the space: Tape waxed paper down to the tabletop since the play dough's salty residue may be left on the surface. An old tray or placemat could work too!

Play dough circles: Roll dough into a long piece to make a circle by joining the two ends of the roll together. Encourage the child to make one too. Tell the child this shape is a *circle*.

Square and triangle: Use the rolls of play dough to make a square and a triangle. Point out to the child that the square and triangle do not have curves. Show the child how a circle can be pinched at four corners with equal distance from each other to form a square.

What if my child eats the play dough? Remind your child at the beginning of play dough time that play dough is not for eating. Nonetheless, if your child eats some play dough anyway, keep in mind that none of the ingredients are toxic. Also, the play dough tastes extremely salty and after experiencing the unpleasant taste, your child will most likely learn that eating play dough is not enjoyable. If your child continues to eat the play dough, you can take the activity away as a consequence and reintroduce it at another time. Be consistent and explain clearly that the reason for the play dough being taken away is because the child made the choice to put the play dough in his or her mouth.

This activity develops:
- Eye hand coordination
- Free exploration to create with play dough
- Independence and confidence
- Awareness of the shapes: circle, square, and triangle
- Enhancement of the sense of touch with the play dough

Age 2 - Activity 3 – Scrunch and Toss Into the Bag

You will need:
- Beanbag or scrunched up balls of paper
- Empty shoe box or brown paper bag

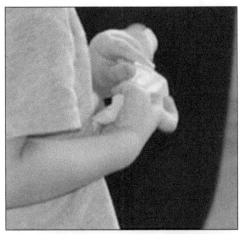

Scrunch into a ball: Show the child how to scrunch up a piece of paper into a ball. Allow the child to do this with a few pieces of paper independently.

Your child may find himself or herself completely content with just doing this activity for awhile, so don't rush the next activities.

Toss into a shoebox: Show your child how to use one hand to toss the scrunched up paper balls into the shoebox. Encourage the child to use one hand. Accept over hand or under hand tosses. The object is to aim for the target with the beanbag or scrunched up paper ball.

> **Reminder**: Make it clear to the child that he or she should aim only for the shoe box and not the furniture, lamps, tables, etc.

Extension: When the child has gained confidence in tossing the bean bag a short distance, the shoebox can be moved farther away from the child. This will offer your child more of a challenge when he or she is ready and will increase his or her skill and confidence.

This activity develops:
- Eye-hand coordination
- Gross motor coordination
- Interest in a game
- Following directions
- An awareness of distance and time in relation to when the bean bag is first tossed and when it stops

Age 2 - Activity 4 – Make a Necklace

You will need:
- 10 construction paper circles
- 10 construction paper squares
- Pipe cleaner
- 36 in. of yarn

Set up: Punch a hole in the center of each circle and square piece of construction paper. Use a pipe cleaner as a needle to tie to the end of a yarn string. Tie a knot at the end of the yarn.

Model: Show the child how to thread the yarn through the holes of the circles and squares.

Child's turn: Allow the child to string the circles and squares in any order. The child should be encouraged to finish this activity even though it may not be completed the same day. A few shapes can be threaded on at a time, depending on the interest of the child.

Necklace to wear: When the child completes stringing all 20 shapes onto the yarn, remove the pipe cleaner needle and tie the two ends together to make a necklace. The child can wear the necklace he or she has made.

Shape talk: Invite the child to tell you which shapes are circles or squares on his or her necklace. The colors that are used for the necklace can also be identified.

Reminder: Go back to the activities from Age 0 and 1 that your child may or may not have been successful or interested in when first attempted. As your child matures, he or she may respond differently to the activities from before.

This activity develops:
- Eye-hand coordination
- Awareness of different colors
- Awareness that a task should be completed
- Differentiating between shapes: circles and squares
- Appreciation of something created

Age 2 - Activity 5 – Box Skating

You will need:
- 2 empty shoe boxes
- Masking tape

Set up: Show the child how to put his or her feet inside the empty shoeboxes like shoes or skates. Establish a "finish line" by taping a straight line on the carpet with masking tape.

Follow directions: Tell the child to go to the finish line by carefully sliding the boxes forward as he or she walks. Show the child what you mean if he or she seems to have difficulty.

Skate to music: Play "The Skater's Waltz" or another classical piece of music while the child "skates." He or she can pretend to be skating on a pond.

This activity develops:
- An awareness of completing a task (finish line)
- Gross motor coordination
- An awareness of something different to do with the feet
- An awareness of left and right laterality
- Independence and confidence

Age 2 - Activity 6 – My Name

Use a rhyme: Teach your child to say his or her name.

Counting books are a great resource for introducing the idea of two and other numbers.

> My name is (child's name)
> I am two
> I am a (girl or boy)
> And I love you!

Hold up two fingers: As you practice this rhyme, hold up two fingers when saying the "I am two" line. When the "I love you" line is said, hug the child.

Fill in the missing words: If the child is reluctant to say the rhyme, repeat the rhyme and pause at the last word of each line. Encourage the child to listen and fill in the missing words.

Count 1, 2: Tell the child that you are going to look for pictures of two things. Hold up two fingers again and ask the child to count the fingers that are up. Count 1, 2. Use two of the child's fingers and count 1, 2.

Look for two things: Sit with the child and look at a book and count objects in pictures of things that you see in the book. Avoid counting higher than two, because the idea is to teach the concept of two.

Play with two things: The child may also enjoy arranging blocks, toys, books, buttons, rocks, shells, or keys in sets of *two*. This is a simple but important activity.

This activity develops:
- An awareness of name, gender, and age
- An awareness of the concept *two*
- An awareness of the rhyming words *two* and *you*
- An interest in memory recall of the rhyme

Age 2 - Activity 7 – Learning Colors

You will need:
- Construction paper squares (red, yellow, blue, orange, green, purple, brown, black, pink)
- Hole punch
- Piece of yarn

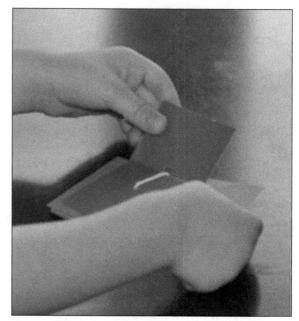

Make a color booklet: Cut the paper into the same-sized squares. Punch a hole in the top left corner of each. String a piece of yarn through the hole and tie a knot to connect the squares together to form a color booklet.

"Read" the booklet to your child by saying the name of the color for each page. Allow the child to turn the pages and repeat the name of each color that you say aloud.

Color of the day: Choose one color from the booklet each day and identify different objects, toys, and pictures that have that particular color in them during the day. Encourage the child to find objects on his or her own that have the color of the day in them. Have the child point out those objects to you.

Color hop: Once the child is familiar with his or her colors, lay down construction paper squares (or foam squares) of the learned colors. Have your child hop to the colored square that you verbally call out.

Food to identify colors:

Brown: pretzel sticks   **Yellow**: banana   **Blue**: blueberries
Orange: orange slices   **Red**: strawberries   **Green**: inside of a kiwi

Book idea: *My Very First Book of Colors* by Eric Carle

This activity develops:
- Skill in naming the colors
- An awareness of clothing and detail
- Listening and observational skills

Age 2 - Activity 8 – Finger Paint Bag

Set up:
- 2 zip lock bags
- Packing tape
- Tempera paint

Free exploration: Squirt some tempera paint into the bag and seal tightly. Use packing tape to reinforce the edges of the bag and then place it on a flat work area. Notice any changes your child makes as he or she explores the paint bag for a second time. As the paint inside moves according to the movement of your child's hands or fingers, does your child stay more focused than before or does he or she use his or her finger to draw in the paint more carefully or purposefully? This is a great activity to pull out over and over as your child grows, so refer back to it when your child shows an interest.

Finger movement directions: Encourage the child to use his or her index (pointer) finger and gently move it from left to right. By showing the child the movement of the left and right progression, the child's eyes and finger movement are being trained for future reading and writing skills.

Kinds of lines: Model making straight lines, curvy lines, and zigzag lines from left to right. Each of these lines should be emphasized one at a time, and then allow your child to copy these lines with your help or on his or her own.

Drawing shapes enrichment: The child may be encouraged to make circles and squares. Some may be big and some little. Talk to the child about the shapes and sizes that he or she has formed to review.

This activity develops:
- A tactile approach to hand movement (feeling)
- More of an awareness of *left* and *right*
- Free exploration and creativity
- An awareness of line variations
- Visual skills (copying)

Age 2 - Activity 9 – Jump and Hop

Set up:
- Take two pieces of rope or yarn.
- Cut one length approximately 2 yards long and the other length 1 yard long.
- On the floor or outside, make a big circle with the longer piece of yarn and a little circle with the shorter piece.
- Talk to the child about the big and little circles.
- Have a beanbag on hand for activity extension.

Model jumping: Show the child how to jump up and down on two feet inside the bigger circle. Then do the same for the little circle. Counting each complete jump will motivate the child to want to jump with you.

One-foot hops: Show the child how to hop on one foot inside the big and little circles. It may help the child to balance better if he or she holds one foot, one at a time, before attempting to hop inside the designated circle. As the child hops, count and clap or use words that rhyme to maintain the child's interest.

Beanbag activity extension: The child can toss the beanbag inside one of the circles and then jump inside the circle to pick it up. Then he or she can jump or hop while holding the beanbag. You should designate the circle (big or little) and the activity (jump or hop) that he or she should use to perform this task.

This activity develops:
- Gross motor coordination
- Recognition of *big* and *little* circles
- Awareness of the difference in jumping and hopping
- Awareness of *inside* and *outside* a boundary
- Listening and following directions
- Awareness of counting sequence or rhyme

Age 2 - Activity 10 – My Family

You will need:
- Photograph of the family or individual pictures of each member
- Construction paper
- Glue
- Stapler and staples (for book assembly)

Point and name the family member: Point and name each family member and allow the child to point to and name each member also.

Family member characteristics: Talk about the family members. Say something unique about each member. Some characteristics of each member can be: size, boy or girl, something they like to do, hair color, and various other characteristics that may be meaningful to the child. Use the words father (daddy), mother (mommy), sister, brother, and baby to ensure that the child can make the proper relationships to the family members.

Make a family book: Pictures of each family member can be glued on a piece of construction paper and stapled together to form a Family Book. Write the name of each family member underneath his or her picture. Explain to the child that the word below each picture is the family member's written name. For interest, the pages can be cut in the shape of a house.

Read the family book: Allow the child to "read" his or her Family Book to you or to another family member when it is complete.

This activity develops:
- Awareness of family members
- Awareness of love and affection in the family
- Awareness of various sizes of family members
- Visual observation of cutting and awareness of gluing
- Awareness of pictures or photographs to represent real people
- Listening and identifying skills

Age 2 - Activity 11 – I Can Paint

You will need:
- Newspaper or old plastic table cloth
- Sharpie or masking tape
- Old shirt (for smock)
- Paint brush
- Tempera paint (one color)
- Paper plate bowl

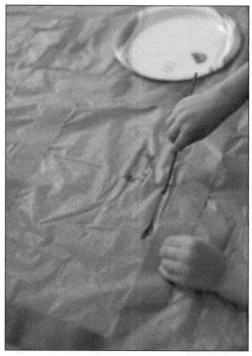

Set up: Draw a square around the edges of the newspaper with a sharpie or with strips of masking tape to create a frame or boundary for the child's picture. Put some tempera paint in a paper plate bowl.

Model: Model for the child how to dip the paintbrush in the paint and smooth it over the newspaper to paint lines, shapes, or pictures. Show the child how to brush against the sides of the bowl to get rid of too much paint on the brush. Encourage the child to paint inside of the boundary lines.

Observe the child's strokes. Are they up and down or back and forth? Does he or she make circular brush strokes? All of these movements are developmental for later control in painting a recognizable object in a picture.

Tell a story about a picture: Invite the child to tell you a story about his or her picture when finished. Accept whatever he or she says about the picture. Praise and encouragement are needed, so avoid negative criticism. You may want to hang the picture up for other family members to admire.

This activity develops:
- Free exploration with paint
- Creativity
- Further awareness of a boundary
- Eye-hand and arm coordination
- Imagination and language in describing his picture

Age 2 - Activity 12 – Farm Animals

Animal recognition: Use the pictures in a children's book to identify and name each animal. Practice the animal names with the child until you feel he or she can successfully name each animal in the pictures.

Animal sounds: Try to make the sound of each farm animal. Encourage the child to repeat the animal sound after you. This will help the child learn to associate different animal sounds with the pictures.

dog	*bow wow*
horse	*neigh, neigh*
cat	*meow, meow*
donkey	*hee, haw*
rooster	*cock-a-doodle-do*
cow	*moo, moo*
lamb	*baa, baa*
pig	*oink, oink*
duck	*quack, quack*
turkey	*gobble, gobble*

Animal sound audio recording: Make an audio recording of the animals' names and their sounds. Play the recording for the child. He or she may attempt to make these animal sounds on his or her own and will be learning to articulate the tongue for further speech patterns.

Sing "Old MacDonald": For enrichment, sing this familiar children's song aloud or find a version of it online to sing along with. The child can fill in the animal names and sounds that he or she has learned.

Book ideas:
- *Baby Animals on the Farm* by Rebecca Heller
- *Who Says That? A First Book of Animal Sounds* by Marguerite Muntean Corsello

This activity develops:
- Listening skills and memory recall
- Skill in naming animals using visual and auditory clues
- Language enrichment

Age 2 - Activity 13 – Put It In a Line

You will need:
Paper bag filled with the following:
- Block
- Key
- Sponge
- Clothespin
- Bottle cap
- Large button
- Rock
- Spool
- Small toy
- Spoon
- Cup
- Food item like a yogurt or cheese stick

Set up: Tape a piece of masking tape in a straight line on a table surface for the child to place items along.

Model putting items on the line: Start on the left and place one of the items from the bag on the line of tape. Encourage the child to continue moving from left to right, placing the objects chosen from the bag on the tape line until the bag is empty.

Pick up from left to right: Direct the child to pick up each item one at a time, from left to right, until all of the objects are back in the bag.

Repeat activities: Repeat this activity on different occasions and substitute other items to place in the bag. Go back to some of the previous activities, because the child needs repetition in order to master these basic concepts and skills.

This activity develops:
- Awareness of left to right progression
- Enhancement of the sense of touch in handling objects in the bag
- Eye-hand coordination
- Skill in following directions and completing a task
- Awareness of *one* object to place at a time

Age 2 - Activity 14 – Jack Be Nimble

You will need:
- Candlestick or cup for a pretend candle holder (an empty sippy cup will do)

> *Jack be nimble, Jack be quick*
> *Jack jumped over the candlestick.*

Repeat the rhyme: Emphasize that the words *quick* and *stick* sound alike. Encourage the child to say the rhyme with you several times. If there is enough interest, motivate the child to add more rhyming words by saying *lick*, *click*, *tick*, *chick*, *pick*, *sick*, *kick*, etc.

Pretend to be Jack: Invite the child to pretend he or she is "Jack" and jump over the "candlestick" as you say the word *jump* during the rhyme. The child should practice jumping with his or her feet close together. Be sure to emphasize the word *over*.

Jumping far: Encourage the child to jump as far as possible. Place an object to show how far the child jumped from a given point. Tell the child to jump again and see if he or she can jump even farther. The child will enjoy seeing his or her progress in jumping distance. This will motivate him or her to practice more.

Book idea:
- *Jack Be Nimble Lap Book* by Josie Stewart

This activity develops:
- Skill in listening and recall
- Further awareness of rhyme
- Role playing
- Language enrichment
- Gross motor coordination
- Awareness of the concept, "over"

Age 2 - Activity 15 – Feely Bag Fun

You will need:
- Two lunch bags or old socks
- Items to fill the bags include:
  - o Two spools
  - o Two bottle caps
  - o Two cotton balls
  - o Two sponge pieces
  - o Two keys
  - o Two large buttons

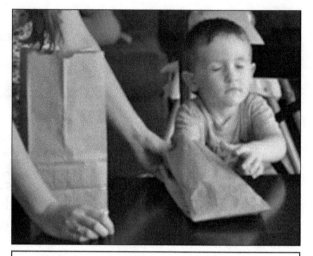

Set up: Put one of each item in both bags, so that they have exactly the same contents.

Matching: Show the child the two bags and match each set of two items one to one. In this way, the child will see and understand that there are two identical items of each kind. Refill the two bags and give one of the bags to the child.

Reminder: Items in the bags may be changed, but the child should be aware of this to avoid confusion, distrust, or frustration.

Feel to find: Take one of the objects out of the bag and show it to the child. Tell the child to close his or her eyes and feel for an object that is just like the one that you took out of your bag. Remind the child to "feel" not to look. Help the child if necessary. Put the matched objects back into the bags. Choose another item and continue until the child loses interest.

This activity develops:
- Further awareness and use of the sense of touch
- Matching skills
- Hand coordination
- Following directions

Age 2 - Activity 16 – The Three Bears

Book idea: *Goldilocks and the Three Bears: A Read Along with Me Book (See and Say Storybook Series)* by Derrydale Publishers

---

The suggested interactive book uses pictures in place of words, so that once your child is familiar with the story a second time, you can point to the picture and have your child say the word the picture represents. In this way, the child begins to actively participate in the reading process.

Any picture book with the story about Goldilocks and the three bears will do for this activity.

Read aloud and ask questions:
- Who came to visit the bears while they were gone?
- Whose food was too hot?
- Whose chair did Goldilocks like best?
- Whose bed did she sleep in first?
- Did I forget something in the story that you would like to tell me about?

Open-ended discussion: The last question leaves this discussion open for any recall or comment the child might have. If the child cannot answer the questions, read the story again and point out the answers to the child.

Props: Big, medium, and little size chairs (around the house); big, medium, small bowls for pretend porridge; big (rough), medium (soft), and small (child's) blankets laid out on the floor for beds.

Pretend to be Goldilocks and count 1-2-3: Invite the child to pretend he or she is the character of Goldilocks from the story. You can provide your child with the "props" listed above. You can use the pictures from the storybook to count the three bears, the three chairs, the three bowls, and the three beds.

This activity develops:
- Listening and memory recall
- Skill in following a sequence
- Role playing
- Language enrichment
- More awareness of counting 1-2-3
- Skill in using visual skills for recall

Age 2 - Activity 17 – Sock Match

You will need:
- Several pairs of socks (of different colors and sizes)
- Magazine with pictures
- Scissors
- Construction paper
- Glue

Model matching: Show the child that there are two of each kind of sock. Mix the socks and display them on a flat surface in front of the child. Pick up one of the socks and tell the child to find its match. Assist the child if necessary.

Pair **means two:** Tell the child that each matched set of socks is called a *pair*. A pair is two. Then count each pair 1-2, 1-2 to help the child establish the concept of two.

Sock matching helper: This activity can be repeated each time you are sorting clean laundry.
Show the child how to match socks and encourage the child to be your sock matching helper. He or she will develop a sense of responsibility through having this "job." It will be beneficial to the child if you allow him or her to help with this task, even if it takes you longer to sort and fold the laundry.

What else comes in pairs? Have a discussion with your child about what else comes in pairs.

- Hands
- Feet
- Ears
- Eyes
- Shoes
- Gloves

Make a pairs booklet: Pictures of these sets of pairs can be cut from a magazine or printed from the internet and glued on construction paper to make a "Pairs Booklet." Write the word *pairs* on the front of the booklet for a title. The child can "read" you his or her booklet by naming each set of pairs in it.

This activity develops:
- Eye-hand coordination
- Awareness of a pair and counting 1-2
- Feeling of helping through responsibility
- Vocabulary enrichment

Age 2 - Activity 18 – Outline the Shape

You will need:
- Several pieces of paper
- Red and blue sharpies
- Yarn
- Straws
- Cooked, colored spaghetti pieces
- Glue
- Crayons

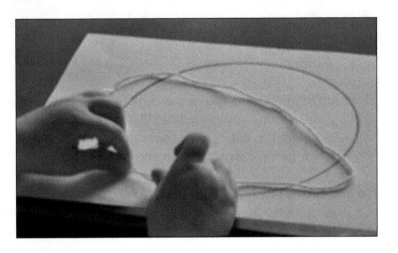

Set up:
1. Draw a circle about the size of a paper plate on the piece of paper with a red sharpie.
2. Draw a 6-inch square with a blue marker on another piece of paper.
3. Cut a piece of yarn the size of the circumference of the circle.
4. Cut several straws in 3-inch lengths so that you have at least 8 pieces.

Model: Show the child how to use the yarn and lay it on the line that was drawn to form the circle. Lay the straw pieces on the lines of the square.

Talk about the circle: Identify the circle with its name. Talk about curved lines. Tell the child that the yarn is curved to form a circle. Hold the child's hand and make a pretend circle in the air. Then ask the child to make a pretend circle in the air all by himself or herself.

Talk about the square: Ask the child to recall the square's name as you point to it. Explain to the child that the square is made up of straight lines. Talk to the child about the square's corners called *points*. Ask the child how many straw pieces were used to form a side of the square. Since the pieces were cut in 3-inch lengths, it will take two of these to form one side of a 6-inch square. Ask the child to make a pretend square in the air.

Spaghetti shapes: The child can form circles and squares using cooked, colored (with food coloring) spaghetti. This can be done on a flat surface.

> This activity develops:
> - Further awareness of the circle and square
> - Eye-hand coordination
> - Awareness of curved and straight lines
> - Following directions

Age 2 - Activity 19 – Up, Down, and the "Simon Says" Game

You will need:
- 10 or 20 Solo or plastic cups
- Long piece of yarn

Stacking exploration: Allow the child to explore with the cups by un-stacking and restacking them. The child may enjoy knocking the stacks over and watching to see what happens. Emphasize the words *up* and *down*.

Up and down pattern: Place the cups up, down, up, down in a pattern. Have the child add on to the row that you have modeled. Continue the pattern with your guidance if needed.

"Simon Says" game directions:
1. Instruct the child to follow a special command that Simon gives and model being Simon first.
2. Simon should say, "Simon Says" before every command.
3. However, if Simon says a command without saying "Simon says" at the beginning, the child should not act on the command given.
4. The child should only move when *Simon says* is said before the command.
5. Start the game off with only the commands of standing up and sitting down until the child has mastered the "Simon Says" game format.

Other command ideas:
- Turn around
- Raise hands above your head
- Touch toes
- Wiggle fingers
- Jump up and down
- Clap your hands

Reminder: At this age, giving too many different commands at one time may tend to confuse or frustrate your child. Try changing the commands one at a time to ensure that your child understands the command and can perform it successfully. Once the child feels confident, reverse roles and allow him or her to play Simon and give you the commands.

> This activity develops:
> - Free exploration, problem solving, coordination
> - Awareness of a pattern of *up* and *down*
> - Listening to directions carefully

Age 2 - Activity 20 – What Belongs in the Drawer?

You will need:
- 2 empty drawers or 2 shoe boxes to represent empty drawers
- Spoons
- Lids
- Socks
- Papers
- Crayons

Sorting items: Make the child aware that we have certain things that we keep in each drawer. Assemble any two sets of safe materials such as spoons, lids, socks, shirts, paper, crayons, etc. Mix the materials that were chosen and point to a drawer and say for example, "This is where the spoons go. Put all the spoons in here." Point to the other drawer and say, "This is the drawer where I keep lids. Put all the lids in here." Repeat this procedure with the other items.

Discussion: Talk about keeping things in special places. Tell the child that this is the way we keep things in order and can remember where things are kept. Invite the child to go with you to observe what is kept in different drawers in the house. Talk about privacy and safety with your child. Remind him or her to ask permission to open drawers that may contain personal or dangerous items.

Organization in the house: Emphasize the need for order in the home. Suggest a special drawer for the child to keep small items in that belong to him or her. Provide a toy box, another large container, or a shelf for the child to keep his or her larger toys or stuffed animals in. In this way, the child should soon learn to keep his or her toys picked up. A room will stay neater if a child is allowed to choose only a few toys at a time to use. He or she should be trained to put those toys away after choosing others with which to play.

This activity develops:
- Awareness of orderliness
- Awareness of sorting items
- Awareness of same and different kinds of items
- A desire to help
- Confidence

Age 2 - Activity 21 – Rub-A-Dub-Dub

You will need:
- Plastic tub or cardboard box big enough for the child to get inside of

Imagine: Tell the child to imagine three men in a tub floating on the water, rocking back and forth.

Read the nursery rhyme.

> *Rub-a-dub-dub*
> *Three men in a tub.*
> *And who do you think they be?*
> *The butcher, the baker, the*
> *candlestick maker*
> *Turn them out, knaves all three.*

Butcher, baker, candlestick maker: Explain to the child that a butcher prepares meat, a baker makes bread, cakes, and pies, and a candlestick maker makes candles. A knave is a servant or a worker. Emphasize *three* men. Name them again and count 1-2-3.

Pretend and repeat: Use the plastic tub or cardboard box as the "tub" in the rhyme. Invite the child to get in the tub or box and to pretend to be one of the three men. Let the child choose which one he or she would like to be. With repetition, the child will soon learn to say the rhyme from memory and may recall rhyming words at random.

Rhyming words: Say the rhyme again and encourage the child to move around in the tub or box and pretend to be floating and safely rocking back and forth on the waves of the water. Ask the child to think of other words that rhyme with tub like: *rub, dub, hub, sub, pub, cub*, etc. Accept nonsensical words the child may develop. This type of response will denote that the child is aware of words that sound alike.

> This activity develops:
> - Listening for a purpose (rhymes)
> - Memory recall
> - Role playing
> - Language enrichment
> - Freedom in making a choice (which man to role play)

Age 2 - Activity 22 – I Spy Red, I Spy Blue

You will need:
- All red objects (sweater, shirt, marker, paper, crayons, yarn)
- All blue objects
- Cardboard shaped "magnifying glass"

Red and blue: If the child does not know the color *red* or *blue* yet, explain and identify these color names.

"I Spy" game: Look around the room and find something that has the color red in it. Then tell the child that you spy something *red*. Allow the child to look around the room for something red and ask him or her to tell you when he or she has spied it. Then play "I Spy" with the color blue in the same way.

Look through the magnifying glass to spy: Look through the hole when you look at something red or blue. This will give the child a clue as to the direction of the red or blue object that you spy.

Warm or cold: If the child is close to the object that is being spied say, "You are getting warm." If the child is going in the wrong direction say, "You are cold."

Reminder: Avoid teasing the child during activities like these. Security and success in finding red or blue objects are essential. Be sure to use only one color at a time. Interchanging the colors will tend to confuse a child of this age. This type of direction involves listening for the color and finding it in a certain place. The child must feel secure with the color to find its location.

This activity develops:
- More awareness of the colors *red* and *blue*
- Skill in using clues for problem solving
- Confidence
- Language enrichment
- Matching skills (finding something else of the same color)

Age 2 - Activity 23 – Slide and Roll

You will need:
- Masking tape
- Small box, block
- Coffee or juice can

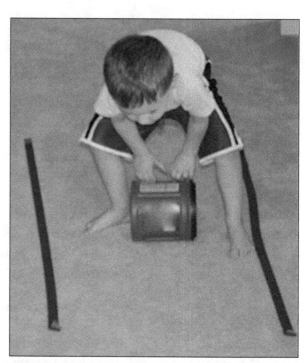

Set up: Use two long strips of masking tape on the carpet or floor for the child to move through the space as he or she rolls and slides the objects toward the finish line. Use a third strip of tape for a finish line at one end.

Slide the box: Tell the child to slide the box toward the finish line without touching the "sides" (masking tape lines).

Roll the can: Instruct the child to roll the can between the two pieces of tape. Remind him or her that he or she must start over if the can touches either of the sides.

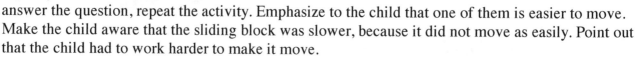

Roll slowly: Explain to the child that he or she must be careful and roll the can to control it.

Compare sliding to rolling: Ask the child which object got to the finish line faster. If the child cannot answer the question, repeat the activity. Emphasize to the child that one of them is easier to move. Make the child aware that the sliding block was slower, because it did not move as easily. Point out that the child had to work harder to make it move.

Discovery: Encourage your child to figure out for himself or herself whether sliding or rolling is faster through repeating the activity.

This activity develops:
- Awareness of fast and slow
- More awareness of boundaries (left and right)
- Awareness that it is easier to roll than slide an object
- Skill in following directions
- Awareness of start and finish

Age 2 - Activity 24 – I Can Dress Myself

You will need:
- Large piece of cardboard (as long and as wide as the child)
- Sharpie
- T-shirt, shorts, socks, and shoes

Trace child's outline: Have the child lie down on top of the cardboard and trace his or her outline with a sharpie. Add eyes, nose, ears, mouth, and hair to the cardboard outline. Review body parts and have the child point to the parts of the body as you name them aloud.

"Dress" the cardboard child: Encourage the child to lay the clothes on the outline of himself or herself in the proper places. You can use different shirts and shorts to make different outfits for the child to "dress" the cardboard child.

Dressing by myself: If the child can place the clothes correctly, let the child dress himself or herself the following morning. You may need to assist, but allow him or her to do as much as possible on his or her own.

Book idea: *We Help Mommy* by Jean Cushman

Doing chores to help: Consider what chores you can give your child to help out around the house that he or she is capable of doing. Always demonstrate what to do first and then give your child a try. Here are a few chore ideas that your child could be responsible for at your house:
- Put pajamas away in the morning.
- Wipe down the outside of the refrigerator with a wet washcloth.
- Wipe down kitchen chair seats after a meal.
- Use a small dustpan and broom to sweep under the table.
- Dry unbreakable dishes with a paper towel.
- Dust furniture.

This activity develops:
- Further awareness of the body parts
- Awareness of body size and shape
- Skill in associating placement of clothing
- Responsibility

Age 2 - Activity 25 – Clapping Hands

Clapping hands with a one-time pattern: Clap your hands once in front of your waist. Ask the child to clap his or her hands just as you did. Next, clap your hands over your head once and encourage the child to do the same. Bend and clap your hands once below your knees and tell the child to do likewise.

Clapping hands with a two-time pattern: Tell the child that this time you are going to clap two times. Count as you clap twice with the hands at waist level. Instruct the child to do the same. Count as you clap twice above your head and encourage the child to copy you. Count as you clap twice below the knees and instruct the child to do likewise.

Watch, listen, and clap: This time, do not speak as you clap once above you head. Did the child copy and clap correctly? Assist the child if necessary so that he or she understands what you want him or her to do. Again, do not speak as you clap once below the knees and at the waist level. Did the child respond correctly?

New patterns: Progress to two claps in the different positions. Once the child is confident in watching, listening, and clapping, enrich the activity by using one or two claps interchangeably. However, be sure and do this only when the child has become confident in following the one-clap activity and then the two-clap activity. This will depend on the child.

> This activity develops:
> - Listening for a purpose
> - Watching for a purpose
> - Awareness of the change in body position
> - Further awareness of the concepts, "one" and "two"
> - Following directions

Age 2 - Activity 26 - Car Roll

You will need:
- 3 spools (same size and different sizes) or colored cars
- Red, yellow, and blue markers
- Sturdy piece of cardboard or book
- 3 books to create an inclined plane

Set up: Make an inclined plane by placing the cardboard or a book slanted up against 3 other books stacked on top of each another. Use different colored cars or spools.

Roll the spools or cars: Identify the three colors of the spools or small cars. Place a car at the top of the inclined plane and let it roll down hill until it stops. Do the same for the other color cars.

Ask questions:
- Which car (spool) went the farthest?
- Which car (spool) went the shortest distance?
- Did they all stop at about the same place?

Repeat the activity and note if there is any change. During this activity be sure to emphasize the three primary colors and concept of distance.

Different sized spools or cars: Use three spools or cars of different sizes and note if there is any change in the distance that each car (spool) rolls.

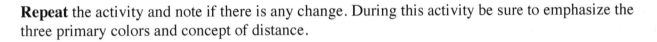

This activity develops:
- More awareness of the three primary colors
- Awareness of distance
- Skill in comparing distance
- Awareness of an inclined plane
- Awareness of change and position in space

Age 2 - Activity 27 – Coat Hanger Hoop

You will need:
- Metal coat hanger
- Masking tape or duck tape
- Doorknob
- Yarn ball, sock ball, or other small ball

Make a coat hanger hoop:
1. Bend the coat hanger hook and hold the neck of the coat hanger, so that it is secure around the knob of a door where you plan to do this activity.
2. Bend the metal of the rest of the coat hanger out until the part where it is fastened together is right up against the door. The metal can then be adjusted to be a round hoop.

"Basketball" activity: Show the child how to toss the ball through the hoop. Model and then allow the child to do it independently. Challenge your child to stand a short distance away from the hoop to practice aiming while shooting a basket.

Count the "baskets": Begin to count each time the ball goes through the hoop. Encourage the child to continue by suggesting a number of times for the child to toss the ball successfully through the hoop. Continue with this activity until the child loses interest. However, leave the hoop on the doorknob for the child to use at other times on his or her own.

Review activities: Don't forget that previous activities should be reviewed! The activities that need further skill development or enrichment should be noted. Choose the appropriate time to re-introduce these previous activities. You should feel free to vary the activity to fit your child's interest and needs as long as it teaches the basic concept that is intended in each activity.

> This activity develops:
> - Gross motor coordination
> - More awareness of aiming at a target
> - Persistence to complete a task
> - More awareness of counting
> - Independence and confidence

Age 2 - Activity 28 – Eggs in the Carton 1-2-3

You will need:
- Empty egg carton
- Raisins or beans
- Green and red markers

Set up:
1. Use a green marker and make a large green dot beside the left-hand cup of the top and bottom rows. *Green represents "go" on the left.*
2. Use a red marker and make a large red dot at the end of the right and bottom cups of the egg carton. *Red represents "stop" on the right.*

One raisin in each cup: Instruct the child to put one raisin in each cup of the carton's top row. Show your child how to start at the top left with the "green light" and stop at the "red light." Check to see if your child has done the activity correctly and empty the raisins from the carton.

Two and three raisins in each cup: Follow the same procedure by placing two raisins in each cup. If the child is interested, have the child place three raisins in each cup. Remember to empty all of the raisins from the carton cups before beginning a new number count.

The concept of three: Counting up to three is sufficient for your child at this age. Counting past three and making sets of objects higher than three can be overwhelming for the child. It is advisable to make sets of one, two, and three with a variety of materials. This will help to build a good foundation for understanding numbers.

Too much too soon can frustrate and confuse the child. Some children have been known to refuse to do activities, because they are challenged before they are ready for a basic concept. Slow and steady is the key to success!

This activity develops:
- An understanding of sets of 1-2-3
- More of an awareness of left and right progression
- Awareness of the color signals to start and stop
- More of an awareness of rows

Age 2 - Activity 29 – Fruits to See, Feel, Smell, and Taste

You will need:

- Red apple
- Orange
- Banana
- Strawberry
- Brown lunch bag
- Vegetables

Show, name, feel, and smell: Show and name each piece of fruit one at a time. Ask the child to repeat the name and identify the fruit's color. Note the specific smell of the fruit.

Observation questions:
- What shape does this fruit resemble?
- How does it feel on the outside?
- Is its outside bumpy or smooth?

Find it: Place each fruit in a row. Name the fruit and have the child find it on the table. Do this until all the fruits have been found. Then ask the child to find a fruit that is a specific color. Match the fruits that have the same color, continually calling each by name.

Feel or smell to find the fruit game: Place each fruit in a separate brown lunch bag and close the bag so that the child cannot see inside the bags. The child must select the fruit by smelling the fruit to find it. Later, the child may select the fruit you name by feeling the fruit to find it.

Introduce the sense of taste: Cut each piece of fruit in half and allow the child to taste and smell the piece of fruit that you have talked about with him or her. In this way, the child is using his or her sense of taste to identify fruit.

Vegetables: This activity should be done many times not only with fruits but also with vegetables. The child's senses will be greatly refined if this activity is consistently done in a casual manner.

This activity develops:
- An awareness of the sense of smell, touch, and taste
- Problem solving and listening skills
- Language enrichment
- Confidence and independence

Age 2 - Activity 30 – Ladder Walk

You will need:
- A wooden or metal extension ladder flat on the floor or in the yard
- Small object

> **Don't have a ladder?** If a ladder will not work, use 2 strips of yarn pulled through paper towel rolls stuffed with newspaper on the floor to resemble the rungs of ladder steps.

Walk between each ladder rung: Model for the child how to walk between each ladder rung. Emphasize the word *between*, and encourage the child to walk without touching the rungs and the sides of the ladder.

Activity extension: Encourage the child to walk again *between* the rungs, picking up an object at the end of the ladder. Then your child can turn around and return to the starting place with the object.

> **Tip:** You may need to hold your child's hand(s) while he or she attempts this activity to keep him or her from losing his or her balance and maintaining safety throughout the activity.

Book idea: *Ten Men on a Ladder* by Craig MacAulay and Helene Desputeaux

> This activity develops:
> - Awareness of the concept *between*
> - Gross motor coordination
> - Body balance
> - Listening and following directions
> - Language enrichment

Age 2 - Activity 31 – Is It Hot or Cold?

Cut out pictures from a magazine or the internet of:

Hot	Cold
Coffee	Milk
Soup	Popsicles
Hot chocolate	Ice cream
Hot dogs	Juice
Something Hot	Something Cold

Talk about hot foods: Talk about coffee and allow the child to smell coffee grounds. Prepare a cup of coffee or other hot drink and allow the child to observe the steam escaping from the hot mug. Be careful, but allow the child to feel the outside of the hot cup, so that he or she understands what the concept of "hot" means. Talk about hot soup, hot chocolate, and hot dogs with your child and how each of these foods is *hot*.

Talk about cold foods: Allow your child to drink a glass of milk or juice and compare the difference between the hot drink discussed earlier. Have the child feel the outside of the cold drink's glass. Talk about cold popsicles, cold ice cream, and other cold foods or drinks your family enjoys.

Sort hot and cold: Put all of the internet cutout pictures in a pile and ask the child to sort between which foods and drinks are hot and which are cold. You can label each pile with a red label written *hot* and a blue label written *cold*.

Appliances that make things cold or hot: Talk with your child about the stove, oven, refrigerator, microwave, and freezer and how these appliances make foods hot or cold.

This activity develops:
- Awareness of "hot" and "cold"
- Sorting
- Awareness that pictures can be used to represent foods
- Listening skills

Age 2 - Activity 32 – Tall and Short, Big and Small

You will need:
- 6 straws cut in half (12 short straws)
- 12 long straws
- 5 small cookies (animal crackers)
- 5 big cookies
- Big bowl
- Little bowl (or cup)

Identify tall and short straws: Identify the tall straw with your child. Then do the same with the short straw so that your child can see the difference. Hold them side-by-side while comparing them.

Tall or short? Instruct the child to find a tall straw from the pile. Then ask the child to find a short straw. Help the child if necessary.

Tall pile, short pile: Tell the child to put all of the tall straws in one pile and all of the short straws in another pile. Model how to sort them if necessary. Each time your child picks up one of the straws, ask him or her whether it is tall or short.

Make a straw line pattern: At another time, the child can create a simple pattern with laying the straws out in the following order: tall, short, tall, short, etc.

Count with big or small cookies: Count the five big cookies, 1-2-3-4-5 and place them in a row. Tell the child to place a little cookie on top of each big cookie and count 1-2-3-4-5. Praise the child if he or she responds correctly. If he or she does not respond correctly, count the big cookies again and repeat the question. Make sure the child is aware that there are just as many big cookies as little cookies. Repeat if necessary.

This activity develops:
- An awareness of tall and short, big and little
- An awareness of sorting for a purpose
- An awareness of a pattern
- Confidence and independence
- Awareness of the concept *five*
- More awareness of one to one matching

Age 2 - Activity 33 – Through the Tunnel

You will need:
- 3 or more cardboard boxes large enough for the child to crawl through
- Sharp knife or razor cutter
- Masking tape or duck tape
- Sandbox
- Coffee or juice can
- Small car

Before putting the boxes together: Allow the child to crawl through each individual box with the top and bottom of the box removed. Then place the boxes together to form a long tunnel. Use masking tape or duck tape to hold them together.

Crawl through the tunnel: Invite the child to crawl through the tunnel. Emphasize the word *through* each time that the child goes through the tunnel. Explain to the child what a tunnel is and that one can be made through rock and underground and even under water.

Make a model tunnel: In the sandbox, assist the child in making a tunnel using a coffee can or other container with both ends removed for support. The child can then drive a small car through his or her tunnel.

This activity develops:
- Awareness of tunnels
- Awareness of the word *through*
- Language enrichment
- Gross motor coordination
- Free exploration
- Independence and confidence

Age 2 - Activity 34 - Bowling

You will need:
- Several empty plastic dish detergent bottles or water bottles
- Tennis ball or other ball to roll
- Blocks, mop handles, masking tape

Set up: Line up the bottles so that they are very close together. Some should be behind the others like bowling pins.

Directions: Instruct the child to aim and try to knock the bottles down by rolling the ball. Direct the child to use both hands if he or she seems to have difficulty managing the ball.

Bowling lane boundaries: Make bowling lane boundaries with blocks, mop handles, or masking tape to offer more of a challenge to the child once he or she has the hang of the game. Change the boundary line depending on how easy or difficult the game is for your child. However, keep the boundary line close enough so that the child is knocking over at least one bottle each time he or she rolls the ball to build confidence.

Count: Count the bottles that are knocked down each time. Set them back in place and encourage the child to roll the ball again. Praise the child for his or her efforts.

Awareness of addition: Build your child's awareness of addition by asking how many bottles were knocked down, and then how many bottles are left standing to be knocked down. Help the child understand that the knocked down bottles plus the bottles still standing make up the total number of bottles in the game. Avoid introducing subtraction concepts until addition concepts are mastered. This will be a gradual process.

This activity develops:
- Eye-hand coordination
- Gross motor coordination
- Skill in aiming
- More of an awareness of *up* and *down*
- More of an awareness of number concepts
- Confidence

Age 2 - Activity 35 – Paper Plate Pull

You will need:
- Paper plate or Styrofoam plate
- Yarn
- Scissors
- Small toys to drag on the paper plate

Set up:
1. Punch a hole in the side of a paper plate with scissors.
2. Push a piece of yarn through the hole and tie it securely.
3. Cut the yarn to a long enough length that the child can hold the yarn and drag the plate around on the floor.

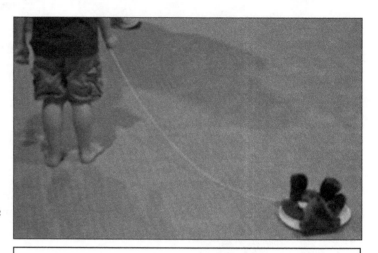

Tip: Start with something that will fill the paper plate and have less potential of falling off like a small teddy bear until the child masters the activity.

Pull a toy to a location: Place a toy on the paper plate and have the child pull the plate to a specified place. The goal is to pull carefully, so that the toy will not fall off the paper plate. If the toy falls off, instruct the child to put it back on the paper plate and continue.

Add a toy: Another toy (and include the child in choosing it) can be added to the paper plate for more of a challenge. Count the toys with your child to make him or her aware that one plus one are two. Indicate how many toys are on the plate and emphasize the word *several* for three or more toys. This would also be a good time to review the concepts of "heavy" and "light."

Pull with a purpose: The child can use his or her paper plate "wagon" to pull trash to the garbage can, toys to the toy bin, or other objects to his or her room that need to be put away. This will boost his or her motivation in helping with putting away things.

This activity develops:
- Gross motor coordination
- Awareness that more objects make the pulling load heavier
- Awareness of the words *one*, *more*, and *several*
- Confidence and independence

Age 2 - Activity 36 – Little Boy Blue

To make a horn:
- Paper towel roll

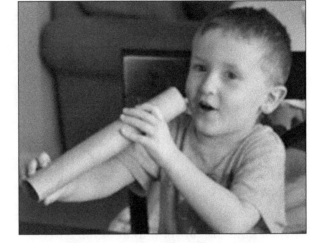

> *Little Boy Blue, come blow your horn.*
> *The **sheep** are in the meadow.*
> *The **cows** are in the corn.*
> *Where is the little boy who looks after the sheep?*
> *He is under the **haystack** fast asleep.*

Listen and respond: Encourage the child to listen for the two animals mentioned in the rhyme as you read it several times aloud to him or her. Ask the child where Little Boy Blue was when someone was looking for him. If your child does not recall the animals or Little Boy Blue's location, read the rhyme again before giving him or her the answers.

Do your best in life lesson: Make the child aware that Little Boy Blue was *supposed* to be taking care of the sheep, but instead he was asleep. Explain to your child that when you have a job to do, you must do the job the best you can. Talk about simple jobs that the child can do to help you such as setting the table, picking up trash in the house, retrieving things in another place for you, and putting his or her toys and clothes away.

Listen and come when called: Explain to the child that Little Boy Blue could blow his horn so that the sheep and cows could listen and come to him. Remind the child that when you call him or her, it is a signal for him or her to come to you. Children should obey parents; therefore, you expect him or her to obey you.

Rhyming words: Encourage the child to help you name rhyming words such as *horn*, *corn*, *born*, and *torn*. Also introduce rhyming words like *sheep*, *sleep*, *keep*, *deep*, and *heap*.

Little Boy Blue's horn: Use a paper towel roll to make a horn for your child to blow, pretending to be Little Boy Blue.

> This activity develops:
> - Listening for a specific purpose
> - Reasoning and memory recall skills
> - Further awareness of words that rhyme (sound alike)
> - Free expression (role playing) when blowing the horn
> - An understanding of obedience and responsibility

Age 2 - Activity 37 – Leaf Matching

You will need:
- 5 different types of tree or bush leaves
- Wax paper
- Iron

Take a walk to collect leaves: On a nature walk in your neighborhood or yard, make your child aware of different kinds of leaves by collecting 5 different kinds that have either fallen from the trees or have been plucked. Collect two of each kind of leaf for a total of ten leaves. Put the leaves in a bag to bring home and examine.

Examine leaves: Talk with your child about the different kinds of leaves that you both collected together.
- What things are **similar** about the leaves? Green, lined veins, pointed ends.
- What things are **different** about the leaves? Shapes, sizes, colors.

Identify: If you are familiar with the names of trees around your home, you may identify the type of leaf that came off of a certain tree.

Matching leaves activity: Place all ten leaves on a flat surface in random order. Have the child find matching leaves that are alike (from the same tree). If the child needs help, pick up a leaf and ask the child to find one like it. Point out to the child similar sets of like leaves or model how to group the sets together if needed.

Make a leaf collection: Preserve the leaf sets by sealing them between two pieces of wax paper. Lay a thin cloth between the wax paper and the hot iron. The heat from the iron will melt the wax of the two pieces of paper and fuse them together when the wax cools.

"I spy something green": Look for things that are green. You can even use the cardboard "magnifying glass" from Age 0 – Activity 35.

This activity develops:
- Skill in matching leaves
- More of an awareness of similarity and differences
- More of an awareness of the color green
- Listening and following directions

Age 2 - Activity 38 – On or Under

You will need:
- Four different but familiar objects
- Piece of furniture like a bed, table, or chair

On: Tell your child that you will be placing the object *on* the piece of furniture that you have selected for this activity. Then place the object *on* the furniture.

Under: Take the other object and place it *under* the same piece of furniture and emphasize to your child that you have placed the object *under*. Ask the child which object was placed *on* and which was placed *under*.

Child's turn: Hand an object to your child and ask him or her to place it *on* the furniture. Then hand another object to your child to place it *under*. If the child understands, switch the positions of the objects and ask him or her which is *on* and which is *under*.

Next, use all four objects and place two *on* and two *under*. Can the child remember the two objects that were placed *under* the furniture without looking?

Repeat: This activity should be repeated at various times and often to strengthen the child's understanding—not only of the concepts *on* and *under*—but also the child's skill in memory recall.

This activity develops:
- Observational skills (number and kind of objects)
- Memory recall
- Listening
- Gross and fine motor coordination in moving and holding selected objects
- Further awareness of the concepts *on* and *under*

Age 2 - Activity 39 – How Far Can You Throw?

You will need:
- A wad of paper secured with a rubber band
- Sock ball, nerf ball, or bean bag (or all 3 for more interest!)

Throw and mark distance: Allow the child to throw the sock ball as far as possible in a designated open area (garage or yard). Mark with a stick or piece of tape the distance the ball was thrown. Tell the child to pick up the sock ball again and throw it to see if he or she can throw it farther than the first time.

How far? Repeat this activity several times and talk to the child about how *far* he or she can throw the sock ball. Emphasize to the child that with practice he or she can throw the sock ball even farther. Praise the child for any positive response.

Other objects to throw: The child may want to use other objects for throwing outside. However, remind the child to throw away from people. Warn the child about the danger of throwing objects at people and animals. Discourage him or her from throwing rocks. Show your child safe objects that he or she can throw and give opportunities to throw them.

Throw rocks in the water: If you are near a pond or creek, allow your child to throw a rock in the water and observe the circular ripples that are made when the rock hits the surface of the water. Remind the child to only throw the rocks in the water and never at people.

This activity develops:
- Eye-hand coordination
- Gross motor coordination
- Awareness of distance
- Awareness of the concept "far"
- Confidence in developing skill in throwing an object

Age 2 - Activity 40 – My Color Booklet

You will need:
- 8 small 2 in. x 2 in. cards out of colored construction paper
- Letter size envelope
- Piece of white paper folded in quarters
- Crayons

Pick out the color game: Put all eight color cards inside of an envelope. Have the child take one color card out at a time and say the color's name aloud. Identify all of the color cards from the envelope.

Picture drawings: Accept and praise the child's drawings, ignoring the apparent scribbling, even though you most likely will not recognize any feature of the specific drawing. Allow and encourage freedom of expression.

Color booklet: Take the piece of white paper folded into quarters and designate each box (4 on front and 4 on back) to the following colors. Then have the child use that colored crayon to draw pictures on each page and say the picture aloud after it is drawn.

Red ball	Green grass	Brown table
Orange pumpkin	Blue water	Black boot
Yellow sun	Purple flower	

Read booklet aloud: Read the color booklet often with the child. The drawn objects' names can be used for memory recall, but keep in mind that this activity is not intended for reading words. Reading the booklet will be meaningful, because the child made it. The goal is for your child to recall the colors and objects from memory when he or she looks at it.

Other booklets: Depending on your child's interest, you can make other booklets with your child including a shape booklet, furniture booklet, nature booklet, or toy booklet. Pictures for these suggested booklets may be drawn by the child or pictures can be cut from old magazines or the internet and glued to the pages of a booklet.

This activity develops:
- Skill in listening and following directions
- More of an awareness of the basic colors
- Skill in identifying objects by color clues
- A feeling of ownership (his or her booklet)

Age 2 - Activity 41 - Belongings

You will need:
- Shirt from each family member
- Pictures of family members
- Shoes from each family member

Explain ownership: Lay the shirts out on the floor and point to each shirt explaining whose it belongs to. For example, "This is Daddy's shirt."

Identify whose shirt: Once all the shirts are identified, hold one up and ask the child whose shirt it is. If the child has difficulty matching the article of clothing with the person, use a picture of that person to help the child. Your child can match the picture of the family member with that person's clothing. When all of the clothing has been identified correctly, repeat the activity so that the child will feel confident and secure.

Identify whose shoe: Ask the child to match the person's name or picture with the correct shoe.

If there are not many family members, use other items of clothing for each family member, so that there are at least 5 items of clothing for the child to identify the ownership of.

This activity develops:
- Skill in matching by association
- Language enrichment
- Listening skills
- Confidence

Age 2 - Activity 42 – What Is Its Use?

You will need:
- Spoon
- Book
- Straw
- Cup
- Toothbrush
- Shoe
- Coins
- Key
- Crayon

Talk about what each household item is used for: Ask the child to tell you its name. Then ask the child what it is used for. Continue in this manner until the child can name each object and tell you its use. Assist the child whenever you feel it is necessary.

Too many objects at one time? If your child is having difficulty remembering the name of an object or its use, you may want to limit the activity to three or four items first and then add more later once he or she has gained more confidence with this.

Which object? Lay the objects out in front of your child and ask your child to identify the object that is used for a specific task.

Example:
- Which one unlocks a door?
- Which one do we stir food with?

Repeat: This activity can be repeated at different times over several days. Choose different items each time. If you feel the child needs additional clarification about any item, discuss it further to enrich the child's knowledge and language development.

This activity develops:
- Language enrichment
- Reasoning and association skills
- Further awareness that objects have a purpose
- Observational skills
- Confidence

Age 2 - Activity 43 – Food and Numbers

You will need:

Meat	Fruit	Vegetable
3 pieces of bite sized hot dog	3 pieces of fruit or raisins	3 peas or green beans

Lay out foods in rows: Count out 3 pieces of hotdog and lay them in a row. Count out 3 pieces of fruit and lay them in a row. Count out 3 pieces of a vegetable and lay them in a row. As you count aloud, the child can count with you 1-2-3.

First, second, third: Instruct the child to eat a piece of meat *first*, a fruit *second*, and a vegetable *third*. While the child is eating the foods, continue to use the words *first*, *second*, and *third* to explain order.

Mealtime: This activity can be done to make eating more interesting at meal time. Foods should be varied, as well as new ones introduced. Identify the foods for the child so that he or she can recall their names. At mealtime, instead of lining the food in rows, suggest that the child eat a spoonful of meat *first*, fruit *second*, and vegetable *third*. Your child can continue using ordinals (first, second, third) until all of his or her food is eaten.

Ordinal application to birthdays: The child should be made aware of his or her *first* and *second* birthdays that have already been experienced. The *third* birthday is coming next. He or she will be three years old. Explain to the child by holding one finger up and saying *first*. Do likewise with the next two fingers saying *second* and *third* to denote those birthdays.

This activity develops:
- An awareness of first, second, and third
- More of an awareness of his or her age and birthday
- Listening and following directions
- Vocabulary enrichment (names of foods)

Age 2 - Activity 44 – Foot Pushing

You will need:
- Sock ball or other ball
- Masking tape for boundaries

Boundaries and finish line: Establish an area inside that will be safe for the child to move a sock ball with his or her feet. Tape masking tape to the floor to mark the boundaries and the finish line.

Only one foot: Instruct the child to use only one foot to push the ball in the designated area. Remind the child not to kick the ball too hard but to control the ball by pushing it gently with his or her foot so that the ball can be pushed to the finish line.

Following directions: The child should be cautioned not to kick the ball randomly during this activity. It should be with controlled short pushes toward the finish line. If the child kicks the ball, stop, and repeat the directions.

How many foot pushes? When the child has developed some coordination, count aloud how many foot pushes he or she makes to get the ball to the finish line. Repeat this activity at various times and change the distance of the finish line or the side boundaries to add interest to the activity.

This activity develops:
- Eye-foot coordination (difference in a kick and a push)
- Further awareness of a boundary in reaching a goal
- Listening (for the count of the foot pushes made)

Age 2 - Activity 45 – Comic Strip Sequence Fun

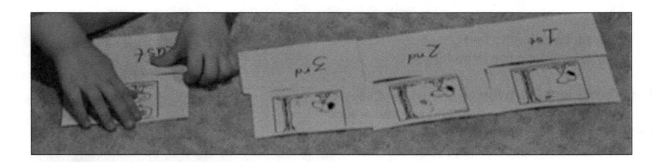

You will need:
- Comic strip from the newspaper
- Scissors
- Index cards (if you desire to draw your own comic strip sequence for the child to order)

Read and explain: Read the comic strip to your child and explain the humor and sequence of events of the chosen comic. Review the sequence with the child to determine if he or she understands what happened *first*, *second*, and *third*.

Order the sequence: Cut the comic strip sections apart. Mix the pieces and tell the child to place the pictures in the proper sequence. The child may enjoy this activity enough to want to repeat the activity several times.

Retell: Encourage the child to retell the story to you and assist him or her whenever necessary, allowing him or her to use words and embellish the story if he or she wishes.

Make your own comic strip sequence: On index cards, draw several simple pictures that have an order to tell a story. You may even want to include your child as a character in the comic for interest. Show the child the correct order of the comic strip cards and tell him or her the story. Then mix up the cards and have him or her place them in the correct sequence while retelling you the story. To aid the child, you may ask questions like, "What comes first, second, third, next?"

This activity develops:
- Memory recall of a brief story in sequence
- Language enrichment
- Eye-hand coordination
- Confidence
- An interest in comics

Age 2 - Activity 46 - Tiptoe

You will need:
- Drum or empty coffee can

Tiptoe with a jingle: Show the child how to tiptoe and say the following:

> *Tippy, tippy tiptoe here we go*
> *Tippy, tippy tiptoe to and fro*
> *Tippy, tippy tiptoe through the house*
> *Tippy, tippy tiptoe like a mouse.*

Tiptoe to a drumbeat: Tap a rhythm out while singing or saying the rhyme while the child tiptoes. Encourage the child to tiptoe on the beat.

Tiptoe hiding game: Encourage the child to tiptoe through the house quietly. Watch to make sure the child walks on his or her tiptoes and not on the sides of his or her feet. When you say the word *mouse* in the rhyme, have the child hide like a mouse as if he or she was hiding from a cat. Suggest that the mouse could hide behind a piece of furniture. Then pretend to be the cat and go looking for the hiding child.

Cat finds hiding mouse: As you hunt for the hidden "mouse," talk about how quiet a mouse must be so that the cat will not find him. When you find the "mouse," tell the child how very quiet he or she was, because you had difficulty finding him or her.

Balancing: Some children have difficulty balancing on their toes. The child may need to practice tiptoeing to develop good balance skills. Repeating this activity will motivate the child to practice balancing.

> This activity develops:
> - Listening and following directions
> - Awareness of the rhythm of the drum beat
> - Confidence
> - Skill in balancing and tiptoeing

Age 2 - Activity 47 – Colored Fish Sort

You will need:
- Red, blue, and yellow construction to cut fish out of (total of 15 fish)
- Glue
- 3 paper plates

Tip: Google a simple fish stencil from the internet to trace it on construction paper. Then cut out the different colored fish.

Set up: Glue one fish of each color on a separate paper plate. Mix the other colored fish and place them individually on the floor.

Extension: If your child enjoyed this activity, you may want to introduce other colored fish such as green, orange, and purple.

Sort by color: Instruct the child to put all of the red fish in the red plate, all of the blue fish in the blue plate, and all of the yellow fish in the yellow plate.

Repeat and count: Repeat this activity several times and praise the child for catching so many fish. Count the four fish in the red plate, the four in the blue plate, and the four in the yellow plate. Do not count the fish that are glued on the plates unless the child mentions it. If he or she does, tell the child that one more than four is the same as five.

Primary colors: Now would be a good time to make sure that the child knows the three primary colors are red, blue, and yellow. All other colors come from mixing these three colors together.

This activity develops:
- More of an awareness of red, blue, and yellow
- Skill in recognizing and matching the colored fish
- Skill in following directions
- Eye-hand coordination
- More of an awareness of four and one more to make five

Age 2 - Activity 48 – Ball Bounce

You will need:
- Ball that bounces and can be held in child's hand

Model dropping and catching: Show the child how to drop the ball and catch it when it bounces up. Emphasis should be placed on watching the ball as it goes down and comes back up so that the child can anticipate the ball's position to catch it at the right time. Say the words *down* and *up* as the ball does these actions.

Child's practice: Allow the child to attempt to bounce the ball on his or her own. Stand behind the child if necessary and help to drop the ball. Assist the child in determining when to catch it. Avoid negative correction.

Count: Once the child has mastered bouncing the ball, count aloud how many times the child can bounce and catch the ball without missing. Encourage the child to count with you. This will help the child become aware of his or her progress, and at the same time enrich his or her understanding of sequential counting.

This activity develops:
- Eye-hand coordination
- Skill in throwing and catching a ball
- Further awareness of *up* and *down*
- Tactile enhancement (feeling when catching a ball)
- More of an awareness of counting in sequence
- Confidence

Age 2 - Activity 49 – Early Skipping Fun

You will need:
- Skipping music

Model how to skip: Tell the child that you are skipping as you skip around the room slowly to show the child how. Skip very slowly and say, "Step, hop." Encourage the child to watch and try to skip slowly with you as you hold his or her hand.

"Step hop" or 1-2 count: You can encourage the child to say "Step hop" with you as he or she skips or it can be a quick "1-2" count. Practice skipping whenever the child shows interest throughout the week(s) either counting "1-2" or saying, "step hop" to establish a rhythmic pattern.

Trot like a pony and/or add music: Instruct your child to be a pony as he or she skips along. You may want to skip with your child to some upbeat music that has a 1-2 rhythm. You can designate a finish line that your child can trot to.

Reminders: If you have had little success with the skipping activity, encourage your child to take short quick steps instead. Practice hopping on one foot if this seems to be preventing the child from skipping successfully.

This activity develops:
- Gross motor coordination (leg and foot)
- A sense of rhythm in skipping and trotting
- Listening and observational skills
- Rhythmic clapping coordination
- Confidence

Age 2 - Activity 50 – Animal Moves

Show the child a picture of each animal and relay facts about each one.
Pictures can be obtained from a book or printed from an internet search.

Snake	Fish	Frog	Bird
No arms or legs Must wiggle to crawl forward Dry scales on its skin and sheds it as it grows	No arms or legs—instead has a tail and fins Swims through the water Mouth and gills for breathing oxygen from the water	4 legs Must hop or jump to move Smooth, sticky tongue to catch insects	2 legs and 2 wings Flies through the air Body is covered with feathers

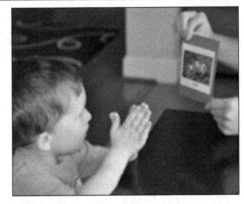

Snake: Encourage the child to wiggle like a snake by laying on his or her stomach and wiggling body muscles to move forward toward a finish line.

Fish: Invite the child to pretend to be a fish by putting his or her hands together and moving them to resemble a swimming fish.

Frog: Place a small pillow on the floor and tell the child to pretend to be a frog and jump over the pillow.

Bird: Invite the child to pretend to fly like a bird by moving his or her arms as wings.

Similar and different: Ask the child how a bird is different from a frog and how a snake is different from a fish. Encourage the child to recall some of his or her favorite facts about each animal discussed.

Field trip idea: Take your child to the zoo where he or she can observe animals and relate facts that he or she has learned about the snake, frog, bird, and fish.

Pet idea: Your child may also enjoy a goldfish of his or her own. Your child can take responsibility by feeding and caring for a pet of his or her own.

> This activity develops:
> - Awareness of different kinds of animals
> - Awareness of how different animals move
> - Keener sense of observation
> - Dramatization

Age 2 - Activity 51 – Matching Pictures

You will need:
- Index cards
- 2 identical magazines (or printed pictures of simple objects from an internet search)
- Glue

Set up: Select and cut out 5 large pictures from each of the two identical magazines. Glue all 10 pictures on index cards, so you have 5 sets of cards to match.

Match together: Lay the pictures face up in two columns and ask the child to find any two pictures that are the same. He or she can make "same" piles with the pictures. For success, you may assist the child by giving clues such as, "It is in this area" as you point to where the matching picture is.

Find the same: Lay 5 different pictures face up and put the 5 matching pictures in a pile. The child can pick a card from the pile and find the picture that is the same.

Concentration **memory game:** To further challenge your child with more picture matching cards, your child can play the memory game *Concentration*. With all the cards face down, the child turns over two cards at a time. If the pair is not a match, he or she turns the cards back down. If the two cards match, they can be put in a "same pile."

Independence and repetition: As your child gains confidence, let him or her do all of the matching. Give verbal clues less and less as you repeat these matching activities with your child.

Book idea: *Matching with Teddy (Fun to Learn Squeaky Board Books)* illustrated by Jenny Tulip

This activity develops:
• Skill in observing and matching pictures
• Eye-hand coordination
• Memory recall
• Further awareness of pictures that are the "same"
• Confidence and independence

Age 2 - Activity 52 – Colorful Fishing

You will need:
- Red, orange, yellow, blue, green, purple, brown, and black construction paper
- Scissors
- Fish stencil (from internet search)
- Hole punch
- 8 paper clips
- Magnet
- Yarn
- Wooden spoon
- Hot glue gun (optional)

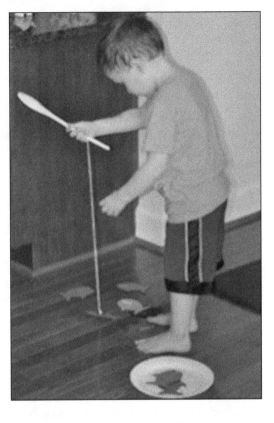

Set up: Trace the fish stencil and cut out a fish from each color of construction paper so that there is a total of 8 fish for this activity. Punch a hole in the "nose" of each fish and put a paper clip through each fish. To make a "fishing pole," tie or hot glue a magnet to a piece of yarn, which you can tie to a wooden spoon.

Review colors and model fishing: Show the child one fish of each color and name each color as you place the fish at random in front of the child. Review each color and ask the child to pick up the color of the fish you name. Then show the child how to "catch" the fish with the magnet. Give him or her a chance to practice.

"Catch" the correct colored fish: Name a color and ask the child to "catch" the fish of that named color. Continue until all of the fish have been caught.

Enrichment ideas: Work with a small number of fish and instruct the child to catch a certain number of fish (1-5) at a time. Count the number of fish that were caught and then ask the child how many are left. Matching stickers, numbers, letters, and words may be used on the fish at different times. Only use a few fish at first and then gradually add more than 8 fish as the child becomes more confident.

Book idea: *Rainbow Fish Big Book* by Marcus Pfister Herbert

This activity develops:
- Further skill in color recognition
- Skill in matching colors
- Listening for the color named in order to find it
- Eye-hand coordination

Age Three: From Three-years-old to Four-years-old

Look at Me!

Three-year-olds are eager for their parent's attention and often beg for it for the wrong reasons. Why not convert those negative attention-getting moments into positive opportunities that focus your child on developing productive skills through the activities in this section?

Curiosity

At this inquisitive age, children are asking many questions about the world around them. The mini lessons in the Age Three section of this book are based on answering and exploring common questions that children of this age often have. Basic scientific ideas like day and night, magnetism, floating, sinking, and shadows are a few of them. Model asking questions in daily conversations with your child and give him or her the freedom to ask questions about what he or she may be curious about.

The Importance of Picture Books

As your child asks more questions, books become an important tool in explaining answers as well as in prompting more questions. Fiction and nonfiction book ideas are suggested at the end of most lessons in this section. These book recommendations connect to the same concepts covered in the lesson's main ideas. Reading aloud to your child regularly (1) jump starts phonemic awareness (sound recognition), (2) increases a child's vocabulary, (3) furthers reading rate and fluency, (4) develops sequencing and questioning skills, (5) makes connections between the child and the world around him or her, (6) builds communication, (7) promotes memory skills, (8) supports attention-focusing habits, and (9) fosters a positive attitude toward learning through the written word.

Conversation

Conversation is the key to continuing this language development with your child. Include him or her in the tasks that you do around the house and explain in words what you are doing and why you are doing it. While driving in the

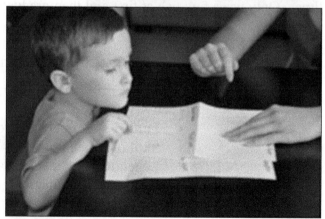

166

car, encourage your child to look out the window and discuss what you see, where you are going, and where you are coming from.

Creativity

Painting, drawing, gluing, cutting, tracing, coloring, etc. are all fine motor skills that your three-year-old child will begin to have better control in doing over the coming months. Three-year-olds are much more self aware, so giving children opportunities to express themselves through these creative outlets is imperative as they develop.

Large Muscle Activities

Active running, jumping, pedaling, hopping, sliding, throwing, catching, and galloping are all skills that three-year-olds are in desperate need of as they abound with insatiable energy. This is why it is essential to go back to many of the activities presented in the Age 1 and Age 2 sections. Just because they are organized in the younger sections, does not mean that your child has "outgrown" these activities. In fact, your child's maturity may have caught up with some of the activities he or she initially had not liked before.

Limit Screen Time

Countless studies show the negative effects of young children watching too much television and glued to video and computer games and iPad apps. As your child's parent, set the example by limiting your own screen time in front of your child. If they see you reading a good book or riding your bike, they will more likely read or ride too. Set limited viewing times and be consistent so that your child knows what is expected of him or her. My hope is that the activities in this book will offer you and your child engaging alternatives to "screen time."

Playing With Others

Playing with other children requires listening, responding, taking turns, and sharing. These are social skills that need to be practiced in safe settings for short amounts of time (no longer than an hour). Do not be surprised if your child has difficulty sharing at first. Monitoring your child and his or her playmate will be necessary until he or she has developed the skills needed for productive play with others.

Note

The author and publisher are not liable for any injury or death incurred due to the misuse of the suggested materials and directions. As with all child-related activities, materials should be selected with careful attention to child safety; adult supervision is essential.

Age 3 - Activity 1 – Spooning, Scooping, and Pouring

You will need:
- Dried beans
- Large spoon
- 2 large bowls
- Rice
- Measuring cup
- Water
- 2 small pitchers

Spoon beans from full bowl to empty bowl: Show the child how to use the spoon to scoop the beans from the full bowl on the left side and pour the beans into the empty bowl on the right side. Allow the child to spoon beans on his or her own. If the beans spill, encourage the child to pick them up and put them in the bowl that he or she is filling.

Scoop rice from full bowl to empty bowl: With the full bowl of rice on the left and the empty bowl on the right, model the correct way to grasp the measuring cup to scoop the rice from the full bowl to the empty one. Allow your child to scoop the rice with the measuring cup on his or her own.

Pour water from full pitcher to empty pitcher: Place the full water pitcher on the left and the empty pitcher on the right. Model the correct way to hold the full pitcher and slowly pour the water into the empty pitcher. Allow your child to pour the water on his or her own.

Separate activities and supervised independence: You may want to do each of these activities on different days or at different times depending on your child's interest level. Repeat these activities so that your child can practice spooning, scooping, and pouring on his or her own with your supervision to gain confidence in completing these tasks independently

---

This activity develops:
- Development of concentration
- Left to right movement
- Eye-hand coordination
- Independence and confidence

Age 3 - Activity 2 – Obstacle Line

You will need:
- Long piece of colored yarn
- Block
- Cup
- Spool
- Small toy
- Small stuffed animal

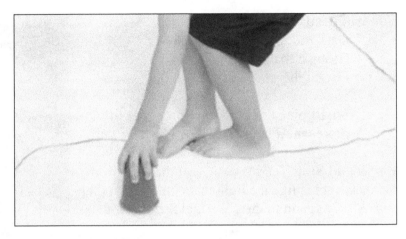

Set up: Lay the yarn on the floor and curve it around at intervals so that it is not in a straight line. Place a small object at each curved indentation. These objects will serve to establish boundaries for the child to go around.

Model: Show the child how to walk with one foot exactly in front of the other. Direct the child to walk from one end of the yarn to the other with one foot in front of the other until he or she gets to the other end.

Pick up: As the child walks the curved yarn line, encourage him or her to pick up the objects at each curved indentation. By slowly bending his or her knees, your child can carefully pick up the cup or block while staying on the line without losing his or her balance.

Colored paper enrichment: To reinforce colors, enrich the activity by placing different colored pieces of paper at the curved indentations of the yarn line instead of small objects. Tell your child to pick up a specified colored piece of paper and bring it back. You may want to introduce new colors like pink, lavender, lime, tan, and gray. Make sure you have identified each new color by name before the paper pick up activity.

Book idea: *Balancing Act* by Ellen Stoll Walsh

> This activity develops:
> - Eye-foot coordination
> - Skill in balance
> - Skill in following directions
> - More awareness of colors
> - Observational skill
> - Confidence

Age 3 - Activity 3 – Day and Night

You will need:
- Dark room
- Globe or ball
- Flashlight
- Tape
- Small piece of construction paper to represent a house

Earth and Sun: Tell the child that the light from the flashlight is like the light that comes from the sun. Also, explain to the child that the globe is round just like the earth that we live on.

Daytime and nighttime: When the sun shines on the earth, we have daytime. When the sun does not shine on the earth, it is nighttime. Show the child the dark side of the globe where the flashlight is not shining.

Day and night at our house: Tape a piece of small construction paper to the globe to represent your house. Allow the child to hold the flashlight and pretend that it is day on this side of the earth where the house is. Slowly turn the globe from left to right. Point out to the child that the part of the earth having day is where he or she lives, and the other side is having night. When the house is on the opposite side of the globe away from the flashlight, explain to the child that it is night.

Application: When it is nighttime, talk to your child again about why it is dark outside. Ask the child where the sun is.

Pretend to be earth: Allow the child to pretend to be earth. He or she can even tape the small construction paper house on the front of his or her shirt. Hold the flashlight and have the child turn or "rotate" slowly around while you hold the light in one position. Through this experience, the child will realize that the light from the flashlight can only shine on one side of him or her at a time.

Book idea: What *Makes Day and Night (Let's-Read-and-Find-Out Science 2)* by Franklyn M. Branley

This activity develops:
- Awareness of day and night
- Awareness that the earth is round and turns
- Awareness that the sun gives us light
- Role playing
- Language enrichment

Age 3 - Activity 4 – Scissors

You will need:
- Children's scissors (with blunt ends)
- Sharpie
- Computer paper
- Cooked spaghetti

Model how to hold scissors: Show the child that the thumb should be placed in the top hole and the middle finger should be placed in the lower hole. The pointer (index) finger should rest just below the rim of the lower hole and provide support to the scissors. Allow the child to hold the scissors correctly on his or her own.

Cut on the line: Draw a line from top to bottom on a half sheet of computer paper with a sharpie. Instruct the child to cut closely beside the line. The child can pretendthat the scissors are "biting" into the paper along the line.

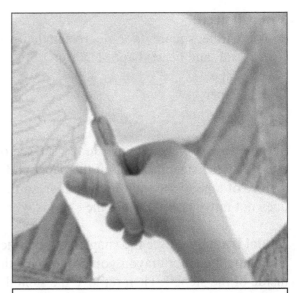

Remind the child that the thumb should always be "up." (top hole of scissors)

The child will need much guidance and patience in learning to coordinate scissors.

Reminders: It is not advisable to leave a child this age alone with scissors. Encourage your child to cut *only* paper that you have given him or her permission to cut.

Cut spaghetti: Allow the child to cut cooked spaghetti (soft) in half. This will give him or her better control of the scissors and help develop more confidence in cutting.

Book idea: *Let's Cut Paper! (Kumon First Steps Workbooks)* edited by Shinobu Akaishi and Eno Sarris

This activity develops:
- Skill in cutting
- Eye-hand coordination
- Visual skill in watching the cutting line
- Skill in following directions
- Confidence

Age 3 - Activity 5 – Shape Stencils

You will need:
- Circle, square, triangle, rectangle, oval, star, and heart shape stencils
- Tape
- Paper
- Crayons

Set up: Tape a piece of paper to the surface of the table. Lay the stencil on top of the paper and use a piece of tape to secure it to the paper, so that it does not move around while the child is working.

Model tracing: Name the shape that you trace and name the color crayon you use to trace the inside of the stencil. Then remove the stencil to reveal the traced shape.

Trace the shape with a stencil: Allow your child to choose a shape stencil to trace. Name the shape and allow your child to choose a color crayon. Make sure that your child is aware of the name of the color crayon he or she has chosen. Then secure

> **Color inside the stencil:** Your child may not be ready for tracing a stencil yet. If this is the case, he or she will enjoy coloring inside of the stencil to create the shape instead.

the stencil to the blank paper with tape and have your child trace the inside of the stencil. Remove the stencil to reveal the traced shape. Repeat this activity with all of the shape stencils available or until the child loses interest.

"I Spy" to review shapes and colors: Reinforce your child's memory recall by playing the game "I Spy" to review colors and shapes around your house and yard.

Book idea: *So Many Circles, So Many Squares* by Tana Hoban

> This activity develops:
> - More awareness of shapes
> - More awareness of colors
> - Freedom of choice in selecting colors and shapes
> - Eye-hand coordination
> - Language enrichment
> - Confidence

Age 3 - Activity 6 – Hit or Miss

You will need:
- Sock ball, nerf ball, yarn ball, or stuffed paper bag
- Piece of yarn or string
- Doorway to suspend the ball with string
- Yardstick or plastic bat

Set up: Hang the ball from the open doorway by attaching a piece of string at the top of the door frame and tying it to the ball. The ball should hang at the child's eye level or slightly above.

Model batting the hanging ball: Show the child how to grasp the bat with the hands and show the child how to bat the hanging ball.

Hit the ball: Instruct the child to keep his or her eyes on the ball as it swings back and forth after the first swing. Remind the child to tap the ball gently and stand in one position so that the ball will swing in clear view for him or her to tap the ball when it returns.

Count the hits: The child will enjoy counting the number of times he or she can hit the ball. Allow the counting to continue as long as the child is interested.

Book idea: *Stop that Ball! (Beginner Books)* by Mike McClintock

---

This activity develops:
- Eye-arm coordination
- Skill in timing or anticipating the return of the ball
- Skill in counting
- More awareness of a boundary

Age 3 - Activity 7 – Hole Punch Row

You will need:
- Index card
- Hole punch
- Marker or pencil
- Paper
- Tape
- Newspaper

Set up: Punch a row of holes in the bottom of the index card to make a stencil. Then use tape to secure the index card to the paper underneath to keep it from slipping.

Color in the row of holes: Give the child a marker or pencil and show him or her how to color in the holes that have been punched. Encourage the child to move from left to right. When the child is finished the row, remove the tape and show him or her the colored circles that he or she made on the paper underneath. Make another row and observe.
- Does your child take time to fill in the entire hole or does he or she just make a mark in each hole?
- Emphasize the word *row*. Make the child aware that he or she is making a row of circles as he or she traces the stencil.

Using a hole puncher: The child can use a metal hole puncher to punch holes at random. This can be done on a newspaper scrap. If your hole puncher is too difficult for the child to grip and punch a hole, assist him or her until he or she develops the necessary strength and coordination to successfully punch holes.

Book idea: *How Many Ducks in a Row? (A Turn & Pop Book)* by Teresa Imperato

> This activity develops:
> - Eye-hand coordination
> - Skill in focusing on detail
> - More awareness of left and right
> - More awareness of a row
> - Awareness of movement along a line
> - Independence and confidence

Age 3 - Activity 8 – Name the Sound

You will need:
- Bell
- Set of keys
- Wooden blocks
- Other objects that make sounds
- 5 brown paper bags
- iPhone (or device that can record sound)

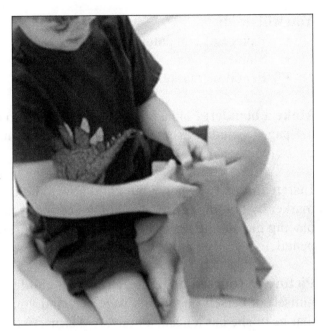

Set up: Place each kind of item in a separate brown paper bag. Name and show the child what is in each bag.

Shake, listen, identify: Shake one of the bags and encourage the child to listen and identify what is in the bag based on the noise that he or she hears. Repeat with the other bags until all of the noises have been identified. Vary the objects for interest. Mix up the bags and allow the child to shake the bag to listen and identify the objects inside on his or her own.

Record familiar home sounds: Record home sounds such as vacuum cleaner, radio, clock, dishes rattling, pouring water, hammering, etc. The recording can be played for the child, so he or she can identify the sounds that are heard. If he or she has difficulty, produce the real sound for the child and then try the recording again.

Book ideas:
- *The Very Quiet Cricket* by Eric Carle
- *Hearing (Rookie Read-About Health)* by Sharon Gordon
- *I Hear Sing and Read (Our Five Senses)* by Joann Cleland

This activity develops:
- Skill in identifying objects
- Listening for a sound to help in making a selection
- Skill in distinguishing different sounds
- Confidence
- Language enrichment

Age 3 - Activity 9 – Listen and Draw Book

You will need:
- 1 piece of computer paper
- Stapler
- Pencil or marker

Make a booklet: Fold a piece of paper in half to create a 4-page (including front cover) booklet and count the pages together.

Listen and draw: Show your child how to hold the marker by holding it with the thumb and index finger placing the middle finger behind to help support the pencil.

Picture of yourself on page 1: Tell your child to draw himself or herself on the first page. Remind your child that he or she has a head, a body, two arms, two legs, etc. Accept whatever the child draws and praise him or her for effort.

Picture of a house on page 2: Suggest that the child should begin with a square. Remind your child that a house has a door, windows, a roof, and a chimney.

Picture of a ball on page 3: If your child asks you for help, draw a circle in the air with your hand and tell the child to draw a ball on the paper.

Keep in mind: These 4 drawings do not all have to be done in one sitting.

Picture of anything you like on page 4: Give your child time to think. If the child says that he or she does not know what to draw, make a few suggestions such as a favorite toy, a tree, a bird, etc. Again, accept what you see and praise the child for effort.

Look at the completed booklet with your child: Ask the child what is on each page and let him or her tell you about his or her drawings. Encourage your child to turn the booklet to the next page as you "read" it together.

This activity develops:
- Skill in listening and following directions
- Eye-hand coordination
- Skill in turning a page

Age 3 - Activity 10 – Guess It! Riddles

Riddles: Children enjoy riddles, and they encourage thinking and reasoning. Simple riddles can be developed quickly and are a great "car activity." Older siblings can participate too!

Book idea: *My First Riddles* illustrated by Judith Hoffman Corwin

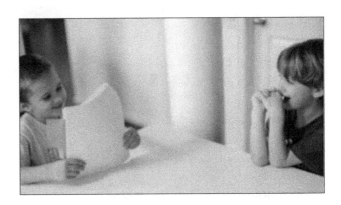

Riddle:	Answer:
What is green and brown and grows very tall?	Tree
What has four wheels and Dad drives it?	Car
What has a front and back and has pages?	Book
What has four legs, a back, and you sit on it?	Chair
What lets you in and out?	Door
What has two wheels, pedals, and handlebars?	Bike
What is yellow and gives us heat and light?	Sun
What is soft and helps you rest your head?	Pillow
What is long and thin, and you can write with it?	Pencil
What is (describe the child)?	Child's Name

Make up your own: Encourage the child to think of some riddles on his or her own to ask you to guess the answers for!

> This activity develops:
> - Active thinking and reasoning
> - Skill in listening for clues
> - Awareness of characteristics of different things

Age 3 - Activity 11 – Create a Picture

You will need:
- Cardstock paper
- Elmer's glue
- Bottle cap
- Cotton swab
- Small pieces of colored paper
- Baggie ties
- Bits of cloth
- Several buttons
- Cotton balls
- Pieces of felt
- String or yarn
- Other materials that can be glued to create a picture

Gather household materials and give directions: Gather an assortment of the above materials for the child to see and feel. Talk about the materials and their uses. Direct the child to use his or her imagination to create a picture using the materials and use glue to paste them on the cardstock paper. The picture can be of something familiar (sheep, house, tree, etc.) or abstract art.

Using glue: Use an overturned bottle cap to fill with Elmer's glue and model using a cotton swab to dip into the wet glue, spread it on the cardstock paper, and press the chosen material down to secure it. You may want to lay down newspaper to keep the area clean in case the glue spills.

Materials from outside: Repeat this activity with outside materials like:
- Leaves
- Sticks
- Small flowers
- Feathers
- Acorns
- Gumballs
- Grass pieces
- Straw

Book ideas:
- *Fisher-Price: Touch & Feel Adventure: Discovering Colors & Textures* by Alexis Barad
- *Pat the Bunny (Touch and Feel Book)* by Dorothy Kunhardt

This activity develops:
- Freedom of choice
- More awareness of textures of a variety of materials
- Eye-hand coordination

Age 3 - Activity 12 – Where Does It Belong?

You will need:

- Key
- Small juice can
- Spoon
- Large button
- Small envelope
- Computer paper
- Sharpie or pen
- 10 buttons of various sizes and shapes
- Clay or play-dough
- Popsicle stick
- Scissors
- Pencils
- Other traceable objects

Set up: Trace the outline of each object on apiece of paper with a sharpie or pen. Start out with 4 items, so the child can master the activity.

Directions: Place the objects in a box and encourage the child to choose an object and place it on the correct shape like a puzzle.

Button extension: Choose ten buttons of various shapes and sizes and trace their outlines on paper. Place the buttons in a container and encourage the child to place the buttons on the correct shape.

Play-dough impressions: Use play-dough to make impressions of the various items in the above activity. Instruct the child to match the objects on the impressions or indentations made in the play-dough with the assortment of objects used.

Book idea: *Shapes (First Learning)* by Jenny Tyler

This activity develops:
- Further awareness of different shapes of objects
- Eye-hand coordination
- Observational skills
- Matching skills
- Awareness of sizes
- Problem solving
- Confidence

Age 3 - Activity 13 – Sponge Painted Turtle

You will need:
- Green paint
- 2 paper plates
- Green construction paper
- Stapler
- Sponge
- Newspaper
- Sharpie

Set up: Cut out 4 legs and the head of a turtle from green construction paper. Staple them to the paper plate. Draw eyes and a mouth with a sharpie on the turtle's head. Lay the "turtle" on the newspaper for the child to sponge paint. Pour some green paint into the other paper plate for the child to dip the sponge into.

Sponge paint the turtle's back: Model dipping the sponge into the paint and then printing it down on the turtle's back and sponge a design.

Finished? When the child is finished with the sponge design, lay the turtle to dry. When the paint is dry, the child can play with his or her turtle!

Print painting with other objects: You can print paint with other objects to create designs and art with your child. Here are a few suggestions:

- Toothbrush
- Bottle cap
- Old comb

- Spool
- Golf ball
- Golf tee

- Pencil eraser
- Clothespin

Book idea: *How the Turtle Got Its Shell (Little Golden Book)* by Justine and Ron Fontes

---

This activity develops:
- Awareness of another way to paint
- Awareness of wet and dry
- Language enrichment
- Awareness of a turtle's characteristics
- Tactile sensitivity when painting
- Confidence

Age 3 - Activity 14 – Penny and a Nickel

You will need:
- 5 pennies and 5 nickels
- 2 cups and sharpie
- Empty grocery items to play "store"

Penny: Have your child hold a penny and explain that President Abraham Lincoln is on the front, and the Lincoln Memorial is on the back. Tell the child that the coin is worth one cent. Count out the 5 pennies together: 1-2-3-4-5.
- How many pennies altogether? 5 pennies.
- How many *cents* is that? 5 cents.

Nickel: Have your child hold a nickel and explain that President Thomas Jefferson is on the front and his home, Monticello, is on the back. A nickel, five cents, is worth (will buy as much as) five pennies. Ask the same questions about the nickel as you did with the penny.

Sort pennies and nickels: Mix the 5 pennies and 5 nickels up and put them in a pile. Use a sharpie to write "1 cent" on a plastic cup and "5 cents" on the other cup. Instruct the child to put all of the pennies in the "1 cent" cup and all of the nickels in the "5 cents" cup.

Pretend store: Write price tag amounts on each grocery store item. Allow the child to use the nickels and pennies to "buy" items at the pretend store. He or she may need your assistance to count out the correct number of pennies or nickels he or she needs to purchase an item. Have your child only buy one item at a time from the store until he or she feels confident. Your child can play the role of "cashier" when he or she gets the hang of the money exchange process.

Book ideas:
- *Penny: The Forgotten Coin* by Denise Brennan-Nelson
- *Benny's Pennies (Picture Yearling Book)* by Pat Brisson

This activity develops:
- Awareness of pennies and nickels
- Sorting skills and counting
- Money exchange
- Role playing

Age 3 - Activity 15 – Two Parts Make a Whole

You will need:
- Poster board or manila folder
- Glue stick
- Pictures from internet or magazine
- Scissors

Set up: Cut out five large colorful pictures. Show them to your child and talk about each picture. Allow the child to help you use a glue stick to glue the picture onto a piece of manila folder. When the glue is dry, cut each picture into two pieces with one or two curves or points in the cutting to create 2-piece puzzles.

Puzzle pieces fit together: Show the child how to take the two puzzle pieces of the same picture and fit them together to make a whole picture. Mix up all the puzzle pieces and tell the child to put them back together again to make two whole pictures.

Left and right sides are different: When the puzzles are complete, pick up the left side of one of the pictures and ask the child to tell you something about it. Then do the same for the right side. Accept whatever answers the child gives you.

Two halves make a whole: During your conversation with the child, refer to the left and right sides of each picture and make the child aware that the picture has two parts. You may mention that each part is called a *half* and that two *halves* make a *whole*.

Repeating activities is important! What may seem simple to you, may not be that simple for the child. That is why it is important to play the same games and repeat activities to firmly instill these concepts and build his or her confidence.

Book idea: *Half or Whole? (Little World Math Concepts)* by Susan Meredith

This activity develops:
- Further awareness of *left* and *right*
- Awareness that the left and right sides of a picture are different
- Eye-hand coordination
- Further awareness that two parts make a *whole*
- Language enrichment

Age 3 - Activity 16 – Box House and Brown Bag Activity

You will need:
- A cardboard box big enough for the child to crawlin and sit down in easily
- Razor or box cutter for making windows and a door
- Sharpie
- Other markers to color the box and decorate it
- 2 brown lunch bags
- Strips of long construction paper (red, orange, yellow, green, blue, purple, brown, and black)

Set up: Turn the box upside down, so that the bottom of the box becomes the roof of the "box house." Cut a door in the front (cutting three sides but leaving the left side intact to "swing open") and windows on the side and/or back. Your child can use markers with your supervision to decorate the outside of his or her "box house."

Review *in* and *out*: You can show your child how to go *in* his or her box house and come *out* of it. He or she can play pretend house and explore going *in* and *out* on his or her own.

Brown bag activity: Put two sets of 8 colored strips of paper in each one. Give one brown bag to your child and keep one for yourself. Choose one color strip out of your bag and ask your child to find that same color strip in his or her bag. The matched color strips should be placed beside each other. Choose another color strip and have the child match it by finding the same color in his or her bag until all of the color strips have been matched together.

Book idea: *Red, Green, Blue: A First Book of Colors* by Alison Jay

---

This activity develops:
- Memory recall
- Skill in color naming and matching
- Gross motor coordination
- Eye-hand coordination
- Confidence

Age 3 - Activity 17 – Tearing Strips

You will need:
- 5 meat trays or paper plates
- Sharpie
- Strips of paper that can be torn

Set up: Number the plates with the sharpie 1, 2, 3, 4, 5. Lay the plates out in a row in number order. Give the child strips of paper.

Tear, count, and place: Instruct him or her to tear off one piece of paper and place it in the tray that has the 1 on it, then have him or her put two pieces in the plate that has a 2 on it and so forth. You may need to model the activity to help your child begin.

Count when finished: Count the pieces in each plate. Emphasize the recognition of 1 for one piece, 2 for two pieces, 3 for three pieces, etc.

Mix the number plates: Once your child is confident completing the activity with the plates in order, mix the five plates for more of a challenge. Instruct the child to find the 1 plate, the 2 plate, the 3 plate, etc. Have the child put the plates in number order.

Book ideas:
- *Rainbow Fish Counting* by Marcus Pfister
- *My First Counting Book* by Lilian Moore

This activity develops:
- Eye-hand coordination
- Further awareness of parts of a whole by tearing from a whole strip to make smaller pieces
- Skill in counting and recognizing 1, 2, 3, 4, and 5
- Matching skill (pieces with numbers)
- Confidence

Age 3 - Activity 18 – Three Triangles

You will need:
- 3 manila folders
- Scissors
- Blank paper
- Sharpie (to make dots)

Set up: Cut out a small triangle on one manila folder, a medium triangle on another manila folder, and a large triangle out of the last manila folder. The remaining pieces from each folder will be used as a frame for each of the three triangles.

Fit into the frame: Show the child the three triangles. Fit the smallest triangle into the frame from which it was cut. Tell the child that this is the *small* triangle. Do the same with the medium and large triangles. Encourage the child to put the triangles in the correct frames like a puzzle. Allow him or her to do it independently but give help if he or she does not seem to understand.

Stacking triangles: Take the three triangles out of the frames and place them on top of each other with the largest on the bottom. Make sure the child sees you do this. Then tell the child to stack the triangles with the largest one on the bottom like you did. Help the child arrange the three triangles to form an evergreen tree.

Triangle talk: Explain to your child that a triangle has three sides and three points. Draw a square on a piece of paper and ask the child how the square is different from a triangle. Point out that a square has 4 sides, but a triangle has 3 sides.

Connect the dots to make shapes: Allow the child to "connect the dots" that you have drawn on a blank piece of paper to form a triangle and a square. Have your child identify each shape by name when he or she is finished.

Book ideas:
- *A Circle Here, A Square There: My Shapes Book* by David Diehl
- *Shapes, Shapes, Shapes* by Tana Hoban

This activity develops:
- More awareness of size
- Eye-hand coordination
- Problem solving
- More of an awareness of the difference between a square and a triangle
- Language enrichment

Age 3 – Activity 19 – Footprint Shapes

You will need:
- A pair of dad's shoes, mom's shoes, and your child's shoes
- Piece of heavy paper, cardboard or manila folders
- Green marker
- Red marker

Set up: Outline the shoe prints of each person's shoes on a piece of cardboard. Trace the left foot of each shoe prints with a green marker and then the right foot with a red marker. Write an "R" on the right footprints and an "L" on the left footprints.

Count and sort: Examine and count the shoes with your child. Tell the child that there are six total shoes but two shoes belong to each person. Instruct the child to match the pairs of shoes with their prints. Explain to the child what the "R" and "L" mean on each shoe print.

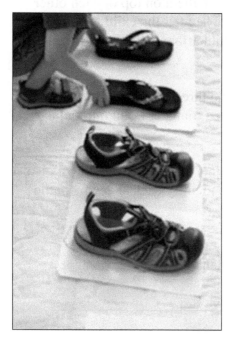

Largest to smallest: Model putting the shoe shapes in order from largest to smallest. Then mix up the shoe shapes and have the child put them in the same order.

Book ideas:
- *Left Shoe Right Shoe* by Yolanda Lopez-Rettew
- *Left or Right? (Little World Math Concepts)* Susan Meredith

This activity develops:
- Eye-hand coordination when matching
- More awareness of left, right, and six
- More awareness of shoes, shoe shapes, sizes, and pairs

Age 3 - Activity 20 – How Does It Taste?

You will need:

- Sugar
- Salt
- Cocoa
- Vinegar or lemon juice
- Dixie cups
- Sharpie to label with

Sweet: Place a little sugar in a Dixie cup labeled *sweet*. Allow the child to wet his or her finger and dip it inside the cup to taste the sugar. Then tell the child that the sugar tastes *sweet*.

Salty: Allow the child to taste the salt from inside the cup labeled *salty* and emphasize the word.

Bitter: Allow the child to taste the cocoa from inside the cup labeled *bitter* and emphasize the word.

Sour: Allow the child to taste the vinegar or lemon juice from inside the cup labeled *sour* and emphasize the word.

Tongue used for tasting: Ask the child to tell you what body part he or she uses to taste with. Use a mirror and allow the child to see his or her own taste buds, which are on the tip, sides, and back of the tongue.

Word labels: Emphasize the four words *sweet*, *salty*, *bitter*, and *sour*. Even though the cups are labeled, do not expect for your child to read or recognize the words. Labels provide a print-rich learning environment for the child to gain familiarity with written words used to express the ideas or concepts being learned.

How do different foods taste? At mealtime, encourage the child to tell how different foods taste using the new vocabulary learned.

Book ideas:

- *Tasting (Rookie Read-About Health)* by Sharon Gordon
- *Tasting (The Five Senses)* by Rebecca Rissman

This activity develops:
- Awareness of the tongue's purpose and sense of taste
- Awareness of different taste groups
- Language enrichment
- Skill in identifying foods by taste

Age 3 - Activity 21 – Set the Table

You will need:

- Forks
- Butter knives
- Spoons
- Container
- Placemat
- Plate
- Napkin
- Cup or glass
- Labels

Sorting and counting silverware: Mix an assortment of forks, knives, and spoons into a container. Ask the child to sort the silverware into three piles with the labels: *forks*, *spoons*, and *knives*. The child can count how many are in each pile.

Empty the dishwasher: You may allow your child to help in sorting the silverware while unloading the dishwasher on a regular basis. Be sure to remove any sharp knives or other dangerous objects from the silverware basket before having your child assist.

Model a place setting: Place the plate in the center of the placemat, the fork on the left of the plate, the knife (closest to the plate) and spoon (on outside) on the right side of the plate underneath a folded napkin, and the cup or glass in the top right hand corner of the placemat. Take one piece away and ask the child to put it back in the correct place.

Child sets the table: Keep your model displayed for the child to refer back to while your child sets other places at the table. With encouragement, he or she will soon learn to do this independently. You will need to supervise your child doing this job until he or she gains confidence. Remind your child to be extra careful with the dishes and glasses, since they can break if they are dropped.

Book idea:

- *Where Everything Belongs: Table Setting and Manners for Children* by Deborah Kane-Wood

---

This activity develops:
- More skill in sorting and counting
- An interest in helping
- More of an awareness of lengths or sizes
- Eye-hand coordination

Age 3 - Activity 22 – Sink or Float

You will need:

- Cork
- Spool
- Plastic block
- Candle
- Jar lid
- Nail
- Pencil

- Shell
- Large button
- Paper clip
- Crayon
- Marble
- Plastic spoon

- Metal spoon
- Tub half filled
  with water
- *Sink* and *Float* labels

Set up: Set the tub half filled with water on the table. Explain to the child that if the object floats on the surface of the water, it will go in the *float* pile. If the object sinks to the bottom of the tub, it will go in the *sink* pile.

Metal spoon sinks: Begin by having the child put the metal spoon in the water. It will sink to the bottom. Ask the child to put the spoon in the correct pile.

Plastic spoon floats: Hand the plastic spoon to the child. Ask the child how the plastic spoon is different than the metal spoon. He or she may think that the plastic spoon is not as heavy as the metal spoon. Allow the child to place the plastic spoon in the water. It will most likely float. Have the child place the plastic spoon in the correct pile.

Test the rest of the items: Allow the child to choose other objects at random to test if they sink or float once they are placed in the tub of water. Depending on whether they sink or float, have the child determine which pile they should be placed in. Allow the child to work independently and only help when necessary.

Book idea: *Who Sank the Boat?* by Pamela Allen

This activity develops:
- More skill in sorting and counting
- An interest in helping
- Eye-hand coordination

Age 3 - Activity 23 – The Alphabet Song

You will need:
- Alphabet written in upper and lower case letters on a piece of paper

Aa	Bb	Cc	Dd	Ee	Ff	Gg	Hh	Ii	Jj	Kk	Ll	Mm
Nn	Oo	Pp	Qq	Rr	Ss	Tt	Uu	Vv	Ww	Xx	Yy	Zz

Now I know my ABC's. Next time, won't you sing with me?

Sing to memorize: Sing the letters slowly and point to each one as it is sung aloud to identify the written letter.

Find the letter while reading: When reading stories to the child, point out a certain letter. Looking for just one letter throughout the book can be fun for the child.

Find the letter on a keyboard: Use a computer or iPad keyboard to help your child find the letter you say aloud.

Alphabet order: Once the child has memorized the song, ask him or her to identify what letter comes before or after a certain letter. For example, "What letter comes before the letter K?" Stick with only asking "before the letter" questions or "after the letter questions," and do not interchange them to avoid confusing your child.

> Explain that each letter has a "mother" and "child" letter." The big (upper case) letter is the "mother," the little (lower case) letter is the "child."

Creative alphabet: The child may enjoy forming the letters with clay, cooked spaghetti, paper strips, or yarn pieces.

Book ideas:
- *Dr. Seuss's ABC: An Amazing Alphabet Book!* by Dr. Seuss
- *Eric Carle's ABC (The World of Eric Carle)* by Eric Carle

> This activity develops:
> - Awareness of upper and lower case letters
> - Awareness of the letter sequence
> - Listening for a specific letter

Age 3 - Activity 24 – Fabric Match

You will need:
- 8 different kinds of colored material (fabric scraps)
- Fabric scissors
- Cardboard or manila folders
- Glue

Types of Fabrics:	
tweeds	plaids
polka dots	stripes
flowers	abstract

Set up: Cut out two 5 in. x 5 in. fabric squares that match and glue them onto cardboard squares that have been cut to the same size.

Mix and match: Mix the fabric squares and ask the child to match the like squares. The activity can be extended by placing the fabric squares face down. Two cards may then be turned over to determine if they match. If they match, the squares can be put in a separate pile. If they do not match, turn them face down again to try to find and remember the right match.

Color, shape, count: Encourage the child to find a certain color in the fabric squares. Ask the child to identify the shape of the fabric square and then make a square shape using all of the fabric squares together. Count all of the fabric squares. Make sets of 2s, 4s, and 8s.

This activity develops:
- Further awareness of a square
- Further awareness of colors
- Matching skills
- Skill in looking for a specific color
- Counting skills
- Memory recall
- Confidence

Age 3 - Activity 25 – Shadow Fun

You will need:
- Flashlight
- Candlestick holder
- Stuffed animal
- Bowl
- Vase
- Box
- Other objects (with interesting shadow)
- Shoe box
- Scissors
- Rubber band
- Pencil
- Paper
- Masking tape
- Semi-darkened room

Set up: Create a hole in a shoebox to hold the barrel of the flashlight that will stabilize the light. Tape a piece of paper on the wall where the object's shadow will be projected. Place one of the objects on the floor near a wall in a semi-darkened room. Move the light back until the shadow of the object is projected clearly on the wall.

Guess the object's shadow: Show all of the objects to the child and name each one. Then randomly choose one of the objects and project its shadow on the wall.

Talk about shadows: Since light *cannot* go through these objects, it goes straight past them and forms an image or shadow on the wall.

Shape shadows: Cut a shape from the center of the paper smaller than the face of the flashlight. Secure the paper to the flashlight with a rubber band. Then shine the flashlight on the wall and ask the child to identify the shape.

See my shadow grow on the sidewalk: When it is sunny, take the child outside in the early morning. Have the child stand at a given point and mark with chalk how the shadow shrinks at noon and grows again in the late afternoon if the child stands in the exact same place at different times.

Book ideas:
- *Whose Shadow Is This? A Look at Animal Shapes* by Clair Berge
- *What Makes a Shadow?* by Clyde Robert Bulla

This activity develops:
- Awareness of light and shadows
- Awareness that outside shadows vary in size during the day

Age 3 - Activity 26 – Gallop Fun

You will need:
- Colored, plain sock
- Newspaper, old stockings, or fiberfill
- Scissors
- Rubber band
- Felt
- (or) Toy stick horse

If you do not have a stick horse to practice galloping with, make your own!

Directions:
1. Stuff an old sock with crushed newspaper.
2. Use different colored felt pieces to cut eyes, nose, ears, and a mouth.
3. Use hot glue to attach the pieces to the sock to make a face.
4. Place a line of glue behind the ears to the neck and attach pieces of yarn for the horse's mane.
5. Insert a yardstick or old broom handle in the cuff of the sock as far up in the stuffed sock as possible.
6. Then use a strong rubber band to tie it together tightly.

Model: Show the child how to gallop. Step forward with one foot and hop as the back foot is brought forward. Step forward with the same front foot and repeat. Do not alternate feet forward. The child can practice these steps and straddle the stick horse and gallop like a cowgirl or cowboy.

Book idea: *Billy and Blaze* by C.W. Anderson

This activity develops:
- Leg-foot coordination
- Awareness of the parts of a horse's head
- Role playing
- Confidence
- Independence

Age 3 - Activity 27 – Trace the Shapes

You will need:
- Jar lid
- Book
- Marker and crayons
- Scissors

How to hold a pencil: Show the child how to hold a pencil or crayon. The thumb and forefinger should be used to grasp the pencil while the middle finger supports the pencil behind.

Activity:
1. **Trace**. Place the jar lid down on a sheet of plain paper. The child can use the pencil to trace around the outside edge. Ask the child to identify the shape.
2. **Retrace**. The child can then trace over the pencil line carefully. Emphasize that speed is not important, but doing his or her best *is* important.
3. **Color** the inside of the circle with a crayon.
4. **Cut** out the circle with scissors. Remind the child to cut closely beside the line, not on it.

Break up the activity steps: Complete each step at 4 different times for more focus and meaning!

Trace other shapes: Follow the same procedure with a book to make a rectangle. Find other objects around the house for the child to trace their shapes, color, and cut out.

Book idea: *Shape (Math Counts)* by Henry Pluckrose

This activity develops:
- More awareness of different shapes
- Skill in tracing and cutting with scissors
- Eye-hand coordination
- More skill in holding a pencil or crayon

Age 3 - Activity 28 – Learn to Tie Your Shoes

You will need:
- Tennis shoes
- Poster board or cardstock paper
- Sharpie
- Hole punch and scissors
- Shoe laces or yarn with masking tape tied

Make two "shoes" to lace:
1. With a sharpie, trace around the outside of a tennis shoe that has been placed on a piece of poster board to create a shoe template.
2. Cut out each shoe and punch four holes with the hole punch in the top middle portion of each shoe.
3. Lace the shoelaces through the holes to represent an untied shoe.

Model and practice:

Step 1: Take a shoelace in each hand and crisscross them to make an X. Pull the top lace through the bottom of the crisscross and pull them tight.

Step 2: Make a loop out of the right lace to create a bunny ear with a long tail!

Step 3: While squeezing the base of the bunny ear, wrap the left lace around the bottom of the bunny ear.

Step 4: Pull the left lace through the bottom hole between the base of the bunny ear and the crisscross underneath.

Step 5: Pull the new bunny ear through and pull both ears to tighten.

Book idea: *All Tied Up: Learn How to Tie Your Shoes in a Fun Way* published by K. H. Simmons, Ltd.

Sung to the Tune of "Splish Splash I was Taking a Bath"

Criss Cross and go under the bridge
Then you got to pull it tight.
Make a loop but keep a long tail
That is how to do it right
Then you take the other string
and you wrap it 'round the loop
Pull it through the hole
Now you got the scoop

Compiled by Linda Cammaroto

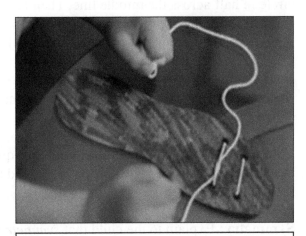

Don't confuse right and left shoes! Draw an arrow with a sharpie inside the heel of each shoe, so the child can look at the arrow to know which foot to put the shoe on!

This activity develops:
- Eye-hand coordination and small muscle refinement
- Confidence in the skill of tying shoes
- Persistence in staying on task and completing it
- Independence

Age 3 - Activity 29 – Fold It and Discover Symmetry

You will need:
- Construction paper
- Sharpie
- Scissors

Shape cuts:
- Cut out a large circle. Draw a line across the middle.
- Cut out two large squares. Draw a line across the middle of one square and diagonally across the middle of the other square.

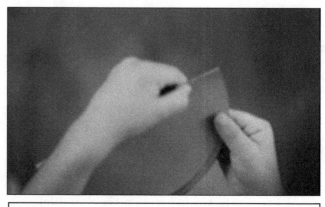

Review all 4 of the shape's names through playing a game! Have the child pick up the shape that you call out.

Fold a circle: Show the child how to fold the circle in half across the middle line. Then let him or her try. Emphasize the difference between *whole* and *half* circle. Point out that the circle has no corners and is the same in size and shape on both sides of the fold.

Fold a square to form rectangles: Fold the square across the horizontal line to make half of a square or two smaller rectangles. Point out that a rectangle has two long sides and two short sides. Count the four corners together.

Fold a square to form triangles: Fold the square with the diagonal line across it in half to form two triangles. Ask the child what shape the folded square has made. Count the sides and the corners of the triangle together.

Symmetry: Explain to the child that *symmetry* is when a shape or picture is folded in half and has the same size/design on both sides as the two halves that face each other.

Book idea: *Symmetry (My Path to Math)* by Lynn Peppas

This activity develops:
- More awareness of basic shapes
- Shape identification through the number of corners and sides
- Eye-hand coordination in folding and connecting dots
- Introduction to symmetry
- Confidence
- Language enrichment

Age 3 - Activity 30 – Magnet Fun

You will need:

- 2 small magnets
- Button
- Paper clip

- Pencil with a metal end
- Hole punch
- Nail clipper
- Rubber eraser

- Piece of chalk
- Clothespin
- Spool
- 2 paper plates

Observe and experiment with magnets: Allow the child to observe and experiment by holding objects up to the magnet that attract and repel the magnet. Talk about the differences between *attracting* and *repelling*. Explain that the objects that are attracted to the magnets are *magnetic*.

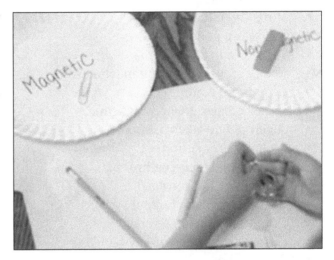

Sort *magnetic* and *nonmagnetic*: Model how to sort between the objects that are attracted to the magnet and those that are not attracted to it. Label one paper plate *magnetic* and have the child draw a picture of a magnet on the top. Label the other paper plate *nonmagnetic*. Allow the child to sort between objects.

Similarities and differences: Guide the child to notice what all the objects on the *magnetic* plate have in common. Count to compare how many objects were attracted by the magnet and which were not. Ask the child which side has more objects. Match the objects one to one to prove which side has more. The child will discover from this experience which number is greater.

Fun with two magnets: Use a paper plate and place one magnet on the top and one on the bottom of the plate in line with the one on the top. Move the bottom magnet slowly across the bottom of the plate. Your child may think it's "magic" how the magnet underneath the paper plate is able to move the magnet on top of it!

Book idea: *What Makes a Magnet?* by Franklyn M. Branley

This activity develops:
- Awareness of magnetism and feeling the pull of magnetism
- Skill in sorting
- Problem solving and free exploration

Age 3 - Activity 31 – True or False

Meaning: Explain the meaning of *true* and *false* and how they are similar to *yes* and *no*. Other statements can be added as the child becomes more confident. *This activity is great to play when travelling in the car!*

Are these statements *true* or *false*?
- The grass is red.
- Birds fly in the water.
- Rocks are good to eat.
- Pages are in a book.
- Plants grow in washing machines.
- Clouds are white.
- Easter comes at Christmas time.
- A cell phone takes medicine.
- A chair is for sitting.
- Mom cooks in the bathroom.
- Fire can be dangerous.
- I can swim in the bathtub.
- I can pour juice in a fork.
- I can wear mittens on my hands.
- Snow is hot.
- Sugar is sour.
- Dad can buy bananas at the grocery store.
- Elephants are little animals.
- Fish live in the water.
- I wear shoes on my ears.
- Cars have doors.
- Lamps give us light.
- Mom washes clothes in the dishwasher.

Older siblings can play along too! This activity enhances the child's thinking and reasoning skills. It also encourages your child to ask more questions.

Book ideas:
- *No, David!* by David Shannon
- *No No Yes Yes* by Leslie Patricelli

This activity develops:
- Listening and thinking skills
- Skill in making a decision
- Language enrichment
- Confidence

Age 3 - Activity 32 – Clothespin Toss and Count

You will need:
- 10 clothespins (colored ones are fun!)
- Brown paper bag
- Masking tape
- Empty pan or trashcan

How to play:
1. Choose one clothespin from the bag.
2. Stand behind the boundary line and show the child how to aim and toss the clothespin so that it will land in the empty container.
3. When the child develops more skill, the container should be moved farther away to challenge the child more.

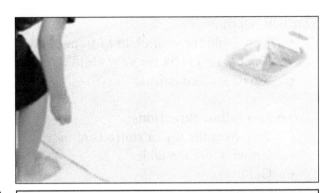

If the child misses the container when tossing the clothespin, encourage him or her to try again. Tell the child that with practice anyone can improve!

Count the clothespins: Once all of the clothespins have been tossed, invite the child to help you count the ones that went into the container first. Then count the clothespins that landed outside the container together.

More or less? Ask the child which number is more: the number of clothespins that went into the container or those that landed outside. Explain the words *more* and *less*. Which word goes with each pile of clothespins? Emphasize the concepts *in* and *out*.

Add them up: Then add both groups together by counting them all to find out the number of total clothespins.

Book idea: *I Can Add (I Can Count)* by Anna Nilsen

This activity develops:
- Eye-hand coordination
- Skill in aiming at a target
- Awareness of a set of ten objects
- More awareness of the concepts "more" and "less"
- Counting and simple addition
- An understanding of "in" and "out" of a container
- Skill in making a decision
- Confidence

Age 3 - Activity 33 – Listen and Move

You will need:
- Low table for your child to sit under
- Strong, large box for your child to sit in
- Small stuffed animal

Listen and follow directions:
- Step over the toy or stuffed animal.
- Crawl under the table.
- Get in the box.
- Get out of the box.
- Open the door.
- Walk around the toy or stuffed animal.
- Stand between the box and the table.
- Stand behind the table.
- Look outside the window.
- Look inside the box.
- Close the door.
- Walk toward the window.
- Walk backwards five steps.
- Stand beside the table.
- Stand beneath (whatever is convenient for the child).

If the child does not seem to understand, calmly repeat the command again and show the child what the command means.

Repeat and change up the directions: These activities should be repeated often. Variations of these commands will encourage more interest and motivation for the child. The materials (props) should also be changed. For example, you can use the bed, dresser, and toy chest to give him or her commands using different selected toys for placement during the activity.

Book idea: *Howard B. Wigglebottom Learns to Listen* by Howard Binkow

This activity develops:
- Listening skills
- Following directions
- More awareness of spatial concepts
- Gross motor coordination
- Tactile enhancement of the various materials used
- Confidence

Age 3 - Activity 34 – What is Missing?

You will need:
- Key
- Cup or block
- Toy car
- Straw
- Button or spool
- Cotton ball
- Other objects
- Tray

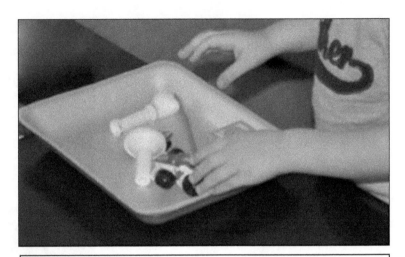

Praise the child if he or she is correct. If he or she is not correct, show the child the missing object and repeat the process.

How to play:
1. Line the objects in a row or on a tray.
2. Name the objects from left to right and encourage the child to name them independently for you.
3. Tell the child to close his or her eyes with no peeking.
4. Remove one of the objects and place it behind you or somewhere else where the child cannot see it.
5. Ask the child to open his or her eyes and figure out what object is missing.

Change it up! As the child becomes more confident in identifying the missing object, change the positions of the objects for more interest and challenge.

Shapes, colors, numbers, and letters: This activity may be varied to use four shapes, four colors, four numbers or four letters, etc. However, I recommend using the shapes and colors first and then introducing the numbers and letters when the child readily recognizes them.

Book idea: *I Spy Little Wheels* by Jean Marzollo

This activity develops:
- Memory recall
- Skill in identifying an unseen object
- Skill in using visual clues for association and identification
- Confidence

Age 3 - Activity 35 – Tell Me How To Make It

Choose an activity: Discuss with the child something simple that can be made in the kitchen. Allow the child to decide what he or she would like to help you make.

Some suggestions are:
- Make a peanut butter and jelly sandwich.
- Make a s'more.
- Make chocolate pudding from a prepared mix.
- Prepare some Jello.

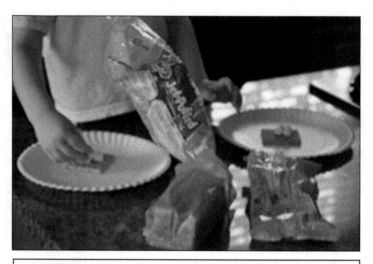

How do you make it? Tell the child to instruct you what should come first, second, third, etc. Listen to the child and attempt to prepare it just as the child tells you to do it.

The sequence may not be in order or a step may be left out, but listen. The child will be watching and helping and may realize mistakes.

Review the sequence and repeat: Review with the child the logical sequence of events and why one step should go before another. Repeat this activity at other times, and you will be amazed at the logical sequence that will develop as you prepare different things with the child. Once your child has developed confidence in making something, he or she can complete the steps and tell you what he or she is doing with your supervision.

Activity extension: Ask the child to tell you how to do things in the proper sequence. You or your child can draw pictures of the following activities on notecards and sort them in order from beginning to end. Some suggestions are:
- Plant a seed.
- Put on a jacket or play clothes.
- Get ready to go on a picnic.
- Set the table.

Book idea: *We Help Mommy* by Jean Cushman

This activity develops:
- Skill in recalling things done in sequence
- Problem solving and language enrichment
- A sense of helping and confidence

Age 3 - Activity 36 – Family Groups

Last name: Explain to your child that all members of the family belong together, because they are related to each other. They are different in many ways, but most families have their last names in common. Say the child's last name and recall the names of all of the family members.

Word groups that belong together: Discuss with your child how 3 different things belong together in a group like a family such as: fork, spoon, and knife. All three of these objects belong in the silverware group. You can use concrete objects and sort them into piles depending on the groups that they belong in to better help the child understand.

Objects:	Group:
coat, hat, mittens	Winter clothing
pencil, pen, crayon	Things to write with
red, green, blue	Colors
banana, apple, orange	Fruit
hands, feet, knees	Body Parts

At this age, your child should know his or her full name, gender, and age. Birthdate, telephone number and address can gradually be taught later, but the child should know these before entering kindergarten.

What does not belong? Talk to your child about objects that may not belong in a particular group. Ask your child to identify which of the three objects do not belong with the other two in the group.

Objects:	Group:
one, two, **lamp**	Numbers
towel, washcloth, **bed**	Bathroom objects
pillow, bear, bunny	Animals
Breakfast, **paper**, lunch	Meals
helicopter, airplane, **spoon**	Things that Fly

This activity develops:
- More of an awareness of a family and the family name
- Skill in associating, reasoning and grouping

Age 3 - Activity 37 – Hopscotch Fun

You will need:
- Yarn or masking tape and index cards (if on carpet)
- Chalk (if on sidewalk)
- Bean bag

Set up:
1. Outline of a hopscotch area with masking tape on the carpet or with chalk on the sidewalk.
2. If on carpet, write a separate number "1, 2, 3, 4, 5 and 6" on index cards and place them consecutively in the top left corner of each box.
3. If this activity is done outside, the numbers can be drawn consecutively in each box of the boundary lines.
4. Identify each number with the child.

With practice, the child will enjoy this activity and at the same time learn to readily recognize the numbers 1 - 6. He or she should also become aware of what number comes before or follows the other.

One version of how to play:
1. Hop on one foot into the first box.
2. Hop to the second box.
3. Hop to the third box and land on both feet in that box.
4. Hop into box four on one foot.
5. Hop to box five on one foot.
6. Land with both feet in box six.
7. Come back and start again.

Add a beanbag: Tell the child to gently throw the beanbag into the first box, play hopscotch and come back, hopping the whole way. Then pick up the beanbag and throw it into the second box, and repeat the activity until the beanbag has been thrown into each of the six boxes.

Book idea: *Let's Play Hopscotch* by Sarah Hughes

This activity develops:
- Gross motor coordination
- More awareness of number sequence
- Skill in balancing and aiming
- Skill in identifying the numbers 1 - 6
- Confidence and independence

Age 3 - Activity 38 – Finish It

This is an activity that allows the child to think and verbalize.

Complete the sentence: Tell the child that you will say a part of a sentence, and he or she should complete it.

Define sentence: *A sentence is a group of words that makes sense and tells a complete thought.*

Sentence suggestions:
> I went to the ___.
> I am going on a vacation to see ___.
> Yesterday I ___.
> Mother and I took a walk and ___.
> Daddy gave me ___.
> A tree is ___.
> My car will ___.
> My name is ___.
> I am ___.
> I like to ___.

This is an activity can be done with a brother or a sister and is a great traveling game. Many different suggestions can be added to the list.

Enrichment activity: Read a familiar book aloud to your child (one that rhymes works well). Read the sentence aloud, pausing before reading the last word of the sentence to the child, so that he or she can guess what word would finish the sentence. You may want to point to a picture on the book's page to guide your child to the right word that would fill in the blank.

Book idea: *Hop On Pop* by Dr. Seuss

This activity develops:
- Listening skills
- Skill in thinking and associating ideas
- Memory recall
- Freedom of expression and language development

Age 3 - Activity 39 – Shape Play

You will need:
- 5 paper plates
- Scissors (Fiskars spring action preschool scissors work best for beginners)
- Pencil or crayon
- Blank paper, magazine, or newspaper
- Masking tape
- Pan
- Uncooked rice
- Straw

Set up:
1. Stencil and then cut out the circle, square, triangle, rectangle, and oval.
2. The size should be approximately five inches at the widest point.
3. Keep the frame (outside edge) of the paper plate intact.
4. Tape the interior of each stencil with masking tape to prevent paper cuts.

Stencil and cut out activity: Give the child a crayon and a sheet of plain white or colored construction paper.
1. **Trace.**
2. **Cut.** Allow the child to use blunt scissors to cut out the drawn circle.

> **Identify shape names** and have the child feel the open cut out shape (stencil) in the middle of each paper plate.

3. Follow the same procedure for the other four shapes and ask the child to name each shape. In addition, evaluate the child's technique of cutting, and if you feel that he or she can do a better job of cutting, encourage him or her to repeat the activity and practice his or her cutting.

"Read the shapes": Place the five cut out shapes in a row from left to right. Ask the child to "read" the shapes. Make sure that he or she starts on the left. Tell the child to turn his or her back while you remove one of the shapes or change the order. The child should then turn around and tell you which shape is missing or what order was changed. This is a game he or she can play independently with a friend.

More cutting practice: Have your child use old newspapers or magazine pages. You may allow him or her to use scissors independently if you feel that the child is sufficiently responsible.

> **Hand Preference:** This is a great activity to notice whether your child is right or left handed!

Color the inside of the stencil shape: Allow the child to select a paper plate stencil. Instead of tracing the edge of the shape, encourage the child to use the side of the crayon to color the entire shape within the stencil's boundary. It may be necessary to secure the stencil with tape to the paper before beginning.

Draw shapes in a pan of rice: To extend the activity, the child can play with a pan of uncooked rice and draw with his or her finger the desired shapes that are being learned. He or she can also use a straw to practice drawing the shapes with a utensil.

Book ideas:
- *Fun with Shapes Stencils* (Dover Little Activity Books) by A. G. Smith
- *Dictionary Stencils (Fun to Learn)* by Brenda Apsley and Jenny Tulip
- *Numbers Stencils (Fun to Learn)* by Brenda Apsley and Jenny Tulip

This activity develops:
- Sensitivity to the feel of the edges of the stencils
- Eye-hand coordination
- Confidence
- Skill in identifying the shapes, tracing and cutting
- More of an awareness of a boundary
- Tracking left to right

Age 3 - Activity 40 – Junk Box

You will need: Junk around the house could include —

- Bolt
- Pencil
- Paper clip
- Feather
- Cotton ball
- Bottle cap
- Button
- Badge

- Key
- Spool
- Magnet
- Eraser
- Dice
- Happy Meal toy
- Comb
- Shell

- Magnifying glass
- Shoebox labeled "Junk Box"

Collect junk from around the house: Your child can collect discarded items (junk) in a plastic grocery bag with handles. More items may be added as the child finds other "special" items.

Activities to do with stuff from the junk box:
1. Feel them.
2. Examine them with a magnifying glass.
3. Sort them.
4. Count them.
5. Trace around the outside edges of them.
6. Talk about them.

Place objects on specific spots: Make red x's in a row on a large piece of newspaper. Instruct the child to choose any item from the junk box and place one of the items on each of the red x's. Show the child which x's were missed, if any.

Book idea: *Cool Junk* by Kathryn Castle, Michael McGuffee, and Patrizia Ahlers-Johnson

This activity develops:
- Freedom of choice
- More awareness of one to one matching
- Skill in following directions
- More awareness of left to right progression

Tell him or her to pretend that each time he or she places an object on an x, he or she is "reading," because people read words from left to right in this order.

Age 3 - Activity 41 – Mail a Letter

You will need:
- Large index card or envelope
- Used stamp re-glued on envelope in top right corner
- Pretend letter inside the envelope
- Pen or pencil
- 2 brown paper bags

Set up (if you don't have a piece of mail already):
1. Print the child's name and address carefully on the middle of the envelope, so it resembles a piece of mail.
2. Use upper case (capital) letters only at the beginning of each word and lower case letters for the remainder of each word.
3. Glue a used stamp in the top right hand corner and write the return address of a special relative at the top left.
4. Write a message on the back of the index card or use a sheet of paper for the message if you are using an envelope. The message should be brief and signed "With love."

To make this activity more realistic, a relative may have already sent a postcard or a letter, or you may suggest that a relative do this especially for the child.

Learning about mail: Show the child a piece of mail with his or her name on it. Point to the child's name as you move your hand from left to right. Show your child where the house number and street name are located below the name. Explain to your child that this is called the family's address, because that is where we live. The mail person (man or woman) knows just where to bring our mail, because he or she can read our address and knows where we live.

Sorting mail activity: Make 5 pieces of mail with the child's name and address on the envelopes. Then make 5 pieces with *other* names and addresses on them to represent letters. To represent mailboxes, mark one paper brown bag with the child's name and leave the other bag unmarked. Mix the envelopes and have the child sort all of his or her mail in the labeled bag and the other mail in the unmarked bag. Show the child how to match the names if he or she does not quite understand. Then allow him or her to work independently.

Learning your address: Read the address several times and ask the child to repeat it after you.

Recall address from memory: Review the child's address with him or her to make certain that he or she can recall it from memory. Encourage the child to repeat the address-matching activity.

Write a letter together: Have your child dictate a letter to a special friend or a relative. This would be an opportune time for the child to begin to express his or her thoughts while you write them on paper. He or she will delight in watching you write what he or she says.

Different types of mailboxes: Show your child different types of mailboxes in the community: blue mail box, house mail box, apartment mailbox, post office mail box, etc.

Field trip idea: Take your child on a "field trip" to your local post office to learn even more about mailing letters.

Book idea: *The Jolly Postman* by Janet and Allan Ahlberg

Vocabulary Words:
- mail
- letter
- envelope
- address
- stamp
- sender
- seal
- return address
- mailman
- post office

This activity develops:
- Skill in recognizing a name in print
- An interest in learning to recall the correct address
- Skill in matching the correct address
- More awareness of mail and delivery of mail
- Language enrichment (mail vocabulary)
- Learning to read from left to right

Age 3 - Activity 42 – Spaghetti Letters

You will need:
- Alphabet set from the internet
- Individual letter templates (printed out on cardstock paper covered in contact paper)
- Cooked spaghetti
- Scissors

Review "The Alphabet Song": Show the child all the letters from an alphabet set as you sing the song.

> **For colorful spaghetti:** You can boil the spaghetti in colored water—using food coloring—to make colorful spaghetti with your child to use in this activity!

Point out:
- Letters are made of straight lines, curved lines or part straight and part curved lines
- There is a capital letter (upper case) and a lower-case letter for each letter we sing in the alphabet
- Letters make sounds
- Letters grouped together form words (like the child's name)
- Letters and numbers are different (numbers tell "how many")

> Allow your child to explore with the spaghetti noodles making straight lines and curves before forming the letters.

Find the letters in child's name: Ask the child if he or she can and the letters in his or her name. Help the child to find them. To make it easier, print out your child's name, so that he or she can match each letter in the printed name.

Upper case and lower case: At this time, point out to the child that his or her name will begin with a letter that is capitalized (big letter) and the rest of the letters will be written with little letters (lower case). This is important for your child to know, because teachers often have to "re-teach" children when they learn to write their names with a mixture of upper and lower case letters.

> The child may be shown the correct way to form letters, but his or her hand coordination may not be refined enough to hold a pencil for making letters.

Spaghetti letters: Allow the child to cut the cooked spaghetti with a pair of blunt scissors. Encourage the child to lay the pieces of spaghetti over top of a stencil of each upper-case letter (you can add the lower-case letters after he or she has mastered the activity with the upper-case letters). Model how to lay the spaghetti to outline each letter. Reinforce the name and sound of each letter as he or she is working. This activity could last over many days/weeks and can also be done in conjunction with later activities that correlate with specific letters.

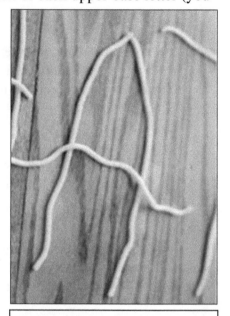

Spaghetti letters on your own: Later, your child can attempt to recreate the shape of the upper case or lower case letters that he or she has traced beforehand on his or her own with the uncooked spaghetti. Allow the child to form non-letters as well to experiment with the spaghetti's shape.

Caution: The child should form only a few letters at a time during an activity, because forming too many letters at one time could be overwhelming for him or her. Frustration may result in the child uninterested in pursuing this activity.

Slow and steady is the way to ensure that the child will be ready (sufficiently skilled) to succeed easily in school.

Book ideas:
- *Abc* by Lesley Clark
- *Curious George Learns the Alphabet* by H. A. Rey

This activity develops:
- More awareness of the names of the letters
- Skill in matching letters in a name
- More awareness of the shapes of the letters
- Eye-hand coordination
- Confidence and independence

Age 3 - Activity 43 – Sewing Fun

You will need:
- 5 pieces of 8 ½ in. x 11 in. poster board or card board
- 5 large pictures (with little detail) from a coloring book, magazine, or the internet
- Scissors
- Glue
- Nail or single hole punch
- Large, blunt tapestry needle (or plastic needle)
- Yarn (1 yd. long)

Make certain the knot is big enough so that the yarn will not slip through the hole around the pictures.

Set up:
1. Cut the pictures out and glue them on the cardboard. Allow the glue to dry.
2. Use a nail or single hole punch to punch holes about two inches apart around the shapes of the pictures.
3. Thread the large plastic needle with the yarn. Make a double length and tie a large knot to join both ends.

Sewing activity: Model how to move the needle in and out of the holes to lace around the pictures. This activity requires a lot of eye-hand coordination, but with practice, the child can develop this skill and become proficient in simple sewing.

Book ideas:
- *Splashy Sea (Lacing Card Book)* by Caroline Davis
- *Playful Pets (Lacing Card Books)* by Caroline Davis
- *Dinosaurs! Lacing Cards* by Bob Barner
- *Busy Bugs (Lacing Card Books)* by Christiane Engel and Caroline Davis

This activity develops:
- Eye-hand coordination
- Skill in the fundamentals of sewing
- More awareness of the different shapes of objects
- Confidence and independence

Age 3 - Activity 44 – Telephone

You will need:
- Phone no longer in use or made from cardboard
- Large piece of paper and sharpie
- 10 small index cards

Activity:
- Name a number and tell the child to find it on the phone.

Learn home phone number: Tell the child your home or parent cell phone number and encourage him or her to repeat it after you several times. You can even put the numbers of your phone number to a chant or jingle to help him or her remember it more easily.

Find the numbers on the phone: Then tell the child to find the same numbers on the phone and make a "pretend" call to that number.

Phone chart: Write your phone number with a sharpie on a large piece of paper. Read each number and point to it as you say the number. Do this several times and then ask the child to recall the phone number from memory. Assist him or her if necessary. Praise him or her for any positive response to help establish confidence.

9-1-1 Emergency Number
Your child should know the emergency number 911 or whatever the emergency number is where you live.

Phone number pattern: Tell the child that this will be his or her phone chart. Then write each number separately on a small index card. Mix the number cards and tell the child to put them in the correct order by using the phone number chart that you made. Put a green mark on the left of the number chart and a red mark on the right. Remind the child that he or she should start on the green side and stop on the red side. Encourage the child to repeat this often so that he or she will know your phone number from memory.

Phone manners: If you know the phone number of your child's friend, allow the child to press or dial the correct number on the real phone. However, before doing this, instruct the child to identify himself or herself by name and then ask to speak to his or her friend by name. For example, the child could say, "This is (child's name) calling. May I speak to (friend's name)?" The child should also be aware that he or she must have a reason to call a person. Discuss and practice proper phone etiquette.

Book idea:
- *My Telephone (My First Book of Sights and Sounds)* by Harriet Ziefert and Laura Rader
- *It's Time to Call 911: What to Do in an Emergency* by Inc. Penton Overseas
- *Hello, Hello* by Fumiko Takeshita

This activity develops:
- Memory recall of a telephone number(s)
- Matching skills with numbers
- More awareness of left and right progression
- Telephone courtesy
- Confidence and independence

Age 3 - Activity 45 – Head, Shoulders, Knees, and Toes

You will need:
- A colorful full view picture of a boy or girl from a magazine or the internet.
- A straw or unsharpened pencil to use as a pointer
- Yarn ball or bean bag or balled up piece of paper
- Blank paper
- Crayons
- Newsprint roll of paper (from the local newspaper) or bulletin board paper

Set up: Cut the picture out and ask the child if the picture is of a boy or girl. The child should be able to answer this question correctly. This should serve to make the child confident before he or she begins the following activity.

Find the body parts: Instruct your child to find the body parts on the picture as you call them by name without talking. Help the child if necessary and praise him or her for any positive response. The body parts to point to are:

> Remind your child that he or she must not talk while you call the words. The child should listen very closely so that he or she does not make any mistakes.

- head/hair
- eye
- nose
- ear
- cheek
- lips
- neck
- arm
- elbow

- wrist
- waist
- stomach (tummy)
- knee
- ankle
- heel
- foot/toes
- hips
- hand/fingers

Beanbag activity: Give the child a beanbag and instruct him or her to use this to point to the different parts of his or her body as you call the same body parts that were previously named. Help the child if necessary but try to allow him or her time to listen, think, and find each body part with the beanbag.

Repeat for accuracy: Make a mental note of those body parts that the child missed or confused. Repeat the activity with the picture and then ask the child to find them again on himself or herself.

Review with a song: Sing "Head, Shoulders, Knees, and Toes" to reinforce the concepts being reviewed.

> *Head and shoulders, knees and toes*
> Knees and toes,
> Head and shoulders, knees and toes,
> Knees and toes,
> Oooh eyes and ears and mouth and nose,
> Head and shoulders, knees and toes,
> Knees and toes.

Draw a boy or girl: Give the child a blank piece of paper and a crayon or pencil. Tell the child to draw a picture of himself or herself. Remind the child to try to include all of the body parts. Accept the results and praise the child for his or her efforts regardless of what the picture looks like.

Progress in pictures: Keep the picture in a safe place and at various times throughout the weeks and months encourage the child to draw other pictures of himself or herself. Date each picture and compare them each time the child draws. You should see gradual progress with each picture.

Full-size picture: Once the child has had practice locating and drawing the parts of the body in his or her own drawings, he or she can locate them on a life-size version! Roll out a piece of newsprint on the kitchen floor and have your child lay down on it. Trace the outline of your child on the paper (be sure to include fingers, etc.). Then have your child get up and add a face, clothing, hair, etc. with crayons. Ask the child to locate the parts of the body on this life size version!

Did you know? *You can obtain large rolls of recycled newsprint from the local newspaper!*

Book ideas:
- *Where is Baby's Belly Button? A Lift-the-Flap Book* by Karen Katz
- *Baby Einstein: Baby da Vinci –My Body* by Julie Aigner-Clark
- *Head, Shoulders, Knees, and Toes* by Annie Kubler
- *Body Parts* by Bev Schumacher

This activity develops:
- Reinforcement of the body parts
- Skill in listening and locating body parts
- Skill in drawing a self "portrait"
- Language enrichment
- Confidence

Age 3 - Activity 46 – Letter Aa Fun

You will need:
- Aa tracing template with arrows printed from an internet search
- Crayons
- Index card
- Popsicle stick
- Masking tape
- Apple (for eating)
- Elmer's glue
- Apple seeds
- Acorns
- Computer keyboard
- Magazine
- Red marker
- 3-ring hole punch
- Binder for creating the alphabet book
- Shoebox for storing letter puppets in

Aa Limerick
Ali O'Malley ambled into an alley
After meeting with Sally, her friend from the valley.
"Alas!" Ali exclaimed, and stood there aghast
For there was an alligator, who came at her fast.

Upper case and lower case letters
You can refer to upper case letters as the "mother" letter. You can refer to the lower case letters as the "child" letter. This will help your child differentiate between the two.

Introduce the letter Aa name and sound: Use an Aa template to introduce the letter Aa. Have the child name the letter and repeat back to you the (short vowel) sound that it makes.

Trace the letter Aa: Have the child use his or her pointer finger to trace the outline of the letter Aa following the arrows.

Letter Aa puppet: Write an upper case and lower case letter Aa on one side of the index card. On the other side of the index card, draw or print a picture of an apple and allow the child to color the apple red. Print the word *apple* in lower case letters below the picture of the apple. Tape a popsicle stick to the bottom of the index card to create a puppet.

Aa is for apple: Tell the child the word *apple* begins with the letter Aa as you point to the word. Also tell the child that there are many words that begin with the letter Aa. Give the child an apple to eat, if possible, for interest and better association of the relationship between the letter Aa and the word *apple*.

Aa page in alphabet book: You can begin making an alphabet book (binder) with a template page printed on cardstock paper and suggested objects glued on the traced outline of the letters. Have your child help you glue the apple seeds or acorns around the upper case and lower case letters. After the glue has dried, use a 3-ring binder hole punch and include it as the first page in the alphabet book that you and your child can create together. You can add things that begin with the letter Aa that you find to the Aa page as you and your child come across them.

Recognizing Aa on a keyboard and in a magazine: At another time, give the child a red marker and an old magazine. Tell the child to put a red circle around every word or letter (Aa) that has the letter Aa in it from a magazine. Guide the child to where the words with Aa's are located on the page. You can also have your child locate the letter Aa on a keyboard. The child will enjoy pressing the Aa button down on the computer in Notepad or Microsoft Word to watch the letter Aa appear on the screen.

Words that begin with the letter Aa: Once the child has mastered recognizing the letter Aa in text and print, have him or her identify words that *begin* with the letter Aa like his or her letter puppet. Try to emphasize the words, *beginning* and *starts with* or *first letter* to impress upon the child what you mean. Praise your child and encourage him or her to find Aa's on several pages.

Book idea: *Apple Pie ABC* by Alison Murray

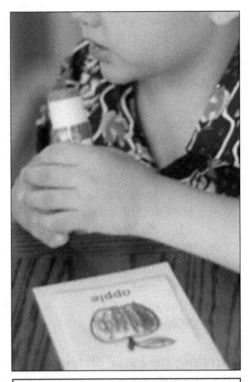

Make your child aware that different fonts on computers print the letter "a" in different ways.

This activity develops:
- Phonemic awareness of the letter Aa's sound as in *apple*
- Name and visual recognition of the letter Aa
- Eye-hand coordination
- Memory recall

Age 3 - Activity 47 – Bouncing Bb

You will need:
- Bb tracing template with arrows from an internet search
- Crayons
- Index card
- Popsicle stick
- Masking tape
- Ball that bounces/balloon
- Elmer's glue
- Buttons or bubble gum pieces
- Computer keyboard
- Magazine
- Blue marker
- Magnifying glass

Introduce the letter Bb name and sound: Use a Bb tracing template from an internet search or made on a word processor (printed on cardstock paper) to introduce the letter Bb. Have the child name the letter and repeat back to you the sound that it makes.

Trace the letter Bb: Have the child use his or her pointer finger to trace the outline of the letter Bb following the arrows.

Letter Bb puppet: Make a letter puppet with the index card and popsicle stick. Draw or paste a picture of a ball or balloon that your child can color. Print the word in lower case letters underneath the picture.

Emphasize the Bb sound in the words when you read them aloud to the child for him or her to recognize the sound.

Listen for the Bb sound in the story: Read the "Betty Burch" story below and have the child hold up his or her Bb puppet every time he or she hears the Bb sound in words from the story! Use this activity with other books too!

Betty Burch had a big, brown button on her blue blouse. Her bike bumped into a big black box. Betty Burch fell with a bash, boom, bang. She nearly broke her back. Betty's brother brought her back home and put her to bed.

Bb is for bouncing ball: Tell the child the words *ball* and *bounce* begin with a letter Bb as you point to the words. Also tell the child that there are many words that begin with the letter Bb. Have your child play with a bouncy ball and remind him or her that *ball* begins with the letter Bb.

Buttons and bubblegum to make the Bb page in alphabet book: You can continue your alphabet book (binder) for the letter Bb. Have your child help you glue buttons or bubble gum pieces around the upper case and lower case letters on the next page.

Recognizing the letter Bb in words in print and on a keyboard: At another time, give the child a blue marker and a magazine. Tell the child to put a blue circle around every word or letter that has the letter Bb in it from a magazine. Guide the child to where the words with Bb's are located on the page. Then have your child identify the letter B on a computer keyboard.

Words that begin with the letter Bb: Once the child has mastered recognizing the letter Bb in text and print, have him or her identify words that *begin* with the letter Bb like his or her letter puppet. You can review identifying the letter Aa and its letter sound in addition to Bb and its letter sound.

The letter Bb is everywhere! At various times throughout each day, allow the child to find Bb's in words on cans, in books, in magazines, on mail, on license plates, signs, etc.

Encourage your child to play with a bouncing ball, emphasizing the sound of the letter Bb that these words start with.

Book ideas:
- *Stop that Ball (Beginner Books)* by Mike McClintock
- *Curious George and the Hot Air Balloon* by H. A. Rey
- *Ben and the Big Balloon (Tadpoles)* by Sue Graves
- *Clifford the Big Red Dog: The Missing Beach Ball* by Sonali Fry

This activity develops:
- Phonemic awareness of the letter Bb's sound as in *ball* or *balloon*
- Visual skills in identifying Bb
- Listening skills
- Eye-hand coordination

Age 3 - Activity 48 – Cc is for Cake

You will need:
- Cc tracing template with arrows from the internet
- Crayons
- Index card and popsicle stick
- Masking tape and glue
- Kernels of corn or birthday candles
- Yellow marker

Cc Limerick
Cathy cooked Christmas cakes
With caramel, carrots and candy canes
Cooks loved the cakes from all around town
And conferred to give Cathy the Cooking Crown!
Cathy continued cooking and would always remember
Her capital Christmas cakes from that December

Introduce the letter Cc name and sound: Use a Cc tracing template from an internet search or made with Word or Pages (printed on cardstock paper) to introduce the letter Cc. Have the child name the letter and repeat back to you the hard Cc sound.

Trace the letter Cc: Have the child use his or her pointer finger to trace the outline of the letter Cc following the arrows.

Letter Cc puppet: Make a letter puppet with the index card and popsicle stick. Draw or paste a picture of a cake with candles that your child can color. Print the word *cake* in lower case letters underneath the picture.

Hint: The cards do not have to be in alphabetical order. However, you can mention that the letter Bb is between the letters Aa and Cc in "The Alphabet Song."

Letter recognition puppet game:
1. The 3 letter puppets that you and your child have made so far can be used with the pictures of the apple, ball or balloon, and cake facing down. All three letters on the puppets should be facing up.
2. Ask the child to pick up the letter that *apple* begins with. Check for accuracy and put the puppet back in place.
3. Follow the same procedure for the *ball/balloon* and *cake*. Change the positions and repeat the activity.
4. Later, the letters can be placed face down and the child can be asked to identify the letters for just the beginning sounds that each studied letter makes.

Missing letter extension game:
- The child may also enjoy turning his or her back while you remove one of the three puppets.
- He or she must then try to identify the missing one by letter and picture name.

Write a Cc story together: Write down a story with your child using many words that begin with the letter Cc. Some words that can be used in the story are *crate, cape, carry, cash, count, cover, coconut, complete, cook, and can*. Read the story you created with your child aloud and have him or her hold up the Cc letter puppet each time a Cc word is read aloud.

Kernels of corn or candles to make the Cc page in alphabet book: You can continue your alphabet book (binder) with the Cc page. Have your child help you glue kernels of corn or pieces of birthday candles around the upper case and lower case letters. Add this page to the alphabet book!

Avoid words such as check, chandelier, and circus. (At another time the child will learn that Cc borrows sounds from other letters and letter clusters.)

Book ideas:
- *Spot Bakes a Cake* by Eric Hill
- *I Like Corn (Good Food)* by Robin Pickering
- *From Kernel to Corncob (Scholastic News Nonfiction Readers: How Things Grow)* by Ellen Weiss
- *Curious George's Big Book of Curiosity* by H. A. Rey
- *Curious George Goes Camping* by H. A. Rey
- *Corduroy* by Don Freeman

This activity develops:
- Awareness of the letter Cc
- Listening skills
- Skill in associating the letters Aa, Bb and Cc
- More awareness of age 3 and 4 and birthday
- Memory recall

Age 3 - Activity 49 – Dig In the Dirt for Dd

You will need:
- Dd tracing template with arrows from internet search
- Crayons and green marker
- Index card and popsicle stick
- Masking tape and glue
- Dimes
- Magazine
- 10 small cardboard pieces

Dd Limerick
Daniel Dodd drove to the dairy
On a dark day, damp, and dreary
He drew up a dipper of milk to drink
Dawdled past dawn and began to think
Of damsels and dangerous dragons of yore
When a darling dame came to the door
Who dared to ask Daniel for a glass of white
And said, "My dear- this milk's a delight!"

Introduce the letter Dd name and sound:
Use the Dd tracing template page (printed on cardstock paper) to introduce the letter Dd. Have the child name the letter and repeat back to you the Dd sound.

Trace the letter Dd: Have the child use his or her pointer finger to trace the outline of the letter Dd following the arrows.

Letter Dd puppet: Make a letter puppet with the index card and popsicle stick. Draw or paste a picture of a door that your child can color. Print the word in lower case letters underneath the picture.

Digging for the letter Dd:
1. Print the letter Dd on ten pieces of cardboard about an inch square.
2. Hide these ten cardboard pieces in sand or dirt.
3. Instruct the child to dig deep and find the ten cards with the Dd on them.

Activity extension: For variation, Aa's, Bb's and Cc's can be hidden in the dirt with the Dd's. No more than three cards of each letter should be used. Too many will be confusing. After the child finds the cards in the sand or dirt, suggest that he or she put all of the Aa's, Bb's, Cc's and Dd's together and sort them into separate piles.

Looking for the letter Dd in print: The child may suggest looking for the Dd's in a magazine. This activity reinforces the visual skills in recognizing the letter many times in words. It also is good for fine motor coordination when the child uses a marker to circle the letters. It also serves to increase the child's attention span and motivates him or her to work independently. If the child shows no interest in looking for the letters in magazines, suggest that he or she look for Dd's when you read a story or when you go to the grocery store. He or she will undoubtedly recognize the letters you have learned together on signs and buildings.

Dimes to make the Dd Page in alphabet book: Continue your alphabet book (binder) with the Dd Template page. Have your child help you glue dimes around the upper case and lower case letters. (This page may be better made on a piece of thick cardstock, since it will be heavy with the weight of the dimes.) Add this page to the alphabet book! This is a great opportunity to talk to your child about coins and money. Emphasize that a dime represents ten cents (ten pennies).

Book ideas:
- *Dig!* by Andrea Zimmerman and David Clemesha
- *Clifford Digs a Dinosaur* by Sonali Fry
- *Curious George and the Dog Show* by H. A. Rey
- *Make Way for Ducklings* by Robert McCloskey
- *Alexander, Who Used to Be Rich Last Sunday* by Judith Viorst
- *Look at the Coins (Content-Area Sight Word Readers)* by Tammy Jones

---

This activity develops:
- Phonemic awareness of the letter Dd sound
- Visual recognition of the letter Dd
- Skill in listening for letter sounds
- Skill in matching letters
- Tactile sensory enhancement
- Confidence

Age 3 - Activity 50 – Eggs in the Basket

You will need:
- Ee tracing template with arrows from internet search
- Crayons and scissors
- Index card and popsicle stick
- Masking tape and glue
- Egg shells from boiled or cracked eggs
- Construction paper
- Basket

Ee Limerick
Ed fried up eleven eggs every other day
Elephants would enter and try to have their way
Ed fled in error because he was so scared
And left the eggs to elephants who consumed four pair
All in all eight edible eggs were in the theft
So when Ed came back how many eggs were left?

Introduce the letter Ee name and sound: Use an Ee tracing template page (printed on cardstock paper) to introduce the letter Ee. Have the child name the letter and repeat back to you the Ee sound.

Trace the letter Ee: Have the child use his or her pointer finger to trace the outline of the letter Ee following the arrows.

Letter Ee puppet: Make a letter puppet with the index card and popsicle stick. Draw or paste a picture of an egg that your child can color. Print the word in lower case letters underneath the picture.

Eggshells to make the Ee page in alphabet book: Continue your alphabet book (binder) with the Ee Template page. Have your child help you glue eggshell pieces around the upper case and lower case letters.

Egg game set up:
1. Draw ten eggs on construction paper about 3 inches long.
2. Allow the child to cut them out.
3. Use a sharpie and write the letters Aa, Bb, Cc, Dd, and Ee on the ten eggs so that you have two eggs with each letter.
4. Put these paper eggs in a small basket.

Directions: Have your child choose the egg with the name of the letter (or the sound the letter makes) called out to him or her.

Extension: The eggs can be hidden in different obvious places in a room. The child should then be encouraged to go and find them. As he or she finds each egg, he or she must identify the letter that is written on it and place it in the small basket.

Book ideas:
- *Green Eggs and Ham* by Dr. Seuss
- *A Dozen Easter Eggs (Jewel Sticker Stories)* by Melissa Sweet

This activity develops:
- Phonemic awareness of the letter Ee sound
- Visual recognition of the letter Ee
- Skill in listening for letter sounds
- Skill in matching letters
- Tactile sensory enhancement
- Confidence

Age 3 - Activity 51 – Let's Go Fishing

You will need:
- Ff tracing template with arrows from internet search
- Crayons
- Index card and popsicle stick
- Masking tape and glue
- Feathers
- Construction paper
- Scissors
- Kitchen magnets
- Paper clips
- Yarn
- Pencil

Introduce the letter Ff name and sound: Use a Ff tracing template page (printed on cardstock paper) to introduce the letter Ff. Have the child name the letter and repeat back to you the Ff sound.

Trace the letter Ff: Have the child use his or her pointer finger to trace the outline of the letter Ff following the arrows.

Letter Dd puppet: Make a letter puppet with the index card and popsicle stick. Draw or paste a picture of a fish that your child can color. Print the word in lower case letters underneath the picture.

Feathers to make the Ff page in alphabet book: Continue your alphabet book (binder) with the Ff Template page. Have your child help you glue feathers around the upper case and lower case letters.

Ff Limerick
Freddie Ferris flew to Paris looking
for a flower
But only had one chance, this flight to
France, to find the Eiffel Tower.
And find he did on Friday while eating fifty
French fries
He flailed and fumbled and fell where a
Parisian garden lies
From falling, Freddie found a flower he
could sever
And for fun he kept the flower in his
Fedora forever

Magnetic fishing activity set up:
1. Draw 12 fish that are each approximately 5 inches long on colored construction paper.
2. Allow the child to cut them out.
3. Letter the fish with the letters Aa through Ff twice.
4. Place a paper clip on the nose of each fish or staple two staples on the nose area.
5. Tie one end of a piece of string or yarn to a stick or pencil.
6. Attach a refrigerator magnet (or one with a cup hook) to the other end of the string or yarn.

Directions:
1. Lay the 12-colored fish on the floor and tell the child the floor represents the "water" where the fish live. Invite the child to go "fishing."
2. The child should hold the stick or pencil as if it were a fishing rod. The magnetic end should be referred to as the "hook."
3. Tell the child that as he or she catches the fish to tell you the name of the letter on the fish or the sound that the letter makes. All correctly named fish may be kept out of the "water."
4. If he or she does not know the name of the letter or its sound, tell him or her the letter name or sound and instruct the child to put the fish back into the "water."

Fishing Game Variations:

Call a letter by its name or by its sound and have the child catch that fish.

The child may also enjoy matching the two fish with the same letter.

Write your own fish story: You and your child can make up a story about a fish. You can write the words as the child makes up the story. Include other words that begin with the letter Ff such as: *funny, flip flop, fins, four, famous, friend, finish,* etc. Then you can read the child his or her story aloud and have your child finish the sentences with the final word that he or she made up when writing it.

Book ideas:
- *The Rainbow Fish* by Marcus Pfister
- *One Fish, Two Fish, Red Fish, Blue Fish* by Dr. Seuss
- *Little Fish Finger Puppet Book* by ImageBooks Staff
- *Dear Fish* by Chris Gall
- *The Story of Ferdinand* by Monroe Leaf

This activity develops:
- Awareness of the letter Ff
- Memory recall skills (letters Aa - Ff)
- Visual discrimination skills
- Eye-hand coordination

Age 3 - Activity 52 – Gg is For Green Grass Grow

You will need:
- Gg tracing template with arrows from an internet search
- Crayons
- Index card and popsicle stick
- Masking tape and glue
- Gum or gumballs
- Green and blue construction paper
- Scissors
- Pair of old sunglasses

> **Gg Limerick**
> Gretchen got a goat that was a gorgeous color green
> When the goat grazed, he seemed to glitter,
> glow, and gleam
> Garbanzo beans, grapefruits, and garlic were in its gruel
> And guys and girls who saw the goat thought,
> "Gosh- that's really cool!"

Introduce the letter Gg name and sound: Use a Gg tracing template page (printed on cardstock paper) to introduce the letter Gg. Have the child name the letter and repeat back to you the Gg sound.

Trace the letter Gg: Have the child use his or her pointer finger to trace the outline of the letter Gg following the arrows.

Letter Gg puppet: Make a letter puppet with the index card and popsicle stick. Draw or paste a picture of grass that your child can color. Print the word in lower case letters underneath the picture.

Gum to make the Gg page in alphabet book: Continue your alphabet book (binder) with a Gg Template page. Have your child help you glue pieces of gum or gumballs around the upper case and lower case letters.

Green grass grow:
- Cut the green construction paper in along strip.
- Show your child how to cut one side of the strip to make fringe, resembling grass.
- Let your child glue the green grass strips onto a piece of blue construction paper.
- You child can draw or cut and glue flowers and other wildlife in the grass.

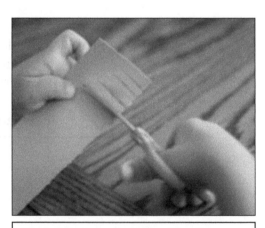

Grass growing science project: Plant some grass seeds in a clear, plastic cup filled with soil. Water it regularly and keep it on the windowsill, so that it will receive lots of sunlight. Watch the grass grow!

Letter Gg sound alliteration poem: Alliteration poems include lines in which all of the words begin with the same letter sound. The lines do not have to rhyme. Have your child help you put together words that begin with the letter Gg sound to form three poem lines. Use words such as: *go*, *great*, *grass*, *green*, *grow*, *gravel*, *good*, *ground*, etc. Read the poem aloud to your child. After your child has become familiar with the lines of the poem, have him or her fill in the blanks with the remaining word at the end of each line.

Game set up:
- Print the letters Aa through Ff twice on separate index cards that have been cut in half.
- Print the letter Gg on four of the cards.
- Two or more people can play this game.

Game directions:
1. The first player turns over a card from a shuffled pile and says the letter sound on the card and places the card upright beside the deck.
2. When someone turns over a Gg card, that person must say, "Glasses get it great" instead of the "Gg" sound.

Game Tips:
- If none of the players has any cards left, that signifies good memory and concentration for all players.
- Be certain to tell the child the sounds of any letters that are missed.
- Practice will help him or her to learn the letter sounds.

Book ideas:
- *Go, Dog, Go!* by P.D. Eastman
- *And the Green Grass Grows All Around: Folk Poetry From Everyone* by Alvin Schwartz
- *Green and Growing: A Book About Plants* by Susan Blackaby

This activity develops:
- Awareness of the letter Gg
- Skill in distinguishing the letters Aa - Gg
- Memory recall skills and listening skills
- Eye-hand coordination and confidence

Age Four: From Four-years-old to Five-years-old

Getting Ready for School

Four-year-old children are excited to learn. Fostering a safe environment for these youngsters to dabble in school-like activities is crucial for their preparedness at school. Cutting, gluing, coloring, drawing, and writing letters are just some of the fine motor skills that pre-kindergartners can practice at home. When children enter K5, they are much more confident when asked to perform these school-like tasks if they are comfortable and familiar with these fine motor skills through practice. That is why many of the activities in this section offer multiple ideas of simple projects that involve these skills.

Mini Lessons

You are your child's first teacher. The activities in this section are designed to guide you in modeling, explaining, and guiding your child in the learning process just like a teacher does. Continue to explore the alphabet with the activities provided in Age 3 Activity 42. The mini lessons in Age Four offer fun, hands-on ways to learn the letters and sounds of the remaining alphabet letters that were introduced in Age Three. Limericks for each letter along with the creation of a finger puppet enable your child to connect with the written letter and the heard sound. Book ideas and other simple activities and projects are suggested as additional resources to help children at this age learn their letters.

Alphabet Book

This section includes ideas for creating an alphabet book with a page devoted to each uppercase and lowercase letter as introduced in the last few lessons of Age Three. A wonderful way to showcase your child's learning! A simple three-ring binder with pages devoted to each letter can be printed on cardstock paper and hole punched to create the pages of the alphabet book. As each letter is introduced in the lessons, objects whose names begin with the letter's sound are suggested to be glued on top of the template to outline the uppercase and lowercase letters.

Letter Recognition and Beginning Sounds

Piggy-backing off of the activities in the latter half of Age Three, the Age Four lessons emphasize letter recognition and beginning sounds. Continue to play the games suggested to help your child recognize both uppercase and lowercase letters of the alphabet. Refrigerator letter magnets are another fun way to help your child recognize letters. Not only should your child be able to recognize the twenty-six letters, but he or she should also be aware of the sound that each makes. You will notice in the lesson that words are given to prompt you in teaching your child how to make the letter's sound and to recognize it when he or she is listening for it.

Attention Span Through Reading

Getting your child ready for the school environment should include stretching your child's attention span to last a little longer every day. Reading stories together is a great way to do this. You may even want to progress toward reading children's chapter books aloud to your child. Books with several characters and continual action keep a child's mind steadily moving along, as it is filled with the imaginative scenes captured in the words of the books being read. As Attention Deficit Disorder and short attention spans are so prevalent at young ages in our world today, reading aloud to your child supports habits that counteract inattention and inability to focus. Focusing on a book requires a child to stay in one place and pay attention, which will help to expand their attention span and focus better in all areas of life.

Reading aloud, even for a short amount of time, enables a child to create the pictures in his or her mind from the words he or she has heard from the story. This mental stimulation takes an amount of concentration that when practiced regularly will gain foundational progress needed to focus on longer tasks and longer periods of read alouds. Focusing habits are essential to future reading development and academic success. As a child listens to a story read aloud, he or she enriches his or her ability to focus on the story for longer and longer amounts of time.

Following Directions

You will notice that the lessons in Age Four suggest giving your child directions for games, projects, and activities. This is because in kindergarten, a child will be required to follow directions to accomplish the tasks he or she is assigned. Even though free play and choice are encouraged, your child needs to practice setting his or her own wishes aside sometimes to follow someone else's directions when asked. Playing Simon Says and other simple games are a great way to make learning how to follow directions fun. Also, incorporate these games with your normal routine. These can include getting dressed in the morning or brushing teeth before bed.

Large Muscle Coordination

Large muscle coordination vastly improves at this age. Some children will still have difficulty with their coordination, but the best thing you can do is to lovingly encourage and support your child by offering multiple opportunities for him or her to practice the skills. These skills include catching and throwing a ball, jumping rope, balancing, and skipping. Practice will serve to refine the necessary coordination your child will need for mastery of these large muscle skills.

Social Skills

Interaction with other children of the same age is advantageous in preparing your child for kindergarten. Set up regular "play dates" with friends both at home and the local playground, so that your child can interact and play for longer stretches of time along with another child. Four-year-olds learn not only how to play fair at this age, but they also will be exposed to others that are different from them, expanding their ideas and imaginations. This also helps in broadening your child's outlook on life and helps in him or her adjusting outside the home environment. Play is a child's way of learning. Children learn from each other.

Lessons from Children's Books
In the same way that many of the activities stem from a connection to the alphabet letter being introduced and taught at the beginning of this section, the activities in the latter half of Age Four are centered on a beloved children's book. The mini lessons that go along with these books develop pre-reading and practical skills that connect with the content of each book. Feel free to spread the activities of each lesson out over several days if needed. Have conversations with your child about the books you read aloud together to remind each other about the stories and the lessons learned.

The Gift of Literacy
The love of literacy is one of the greatest gifts we can give to our children to help them succeed as a future reader and life-long learner. Reading aloud to our children has a plethora of benefits as on-going research, observation, and study proves. Research shows that children who have been read to on a regular basis during their infant, toddler, and preschool years have a significant advantage over other children who attend kindergarten. Reading aloud takes time, but this time is meaningful and proven to have advantages that will follow our children throughout the rest of their lives.

Note
The author and publisher are not liable for any injury or death incurred due to the misuse of the suggested materials and directions. As with all child-related activities, materials should be selected with careful attention to child safety; adult supervision is essential.

Age 4 - Activity 1 – The Hh Hat Game

You will need:
- Hh tracing template with arrows from an internet search
- Crayons
- Index card and popsicle stick
- Masking tape and glue
- Pieces of hay
- Hat that the child can wear
- Yellow construction paper

> **Hh Limerick**
> Helga was a healthy horse who hated haughty hounds.
> They'd heckle her with horrible howls whenever they came around.
> But hawks would help her by holding up their ears, which were hairy and flappy
> So the hounds heckled Helga no more, and the hawks' help made her happy.

Introduce the letter Hh name and sound:
Use the Hh tracing template page (printed on cardstock paper) to introduce the letter Hh. Have the child name the letter and repeat back to you the Hh sound.

> **Wear a Hat and Sing a Chant!**
> When the child is playing with the letter Hh puppet, he or she can use the following chant: "(child's name) says this and that. Did you know that rhymes with hat?"

Trace the letter Hh: Have the child use his or her pointer finger to trace the outline of the letter Hh following the arrows.

Letter Hh puppet: Make a letter puppet with the index card and popsicle stick. Draw or paste a picture of a hat that your child can color. Print the word in lower case letters underneath the picture.

Hay pieces to make the Hh page in alphabet book: Continue your alphabet book (binder) with the Hh Template page. Have your child help you glue strands of hay around the upper case and lower case letters.

Hat match game set up:
- Use yellow construction paper to draw and cut out 16 hats that are approximately 5 inches wide. Allow the child to help you draw and cut out the paper hats if he or she is interested.
- Print the letters Aa through Hh so that there are 2 hats with each uppercase and lowercase letter.

Hat match:
1. Place the hats with the letters face down.
2. Each player turns over 1 hat and then another in search of the 2 hats that have the same letter.
3. If the player finds 2 hats that are the same, he or she puts the matched hats in a pile and continues to search for 2 more that are the same.

4. If he or she turns over 2 hats that are not the same, then the 2 hats must be turned back over face down.
5. The next player then has a turn.
6. When all of the hats have been matched, count the hats with the child. The player with the most hats wins.

> **Memory:** Remind the child to try to remember where the replaced hats are.

Simplify the game: If the memory matching game seems too difficult for your child, play the matching game with all of the hats facing up. Count all of the hats when the game is over. The child will delight in noting how many hats he or she has matched.

> **Learning about winning and losing:** Emphasize to the child that even though the object of a game is to win, there is only one winner. Games should be played for fun, because everyone cannot win.

Write your own hat story: Ask the following questions to help your child brainstorm some ideas to include in his or her story about a big hat.
- *What is special about the hat?*
- *Who wears the hat?*
- *Why is the hat important?*
- *Where is the hat?*
- *How did the owner of the hat get his or her hat?*

Have the child verbally create short sentences with the answers he or she gave above to make the story. This helps the child to formulate sentences in order for him or her to speak in complete thoughts.

Book ideas:
- *The Little House* by Virginia Lee Burton
- *Old Hat, New Hat* by Stan and Jan Berenstain
- *Who's Under That Hat? (Gulliver Books)* by Sarah Weeks

> This activity develops:
> - Awareness of the letter Hh
> - Visual discrimination of the letters Aa - Hh
> - Association skills (matching letters)
> - Memory recall of the letter names

Age 4 - Activity 2 – Ii For Inchworm

You will need:
- Ii tracing template with arrows from an internet search
- Crayons and scissors
- Index card and popsicle stick
- Masking tape and glue
- Paint brush and ink or fountain pen or gummy sour worm candies
- Egg carton
- Construction paper
- Pipe cleaner and googly eyes

> **Ii Limerick**
> Ian was an Eskimo who grew up illiterate
> And everyone insisted that he was an idiot.
> So to improve his image to himself he thought,
> "If only I can win this year's Iditarod!"
> With intense iteration, win it he did
> And now Ian is known as The Ingenious Inuit.

Introduce the letter Ii name and sound:
Use the Ii tracing template page (printed on cardstock paper) to introduce the letter Ii. Have the child name the letter and repeat back to you the Ii sound.

Trace the letter Ii: Have the child use his or her pointer finger to trace the outline of the letter Ii following the arrows.

Letter Ii puppet: Make a letter puppet with the index card and popsicle stick. Draw or paste a picture of an inchworm that your child can color. Print the word in lower case letters underneath the picture.

Name the letter puppets! At another time, allow the child to play with all of the letter puppets and suggest that he or she name all of them for you. Help your child if necessary.

What's missing? Letter game: With the letter puppets, ask the child to identify the letters on the puppets that you plan to use (only 4 to begin with). Tell the child to turn around while you remove one of the puppets. When the child turns back around, ask him or her to tell you what puppet is missing. Tell the child the name if he or she does not recall it. Continue to play the game with any of the 4 puppets. This is good for the child's memory recall.

Ink to make the Ii page in alphabet book: Continue your alphabet book (binder) with the Ii Template page. Have your child help you use the paintbrush and colorful ink or a fountain pen's ink to outline the upper case and lower case letters. Another idea is to use gummy sour worm candies to represent "inchworms" glued on the outline of the letters for your child's alphabet book.

Make an inchworm:
- Cut an egg carton lengthwise.
- Allow the child to cut 5 circles from different colored construction paper.

- Encourage the child to glue the circles together in a row. Each circle should overlap each circle slightly to resemble an inchworm.
- Use pipe cleaner for antennae.
- Glue googly eyes to the inchworm's head.

> **Why is it called an inchworm?** The inchworm gets its name because it brings the end of its body up to meet the front of its body and stretches (inches) forward as if measuring the ground.

Measure an inch with a ruler: Your child may enjoy using a small ruler. Explain to your child how long an inch is. You may want to draw a colored mark where the inch begins and ends on the ruler, so that he or she can better visualize its length. Model how to measure with the ruler in inches. With some guidance the child can begin to measure simple things such as a finger, hand, foot, shoe, book, etc.

Book ideas:
- *Inchworm and a Half* by Elinor J. Pinczes
- *The Inch Book: With 60-Inch Tape Measure (I Can Do It Books)* by Elise Richards
- *Inch by Inch* by Leo Lionni
- *Igloo (Bookworms: The Inside Story)* by Dana Meachen Rau

This activity develops:
- Awareness of the letter Ii
- More skill in distinguishing the letters
- Eye-hand coordination
- Awareness of an inch
- Beginning skills in measuring
- Confidence

Age 4 - Activity 3 – Jj For Jack-in-the-Box

You will need:
- Jj tracing template with arrows from an internet search
- Crayons and scissors
- Index card and popsicle stick
- Masking tape and glue
- Jelly beans
- Large box with top attached (that the child can fit in)
- Construction paper
- Pipe cleaner and googly eyes

> **Jj Limerick**
> In June, Jack jumped jump-rope
> And jauntily jumped so high
> That he fell on his rump and could no longer jump
> Come the month of July.

Introduce the letter Jj name and sound: Use the Jj tracing template page (printed on cardstock paper) to introduce the letter Jj. Have the child name the letter and repeat back to you the Jj sound.

Trace the letter Jj: Have the child use his or her pointer finger to trace the outline of the letter Jj following the arrows.

Letter Jj puppet: Make a letter puppet with the index card and popsicle stick. Draw or paste a picture of a jack-in-the-box that your child can color. Print the word in lower case letters underneath the picture.

Jack-in-the-box activity: The top of the box should be attached on one side with the other three sides free so that the child can push the lid up when he pretends to pop up like a Jack-in-the-box. A large Tupperware box with a lid loosely put on the top would also work. Then invite your child to get inside. Chant, "*Jj, Jj, Jack-in-the-box, open the lid and out he pops.*" Tell the child to open the lid when you say *pops* and jump up like a Jack-in-the-box.

Jj, Jj, Jack-in-the-box, open the lid and out he pops.

Jellybeans to make the Jj page in alphabet book:
Continue your alphabet book (binder) with the Jj template page. Have your child help you use the jellybeans to outline the upper case and lower case letters.

"I Spy" things that start with the letter Jj: You can make your child a spy glass by cutting cardstock paper in the shape of a magnifying glass and cutting out the center circle to see through. Model how to use the spy glass to find things around your house or outside that begin with the letter Jj.

Book ideas:

- *The Jelly Bean Fun Book [Board Book]* by Karen Capucilli
- *Jeremiah Jellyfish Flies High* by John Fardell
- *Jack and the Beanstalk (Pudgy Pals)* by Benrei Huang

This activity develops:
- Awareness of the letter Jj
- Skill in distinguishing letters
- Role playing
- Listening skills

Age 4 - Activity 4 – Kk For Kite

You will need:
- Kk tracing template with arrows from an internet search
- Crayons and scissors
- Index card and popsicle stick
- Masking tape and glue
- Cardstock paper or cardboard
- Yarn
- Leftover keys or Hershey's "kisses"
- Construction paper

Introduce the letter Kk name and sound: Use the Kk tracing template page (printed on cardstock paper) to introduce the letter Kk. Have the child name the letter and repeat back to you the Kk sound.

Trace the letter Kk: Have the child use his or her pointer finger to trace the outline of the letter Kk following the arrows.

Letter Kk puppet: Make a letter puppet with the index card and popsicle stick. Draw or paste a picture of a kite that your child can color. Print the word in lower case letters underneath the picture.

Make a pretend kite: Cut off the corners of a piece of 8½ in. x 11 in. piece of cardstock paper or cardboard. Allow the child to decorate the kite before he or she cuts off the corners. Staple a piece of yarn to the middle of the top section. Staple another piece of yarn to the bottom tip of the kite to represent a tail. Tie a knot at the end of the two pieces of yarn before stapling them to the kite. This will prevent that yarn from slipping under the staple. Give the kite to the child and allow him or her to pretend to fly his or her kite indoors.

Leftover keys or Hershey's "kisses" to make the Kk page in alphabet book: Continue your alphabet book (binder) with the Kk Template page. Have your child help you use leftover keys or Hershey's "kisses" to outline the upper case and lower case letters.

"I Spy" things that start with the letter Kk: Use the spyglass (made in the previous lesson) to find things around your house or outside that begin with the letter Kk.

> **Kk Limerick**
> Kayla was a killer whale
> Who loved to snack on sea
> turtle bales.
> One day Kayla got caught up in kelp
> But her kin, Kyle, was there to help.
> The turtles escaped because of
> their skill
> And Kayla was reduced to just
> eating krill.
> Though her eyes were keen and
> demeanor was mean,
> She could not find any turtles afoot
> So Kayla wept for the life
> that she kept
> Because her killing days were kaput.

Book ideas:
- *Curious George and the Kite* by H.A. Rey
- *The Flyaway Kite* by Steve Bjorkman
- *The Hershey's Kisses Addition Book* by Jerry Pallotta

This activity develops:
- Awareness of the letter Kk and its initial sound as in the word *kite*
- Eye-hand coordination
- Dramatization as in pretending to fly a kite

Age 4 - Activity 5 – Ll is For Lollipop

You will need:
- Ll tracing template with arrows from an internet search
- Crayons and scissors
- Index card and popsicle stick
- Masking tape and glue
- Construction paper
- Small bottle cap, large bottle cap, cup, bowl, large bowl

Ll Limerick

Lola loved lollipops almost as much as lindy-hops
She liked to lick, and she liked to dance
And loved to go out with her friend named Lance.
They laughed out loud, and leapt around
in the crowd
And then they left for a Cola
Lance liked this girl and the way she would twirl
And called her Lovely Lola.

Introduce the letter Ll name and sound: Use the Ll tracing template page (printed on cardstock paper) to introduce the letter Ll. Have the child name the letter and repeat back to you the Ll sound.

Trace the letter Ll: Have the child use his or her pointer finger to trace the outline of the letter Ll following the arrows.

Letter Ll puppet: Make a letter puppet with the index card and popsicle stick. Draw or paste a picture of a lollipop that your child can color. Print the word in lower case letters underneath the picture.

Make a lollipop with circles: Cut several sizes of circles out of different colored construction paper and glue them on top of each other. Start by tracing and cutting out the largest circle out of a large bowl, then use a smaller bowl, a cup, a large bottle cap, and finally a small bottle cap for the center.

Lollipops to make the Ll page in alphabet book: Continue your alphabet book (binder) with the Ll Template page. Have your child help you use lollipops to outline the upper case and lower case letters.

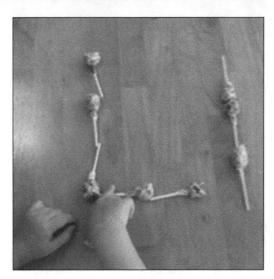

Toothpicks or lollipop Ll's: Your child may enjoy lining up toothpicks or lollipops to form uppercase L's and lowercase l's.

"I Spy" things that start with the letter Ll: Model how to use the home-made spyglass to find things around your house or outside that begin with the letter Ll.

Book ideas:
- *Big Red Lollipop* by Rukhsana Khan
- *Amanda Pig and Her Best Friend Lollipop* by Jean Van Leeuwen
- *Are Lemons Blue?* by DK Publishing
- *The Lemon Drop Jar* by Christine Widman

This activity develops:
- Awareness of the letter Ll
- Skill in distinguishing letters
- Listening skills
- Memory recall
- Awareness of the letters that are made primarily of straight lines

Age 4 - Activity 6 – Mm For My Mittens

You will need:
- Mm tracing template with arrows from an internet search
- Crayons and scissors
- Index card and popsicle stick
- Masking tape and glue
- Construction paper

Introduce the letter Mm name and sound: Use the Mm tracing template page (printed on cardstock paper) to introduce the letter Mm. Have the child name the letter and repeat back to you the Mm sound.

Trace the letter Mm: Have the child use his or her pointer finger to trace the outline of the letter Mm following the arrows.

Letter Mm puppet: Make a letter puppet with the index card and popsicle stick. Draw or paste a picture of a mitten that your child can color. Print the word in lower case letters underneath the picture.

Read "Three Little Kittens" rhyme: Read the rhyme aloud once. Read the rhyme again, and this time have your child fill in the blanks where you pause at the end of a familiar line to provide the missing rhyming word like *mittens*, *cry*, and *pie*. Talk about the words that rhyme. This may also be an opportune time to slip in a life lesson with your child about obedience and the meaning of the word *naughty*.

Make play mittens and make them match:
1. Fold a piece of construction paper in half and trace around one of the child's hands.
2. Cutting through both thicknesses of the paper will produce two paper mittens.
3. Turn one of the paper mittens over so that the left and right thumbs face inside toward each other.
4. Point out the left and right mitten to the child and tell him or her that he or she has a pair of mittens to decorate.
5. Tell your child to decorate each mitten the same so that both mittens "match."

> **Mm Limerick**
> Milly the moose and Gilly the goose moved
> into a mansion for lease
> "Me oh my!" Gilly said and sighed, "There's
> not much money for my geese!"
> "Maybe," mooned Milly, "If we move
> Monday, we won't be in such a mash,
> We may market some meat for the men in
> the street, and then sell it for cash!"

> **Three Little Kittens**
> *The three little kittens, they lost their mittens,*
> *And they began to cry,*
> *"Oh, mother dear, we sadly fear,*
> *That we have lost our mittens."*
> *"What! Lost your mittens, you naughty kittens!*
> *Then you shall have no pie."*
> *"Meow, meow, meow."*
> *"Then you shall have no pie."*

Macaroni pieces to make the Mm page in alphabet book:
Continue your alphabet book (binder) with the Mm Template page. Have your child help you use macaroni pieces to outline the upper case and lower case letters.

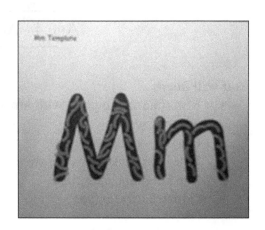

Book ideas:
- *Three Little Kittens* by Jerry Pinkney
- *Mike Mulligan and His Steam Shovel* by Virginia Lee Burton
- *M is For Mitten: A Michigan Alphabet (Discover America State By State Alphabet Series)* by Annie Appleford
- *Toby Counts His Marbles* by Cyndy Szekeres
- *Glad Monster, Sad Monster* by Ed Emberley
- *Goodnight, Little Monster* by Helen Ketteman

This activity develops:
- Awareness of the letter Mm
- Listening skills
- Rhyming skills
- More awareness of left and right
- More awareness of a pair
- Confidence

Age 4 - Activity 7 – Nn is For Night Time

You will need:
- Nn tracing template with arrows from an internet search
- Crayons and scissors
- Index card and popsicle stick
- Masking tape and glue
- Black and yellow construction paper

Introduce the letter Nn name and sound: Use the Nn tracing template page (printed on cardstock paper) to introduce the letter Nn. Have the child name the letter.

Trace the letter Nn: Have the child use his or her pointer finger to trace the outline of the letter Nn following the arrows.

Letter Nn puppet: Make a letter puppet with the index card and popsicle stick. Draw or paste a picture of a nighttime sky that your child can color. Print the word in lower case letters underneath the picture.

Nutshells, nails, noodles, or nickels to make the Nn page in alphabet book: Continue your alphabet book (binder) with the Nn Template page. Have your child help you use nutshells or other options listed above that begin with the Nn sound to outline the upper case and lower case letters.

Nn Limerick
Nancy never navigated by using maps on treks,
Instead she wore a GPS that fastened
around her neck.
From Nevada to the Netherlands,
She left everyone perplexed.
Now no one knows where Nancy goes
Or where Nancy's going next.

Nn chant: Nn is for night when I sleep tight.

Alphabet puppet box: Allow the child to play with the Nn puppet and repeat the chant several times. Give the child the shoebox or container with the other puppets and ask what the letters are and the associated words that begin with those letters. Example: Nn is for night or Mm is for mittens. This type of skill will be helpful to the child when he or she begins to read. This sound awareness will also be helpful to the child in spelling.

Over 80% of the words in the English language are spelled phonetically (sound reading).

Book ideas:
- *Day and Night* by Teddy Newton
- *Goodnight Cowboy* by Glenn Dromgoole
- *The Perfect Nest* by Catherine Friend
- *The Nutcracker: A Pop-Up Book Adapted From the Classic Tale by E.T.A. Hoffmann* by Patricia Fry

This activity develops:
- Awareness of the letter Nn
- More of an understanding of letter/sound relationships
- Vocabulary enrichment
- Eye-hand coordination
- More awareness of rhyming in the chant
- Listening skills

Age 4 - Activity 8 – Oo is For Octopus

You will need:
- Oo tracing template with arrows from an internet search
- Crayons and scissors
- Index card and popsicle stick
- Masking tape and glue
- Construction Paper
- Paper plate
- Hole punch
- Strips of cloth or yarn
- Stapler and sharpie

> **Oo Limerick**
> Ollie the octopus lived offshore and operated an office for eyes.
> Fish would opt for optimum options and were never caught by surprise
> For Ollie was great in granting their wish
> And became opulent for fixing eyes for fish.
> Their sight- no longer obstructed or obscure-
> Was owed to Ollie's optometry for sure!

Introduce the letter Oo name and sound: Use the Oo Tracing Template page (printed on cardstock paper) to introduce the letter Oo. Have the child name the letter and repeat back to you the short vowel Oo sound.

Trace the letter Oo: Have the child use his or her pointer finger to trace the outline of the letter Oo following the arrows.

Letter Oo puppet: Make a letter puppet with the index card and popsicle stick. Draw or paste a picture of an octopus that your child can color. Print the word in lower case letters underneath the picture.

Suggested chant: *Oo is for octopus that swims along. His body and his tentacles are very strong.*

Make a model octopus for your child to play with:
1. Punch eight holes around the rim of the paper plate.
2. Strips of cloth or yarn can be woven through to make the tentacles.
3. The eight tentacles can then be attached through the holes in the plate and secured with a knot or they may be stapled to the plate.
4. The strips of cloth or yarn may be knotted at the ends to represent the octopus' suckers.
5. The child can then add two eyes on the top with a crayon or Sharpie.
6. It can be hung with a string or rubber band for the child to hold and play with. This will give the illusion of a swimming octopus.

Facts of interest about the octopus to share with your child:

- An octopus has two large, shiny eyes.

- An octopus has strong hard jaws that come to a point like a bird's beak. These help him to get his food.
- The octopus can squirt a liquid in the water to make it cloudy, so other animals that would eat the octopus cannot see him in the water.
- The octopus has no bones and his body is soft.
- His eight arms or tentacles have suckers on them that allow the octopus to attach himself to an object or to capture his food.
- The octopus draws water into his body and squeezes it back out with a strong force. This causes his body to move through the water.

Counting with the octopus: Your child will enjoy counting the tentacles of the octopus. Show the child the number 8 so that he or she can associate the symbol with the eight tentacles.

Order the alphabet puppets activity: The letter puppets should be placed in order from Aa to Oo and identified at different times. The letter games from past activities can be played and the chants repeated to reinforce the letters and the sounds without the child feeling pressured to do so.

Cheerios or orange peel slices to make the Oo page in alphabet book: Continue your alphabet book (binder) with the Oo Template page. Have your child help you use Cheerios or orange peel slices to outline the upper case and lower case letters.

Book ideas:
- *The Ox Cart Man* by Donald Hall and Barbara Cooney
- *My Very Own Octopus* by Bernard Most
- *The Biggest Thing In the Ocean* by Kevin Sherry

This activity develops:
- Awareness of the letter Oo
- Language enrichment
- Dramatization (playing with the swimming octopus)
- Eye-hand coordination
- More skill in sound/letter relationships

Age 4 - Activity 9 – Pp is For Pickle

You will need:
- Pp tracing template with arrows from an internet search
- Crayons and scissors
- Index card and popsicle stick
- Masking tape and glue
- Construction paper

Introduce the letter Pp name and sound:
Use the Pp tracing template page (printed on cardstock paper) to introduce the letter Pp. Have the child name the letter and repeat back to you the Pp sound.

Trace the letter Pp: Have the child use his or her pointer finger to trace the outline of the letter Pp following the arrows.

Letter Pp puppet: Make a letter puppet with the index card and popsicle stick. Draw or paste a picture of a pickle that your child can color. Print the word in lower case letters underneath the picture.

Sequence the alphabet letters activity:
Encourage your child to place all of the letter puppets in a row, starting with *Aa for apple* and so on. Call the letter sound that comes next and have the child find the puppet and place it in the correct order to practice the phonetic sounds of the letters and match the sound with the printed letter. Sing the alphabet song once the puppets are all lined up and point to each one as you sing them in the song with your child.

> **Pp Limerick**
> Paul was pale as paper when something pawed outside his door
> "It could be a pauper or a prisoner- for sure!"
> Paul peered into the peephole, prepared to phone the police
> But it was just a precious puppy that pleaded for a place of peace.

Repetition and reinforcement of these letter games and activities will provide your child with a firm foundation for future reading skills!

Pickle jar game set up:
1. Invite your child to help you make sixteen big and sixteen little pickles by drawing them with a Sharpie on green construction paper.
2. Allow the child to help you cut out all of the paper pickles.
3. Print one upper case letter (from *A* through *P*) on each of the big paper pickles.
4. Similarly, print one lower case letter (*a* through *p*) on each of the little paper pickles.
5. Make a reference chart by printing the letters (*Aa* through *Pp*) on a piece of paper.

Directions:
1. Place all of the big (pickles) letters face up in a row on a table or the floor.
2. The little (pickles) letters should all be in a large plastic jar or other container, which should be referred to as the "pickle jar." You may even want to label it with a Sharpie.
3. The object of the game is to draw a little pickle from the pickle jar and match it with the big pickle on the floor.
4. The game is over when all of the little pickles have been matched with the big pickles.
5. Help the child if necessary and encourage him or her to use the alphabet reference chart.

> Make a note of the letters that seem to confuse the child and work with only those at another time.

Count the pickles: For further enrichment, count the little pickles, then count the big pickles, and then count all thirty-two of them together.

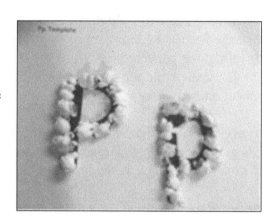

Popcorn to make the Pp page in alphabet book: Continue your alphabet book (binder) with the Pp Template page. Have your child help you use popped popcorn to outline the upper case and lower case letters.

Book ideas:
- *Pickles, Please! A Dilly Book* by Andy Meyer
- *Picky Mrs. Pickle* by Christine M. Schneider
- *The Popcorn Book* by Tommie DePaola

> This activity develops:
> - Awareness of the letter Pp
> - Skill in matching letters
> - More awareness of alphabetical order
> - Memory recall of the letters
> - More awareness of upper and lower case letters
> - Counting skills

Age 4 - Activity 10 – Qq is For Quilt

You will need:
- Qq tracing template with arrows from an internet search
- Crayons and scissors
- Index card and popsicle stick
- Masking tape and glue
- Construction paper

Introduce the letter Qq name and sound: Use the Qq tracing template page (printed on cardstock paper) to introduce the letter Qq. Have the child name the letter and repeat back to you the Qq sound.

Trace the letter Qq: Have the child use his or her pointer finger to trace the outline of the letter Qq following the arrows.

Letter Qq puppet: Make a letter puppet with the index card and popsicle stick. Draw or paste a picture of a quilt that your child can color. Print the word in lower case letters underneath the picture. Q-tips can be glued to the outline of the Qq's for your child's alphabet book.

Count the quilt squares: Encourage your child to count the squares on the quilt with you. Show the child that there are 3 squares across and 3 squares down. Write the number 9 on a piece of paper, so that he or she will relate the concept of nine with the numeral 9.

Book ideas:
- *Patchwork Quilt* by Valerie Flournoy

> **Qq Limerick**
> Quinn the quail was quite quixotic
> For he fancied a queen who was quite exotic
> He had qualms for her feather, a quaint shade
> of heather
> And quickly asked to be whom she doted
> And like a work of art, he won her heart
> From *Don Quixote* like he quoted.

This activity develops:
- Awareness of the letter Qq
- More skill in identifying and associating letters
- Language enrichment and eye-hand coordination
- More awareness of the number concept "9"

Age 4 - Activity 11 – Rr is For Rocket

You will need:
- Rr tracing template with arrows from an internet search
- Crayons and scissors
- Index card and popsicle stick
- Masking tape and glue
- Construction paper
- Paper towel roll
- Stapler or glue
- Two small rectangular cardboard pieces
- Raisins

> **Rr Limerick**
> Randy the rabbit had a very bad habit of running through rows of roses
> Rearing and roaring, the farmer came storming with his hoe and hoses
> "Get your rear out of here!" he roared with a sneer,
> "You're rooting and ruining my crop!"
> But Randy returned, for the roses he yearned,
> And romped with his rough rabbit hop.

Introduce the letter Rr name and sound: Use the Rr tracing template page(printed on cardstock paper) to introduce the letter Rr. Have the child name the letter and repeat back to you the Rr sound.

Trace the letter Rr: Have the child use his or her pointer finger to trace the outline of the letter Rr following the arrows.

Letter Rr puppet: Make a letter puppet with the index card and popsicle stick. Draw or paste a picture of a rocket that your child can color. Print the word in lower case letters underneath the picture.

Rr is for rainbow: To reinforce the letter Rr and its sound, your child may enjoy drawing a large rainbow with red, orange, yellow, green, blue, and purple colors.

Recognizing Rr words: Encourage your child to recognize that the word *rainbow* starts with the same letter and sound that *rocket* does. Name other words that begin with the letter Rr and the sound that it makes.

Rr is for rocket that blasts so high. It moves very fast in the big, blue sky.

rain	*ring*	*ripple*	*rhyme*
rip	*ram*	*roar*	*rich*
rough	*rag*	*riddle*	*roll*

Count backwards for blast off! Have your child pretend that he or she is a rocket ready for blast off by squatting down on the floor. Encourage your child to count backwards with you, "*10, 9, 8, 7, 6, 5, 4, 3, 2, 1, Blast off!*" Then your child can jump up as if he or she were a rocket.

Build your own model rocket:
Step 1: Draw a circle a little larger than the circumference of the paper towel roll on a piece of paper.
Step 2: Draw a line from the edge of the circle to the center.
Step 3: Allow your child to cut out the circle and the line that was drawn to the center.
Step 4: Overlap the cut edge of the circle and staple or glue this to form a cone.
Step 5: Attach the cone to the paper towel roll with tape.
Step 6: Cut several slits at the bottom of the paper towel roll.
Step 7: Slide the two rectangular cardboard pieces to form the base.

Raisins to make the Rr page in alphabet book: Continue your alphabet book (binder) with the Rr Template page. Have your child help you place raisins side by side to outline the capital R and lowercase r.

Book ideas:
- *On The Launch Pad: A Counting Book About Rockets (Know Your Numbers)* by Michael Dahl, Denise Shea, and Derrick Alderman
- *Curious George And the Rocket* by H.A. Rey
- *Roaring Rockets (Amazing Machines)* by Tony Mitton and Ant Parker
- *A Rainbow Of My Own* by Don Freeman
- *Miss Rumphius* by Barbara Cooney

This activity develops:
- Awareness of the letter Rr
- Role playing
- Memory recall
- More awareness of words that begin with the letter Rr
- Confidence and eye-hand coordination

Age 4 - Activity 12 – Ss is for Snake

You will need:
- Ss tracing template with arrows from an internet search
- Crayons and scissors
- Index card and popsicle stick
- Masking tape and glue
- Construction paper
- Marker or Sharpie
- String

Ss Limerick
Sam saw seventeen snakes under a sign saying, "Snakes for sale"
"Sir," said Sam, "Is it true that you can sell me some snakes with scales?"
"Sure!" said the sir, and slid his hand into stir the snakes for sale today.
"On second thought, I've decided to not" said Sam as he skipped away.

Introduce the letter Ss name and sound: Use the Ss tracing template page (printed on cardstock paper) to introduce the letter Ss. Have the child name the letter and repeat back to you the Ss sound.

Trace the letter Ss: Have the child use his or her pointer finger to trace the outline of the letter Ss following the arrows.

Letter Ss puppet: Make a letter puppet with the index card and popsicle stick. Draw or paste a picture of a snake that your child can color. Print the word in lower case letters underneath the picture.

Make a paper snake:
Step 1: Cut out a circle from construction paper.
Step 2: Use a pencil to draw a continuous spiral line from the outside of the circle to the center leaving about one inch between the line as you draw the spiral line to the center.
Step 3: Use a marker or sharpie to trace over the pencil line.
Step 4: Assist the child in cutting on the spiral line to the center leaving a small section to represent the head in the middle.
Step 5: Add eyes, mouth, and spots!

Slither like a snake: Encourage your child to move like a snake by slithering on the floor. You can even have a starting or stopping boundary, so that your child has an end goal as he or she slithers.

Ss word hunt: Look for words with your child in a magazine that begin with the letter Ss. He or she should also be motivated to try to name words that begin with the letter Ss.

seal	sew	same	sip	sick	some
soup	sing	sister	sound	story	sort

Keep in mind: Words that begin with the /sh/ sound should not be included at this time, since the Ss sound is changed when it is followed by the letter h. This is a skill that should be taught later.

String to make the Ss page in alphabet book: Continue your alphabet book (binder) with the Ss Template page. Have your child help you use string to outline the capital S and lowercase s.

Book ideas:
- *The Splendid Spotted Snake: A Magic Ribbon Book* by Alexander Wilensky
- *The Sand Castle Contest* by Robert Munsch

This activity develops:
- Awareness of the letter Ss
- More skill n distinguishing letters
- Memory recall
- Gross motor coordination (moving like a snake)
- Language enrichment
- More awareness of words that begin with the same letter
- Confidence

Age 4 - Activity 13 – Tt is for Treetops

You will need:
- Tt tracing template with arrows from an internet search
- Crayons and scissors
- Index card and popsicle stick
- Masking tape and glue
- Green and brown construction paper
- Sharpie

Tt Limerick

Tommy Tuck drove a truck with really big tires so he'd never get stuck
In the mud or in the muck, Tommy travelled with his truck.
On Tuesday, a tire tore from a tool in the road
And Tommy had to get his tiny truck towed.
He got tired of tires and took a loan from a bank
To buy a tremendous tire-less tank.

Introduce the letter Tt name and sound: Use the Tt tracing template page (printed on cardstock paper) to introduce the letter Tt. Have the child name the letter and repeat back to you the Tt sound.

Trace the letter Tt: Have the child use his or her pointer finger to trace the outline of the letter Tt following the arrows.

Letter Tt puppet: Make a letter puppet with the index card and popsicle stick. Draw or paste a picture of a tree that your child can color. Print the word in lower case letters underneath the picture.

Tree talk: Go on a walk with your child outside and talk about trees. Ask simple questions and give your child "wait time" to answer with his or her responses.
- What colors do you see?
- How does the tree trunk feel?
- How do the leaves feel?
- What happens to the tree when the wind blows? What do you hear?

"Tree Tops" game assembly:

Step 1: Draw 20 green scalloped ovals to represent treetops.

Step 2: Draw 20 brown tree trunks. Encourage your child to help you cut them out!

Step 3: Use a sharpie to write upper case letter (A through T) on the green treetops, and write the lower case letters (a through t) on the brown tree trunks.

"Wait Time" can be about 3-10 quiet seconds, while your child thinks of what words to come up with in his or her answer.

How to play the "Tree Tops" game:
1. Line the tree trunks in a row and have your child arrange them in alphabetical order on the floor.
2. Place the green treetops in a separate container and encourage him or her to draw one out and place it on the tree trunk with the letter that matches.
3. If your child needs help, refer him or her to an alphabet chart printed off from the internet.
4. Continue with this activity until all of the trees are complete with top and trunk.

Count to twenty! Use the game pieces to count to twenty, encouraging your child to repeat after you. If there is no interest, suggest that the child place them in a container for later use.

Keep in mind: Some of the alphabet games using the puppets may be reintroduced. You may be tired of reviewing these, but a young child needs much repetition in order to feel secure. The more comfortable a child feels with the letters and sounds, the more freely he or she will begin to use them.

Be a tree! Encourage your child to pretend to be a tall tree. To do this, the child should try to stand as tall as possible. Then tell the child to pretend to be a short tree. The child should then be encouraged to squat as low as possible to resemble a short tree.

Toothpicks to make the Tt page in alphabet book: Continue your alphabet book (binder) with the Tt Template page. Have your child help you use toothpicks to outline the capital T and lowercase t.

Book ideas:
- *The Giving Tree* by Shel Siverstein
- *Thomas the Tank Engine's Big Lift-And-Look Book* by Owen Bell

> This activity develops:
> - Awareness of the letter Tt
> - Skill in distinguishing letters and language enrichment
> - Skill in matching upper and lower case letters

Age 4 - Activity 14 – Uu is for Umbrella

You will need:
- Uu tracing template with arrows from an internet search
- Crayons and scissors
- Index card and popsicle stick
- Masking tape and glue
- Construction paper
- Umbrella
- Pictures of mini umbrellas

Uu Limerick
My uncle lived under a bridge when it rained
And understood that others called him insane
But he had no umbrella, and his hair would get wet
And unkempt and ugly, and it made him upset.
So to underneath the bridge he went
And when it rained he still looked like a gent
Because his hair stayed upright and dry
Even when rainclouds covered the sky.

Introduce the letter Uu name and sound: Use the Uu tracing template page (printed on cardstock paper) to introduce the letter Uu. Have the child name the letter and repeat back to you the short vowel Uu sound.

Trace the letter Uu: Have the child use his or her pointer finger to trace the outline of the letter Uu following the arrows.

Letter Uu puppet: Make a letter puppet with the index card and popsicle stick. Draw or paste a picture of an umbrella that your child can color. Print the word in lower case letters underneath the picture.

Talk about an umbrella: Show your child a real umbrella. Ask simple questions and give your child "wait time" to answer with his or her responses.
- What color is the umbrella?
- What is it used for?
- How do you open the umbrella? Close it?
- Why do you think the umbrella has "ribs" on it?

"Under the umbrella" game:
Step 1: Open the umbrella and set it on the floor.
Step 2: Ask the child to take out one of his or her alphabet puppets from the box.
Step 3: The child must name the letter on the puppet before placing it under the umbrella on the floor.

Keep in mind: If the child has difficulty with a letter, he or she can be told the letter name again, and the picture clue on the other side of the puppet should be identified for reinforcement.

Game variation: Use the pictures on the puppets instead of the letters. The child then should be challenged to name both the picture and the letter before placing the puppet under the umbrella.

Umbrellas or unicorns to make the Uu page in alphabet book: Continue your alphabet book (binder) with a Uu template page. Have your child help you glue down mini pictures of umbrellas or unicorns to outline the capital U and lowercase u.

Book ideas:
- *My Red Umbrella* by Robert Bright
- *Umbrella* by Jan Brett
- *The Umbrella Party* by Jamet Lunn
- *Who Likes Rain?* by Wong Herbert Yee

This activity develops:
- Awareness of the letter Uu
- More skill with letter recognition
- More skill with picture clues to reinforce the initial sounds
- More awareness of the concepts, *open*, *close*, and *under*
- Memory recall
- Language enrichment

Age 4 - Activity 15 – Vv is for Vase

You will need:
- Vv tracing template with arrows from an internet search
- Crayons and scissors
- Index card and popsicle stick
- Masking tape and glue
- Construction paper
- Pipe cleaners
- Sharpie
- Strips of Velcro or velvet

> **Vv Limerick**
> Vera vowed to vote today
> But her van was vexing her on the way.
> It became a vicious and violent device
> And its vibrating velocity wasn't so nice.
> So Vera veered the van off the road
> And voluntarily walked to vote.

Introduce the letter Vv name and sound: Use the Vv tracing template page (printed on cardstock paper) to introduce the letter Vv. Have the child name the letter and repeat back to you the Vv sound.

Trace the letter Vv: Have the child use his or her pointer finger to trace the outline of the letter Vv following the arrows.

Letter Vv puppet: Make a letter puppet with the index card and popsicle stick. Draw or paste a picture of a vase that your child can color. Print the word in lower case letters underneath the picture.

Fill a vase with flowers: Show the child a vase. If possible, collect some flowers with the child and help him or her place them in the vase. If you do not have any real or artificial flowers, make some from construction paper from the activity below. Count the flowers as you put them in the vase.

Make alphabet flowers:
Step 1: Cut out flowers with petals from colored construction paper. Allow your child to help cut them out after tracing a flower shape with a pencil.
Step 2: Use a sharpie to write a letter from Aa through Vv on each of the paper flowers that have been cut out.
Step 3: Attach the paper flowers to pipe cleaners to represent stems.

Flowers in a vase game: Tell the child to put the flowers in the vase one at a time. Help the child count the flowers as each one is placed in the vase. Then instruct the child to identify the letter on each flower as he or she removes them one at a time from the vase.

Reverse the game! The child can name the letter on the flower as he or she places it in the vase. Similarly, he or she can count the flowers as he or she removes each one from the vase.

Velcro or strips of velvet to make the Vv page in alphabet book: Continue your alphabet book (binder) with the Vv template page. Have your child help you use Velcro pieces or strips of velvet to outline the capital V and lowercase v.

Book ideas:
* *Flowers and Showers: A Spring Counting Book (A+ Books: Counting)* by Rebecca F. Davis
* *The Magic Violin* by Mayra Calvani

This activity develops:
* Awareness of the letter Vv
* Skill in identifying the letters Aa-Vv
* Skill in identifying the initial sound of Vv as in vase
* Skill in counting to twenty-two
* Confidence

Age 4 - Activity 16 – Ww is For Wagon

You will need:
- Ww tracing template with arrows from an internet search
- Crayons and scissors
- Index card and popsicle stick
- Masking tape and glue
- Construction paper
- Cardboard box
- 4 paper plates
- Brass paper fasteners
- String
- Mini wheels or pictures of wheels printed from the internet

Ww Limerick
Willy went whale watching and waded
By wetting his feet in the water while he waited
For a whale to make waves before the
sunlight faded
But Willy witnessed none and went home jaded.

Introduce the letter Ww name and sound: Use the Ww tracing template page (printed on cardstock paper) to introduce the letter Ww. Have the child name the letter and repeat back to you the Ww sound.

Trace the letter Ww: Have the child use his or her pointer finger to trace the outline of the letter Ww following the arrows.

Letter Ww puppet: Make a letter puppet with the index card and popsicle stick. Draw or paste a picture of a wagon that your child can color. Print the word in lower case letters underneath the picture.

Make a play wagon: Use a cardboard box large enough for the child to fit inside. Attach 4 paper plates to the box with brass paper fasteners to resemble the wheels. A string can also be taped in the front to be used as a handle for pulling the cardboard wagon.

Alphabet puppets go for a ride! Your child can choose special letter puppets to ride in the wagon. For example, only those upper case (big) letters with straight lines can ride in the wagon. The letters that can ride are A, E, F, H, I, K, L, M, N, T, V, and W. Encourage your child to find other ways of sorting the letters to take them for rides in the homemade wagon.

Wagon alternative: You can also use a Tupperware container with cut out construction paper circles for wheels.

Other sorts include:

1. Lower case (small letters) that have tails (those that hang below the line) like: g, j, p, and q.
2. Letters whose names sound alike and rhyme like: Bb, Cc, Dd, Ee, Gg, Pp, Tt, Vv.
3. Letters that are all curved lines such as: Cc, Oo, and Ss.
4. Letters that are partly straight and partly curved like: Bb, Dd, Gg, Jj, Mm, Nn, Pp, Qq, Rr, and Uu.

> These sorting activities should be encouraged so that the child becomes well aware of the letters, their sounds, their shapes, those that rhyme, and any other ways that the child may choose to separate the letter puppets for a particular purpose!

Mini wheels or pictures of wheels to make the Ww page in alphabet book: Continue your alphabet book (binder) with the Ww template page. Have your child help you use mini wheels or pictures of wheels printed from the internet to outline the capital W and lowercase w.

Book ideas:

- *Red Wagon* by Renata Liwska
- *Where the Wild Things Are* by Maurice Sendak

> This activity develops:
> - Awareness of the letter Ww and the sound it makes
> - Differentiating between uppercase and lowercase letters
> - Sorting between straight lines and curves

Age 4 - Activity 17 – The Musical Xylophone

You will need:
- Xx tracing template with arrows from an internet search
- Crayons
- Index card and popsicle stick
- Masking tape and glue
- Scissors
- Construction paper
- Shoe box or Tupperware container
- Large colored rubber bands

Xx Limerick
X-Ray Express was out to impress
"Expert X-Rays done in five minutes or less!"
Excellent service with no extra expense
Excited their customers to extreme extents
Exactly what would you expect to see
In an X-ray exhibit of you or me?

Introduce the letter Xx name and sound: Use the Xx tracing template page (printed on cardstock paper) to introduce the letter Xx. Name the letter and explain that the Xx sound comes at the end of words like *box* and *fix*. When Xx is at the beginning of a word, it has no true sound of its own and borrows the sound from the letter "Zz" except when it says its name in a word, such as *x-ray*. Have the child name the letter and repeat back to you the Xx sound.

Trace the letter Xx: Have the child use his or her pointer finger to trace the outline of the letter Xx following the arrows.

Letter Xx puppet: Make a letter puppet with the index card and popsicle stick. Draw or paste a picture of a xylophone that your child can color. Print the word in lower case letters underneath the picture.

Make a play xylophone: Stretch several large different colored rubber bands around the shorter sides of the empty shoebox or Tupperware container to resemble a xylophone. Show the child how to pluck the "strings" of the pretend xylophone. Encourage the child to sing the "Alphabet Song." The child may even enjoy trying to produce the same sound as the rubber bands make when they are plucked on the pretend xylophone.

Show a real xylophone to the child with a video from the internet and explain that a real xylophone has wood, metal, or plastic pieces that make a sound when they are tapped with a mallet.

Musical instruments: Introduce your child to the many different kinds of musical instruments. Some instruments make music when a person blows and controls air. Others make music when special strings are plucked or moved, while others make music when something is tapped on a special material. Show the child some pictures of different kinds of musical instruments from a book or online and possible videos of what they sound like from short video clips from the internet.

Mini pictures of xylophones or x-rays to make the Xx page in alphabet book: Continue your alphabet book (binder) with the Xx template page. Have your child help you use mini pictures of xylophones or x-rays from the internet to outline the capital X and lowercase x.

Book ideas:
- *Xavier Ox's Xylophone Experiment (Animal Antics A to Z)* by Barbara deRubertis
- *Meet the Orchesta* by Ann Hayes
- *Musical Instruments (First Discovery Books)* by Claude Delafosse and Gallimard Jeunesse

This activity develops:
- Awareness of the letter Xx
- More awareness of the colors of the rainbow
- Eye-hand coordination in moving the show box "strings"
- Awareness that the letter Xx sounds like the letter Zz
- Confidence in letter and sound recall

Age 4 - Activity 18 – Wind the Yarn

You will need:
- Yy tracing template with arrows from an internet search
- Crayons and scissors
- Index card and popsicle stick
- Masking tape and glue
- Construction paper
- A ball of yarn that the child can play with

Introduce the letter Yy name and sound: Use the Yy tracing template page (printed on cardstock paper) to introduce the letter Yy. Have the child name the letter and repeat back to you the initial Yy sound.

Trace the letter Yy: Have the child use his or her pointer finger to trace the outline of the letter Yy following the arrows.

Letter Yy puppet: Make a letter puppet with the index card and popsicle stick. Draw or paste a picture of a ball of yarn that your child can color. Print the word in lower case letters underneath the picture.

Winding and unwinding a ball of yarn: Show the child some yarn and allow him or her to wind it into a ball. When he or she finishes, let him or her rewind the yarn. This is an excellent coordination skill for a young child. A fun, little chant to say while he or she is winding is: *"Yy is for yarn to wind in a ball. But it will unwind if you let it fall."* Your child may want to allow the yarn ball to fall and will observe that the yarn unwinds on its own.

Alphabet game and memory recall: Allow your child to suggest one of the alphabet games introduced in previous lessons for you to play together, reinforcing letter names and recognition. You can name or show the child a letter and wait to see if he or she can recall the game suggested for that letter. If not, perhaps you can give him or her some clues to help with his or her memory recall.

Yy Limerick
You yawned yesterday while you were young
And let oxygen come and fill up your lung.
Yet you didn't yearn for this yawn to take place,
It just opened your mouth and
stretched out your face.
Yet yawns keep you healthy from year to year.
Let's see if we'll yawn after reading this here.

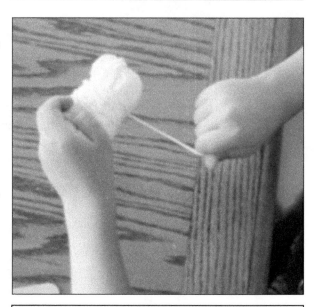

Avoid tangles: Encourage your child while he or she is playing with the yarn ball to rewind it before he or she has a mess of tangles.

Avoid telling the child at this time that the letter Yy has different sounds at the ends of some words like in *baby* or *fly*. It is better for your child to master the beginning sounds of words at this age.

Children of this age often select the same game over and over, so encourage him or her to try to recall other games.

Keep it simple: Naming the letter puppets at random is a good game to play. Make a separate pile for the letter puppets that the child has difficulty naming. At another time, ask the child to recall each initial letter sound as the letter puppet is presented. Again take note of the sounds that need reinforcement, and emphasize those letter sounds later.

Yarn to make the Yy page in alphabet book:
Continue your alphabet book (binder) with a Yy template page. Have your child help you use yarn to outline the capital Y and lowercase y.

Book ideas:
- *Extra Yarn* by Mac Barnett
- *Noodle's Knitting* by Sheryl Webster

This activity develops:
- Awareness of the letter Yy
- More skill in letter recognition
- Eye-hand coordination in winding yarn
- Confidence

Age 4 - Activity 19 – Zero

You will need:
- Zz tracing template with arrows from an internet search
- Crayons and scissors
- Index card and popsicle stick
- Masking tape and glue
- Construction paper
- Circle pretzels or Cheerios
- Alphabet chart
- Zipper strips or mini zeroes

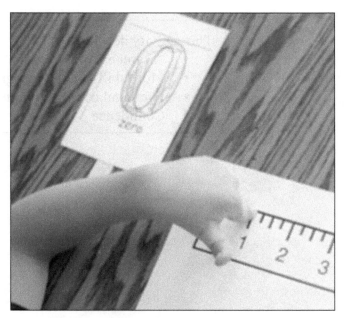

Zz Limerick
Zebras like to zig and zag all around zoos.
They zip with zest to be the best and
never want to lose.
But sometimes they lose zeal and
curl up around their knees
And zone out of the zooming world and
zero in on catching zzzzzzzzzzzz's.

Introduce the letter Zz name and sound:
Use the Zz tracing template page (printed on cardstock paper) to introduce the letter Zz. Have the child name the letter and repeat back to you the initial Zz sound.

Trace the letter Zz: Have the child use his or her pointer finger to trace the outline of the letter Zz following the arrows.

Letter Zz puppet: Make a letter puppet with the index card and popsicle stick. Draw or paste a picture of a zero that your child can color. Print the word in lower case letters underneath the picture.

Zero talk: Tell the child that zero comes before one in counting. It means nothing, and it is a beginning point before we count to one. Use circle pretzels or Cheerios shaped like zeros

Zz Chant: *Zz is for zero where we begin. But when using letters, its name's at the end.*

laying out three or four and then taking away all of them to demonstrate how zero means none.

Illustrate zero with a ruler: Show your child the end of the ruler on the left. Then point to the marking for one inch. Move your hand and show the child two inches, three inches, and continue up to twelve inches. Then go back to the beginning and touch the left ruler edge. This is *point zero* which comes before the one inch even starts! Allow the child to repeat this independently if he or she seems to understand. If not, try again later.

Alphabet chart and Zz words: Show the child an Alphabet Chart from the internet and point out that the letter Zz is the last letter in the series of letters. Use the chart and say the letters slowly. Encourage your child to say them with you. Point out that the words: *zoo*, *zebra*, and *zipper* begin with the letter Zz.

- Zip a **zipper**!
- Count a **zebra's** stripes!
- Plan a family field trip to the **zoo**!

Alphabet game: Empty all of the alphabet puppets from the shoebox and tell the child to put them in alphabetical order. Be certain to give him or her the Alphabet Chart or write a letter at a time on a piece of paper and tell the child to look for that letter. The child can be instructed to move his or her eyes from left to right in each row as he or she searches for the correct letter. This method will serve to avoid confusion, because it is an organized way to look for a specific letter.

Face up alphabetical order! At another time, the letter puppets can be used with the pictures facing up. The child can then be instructed to put the pictures in alphabetical order. Allow the child to use the Alphabet Chart and assist the child if necessary. Use the picture clues to help reinforce the initial sounds of the letters. Tell the child that we use these letters and sounds to help us read, write, and spell words!

Zipper strips or zeroes to make the Zz page in alphabet book: Continue your alphabet book (binder) with the Zz template page. Have your child help you use zipper strips or zeroes printed off the internet or represented by Cheerios to outline outline the capital Z and lowercase z.

Book ideas:
- *Zero* by Kathryn Otoshi
- *Length (Math Counts)* by Henry Arthur Pluckrose
- *Mr. Toggle's Zipper* by Robin Pulver
- *How the Zebra Got Its Stripes (Little golden Book)* by Justine Fotes, Ron Fontes, and Peter Grosshauser
- *Dear Zoo: A Lift-the-Flap Book* by Rod Campbell

This activity develops:
- The awareness of Zz as a letter and the last letter of the alphabet
- More skill in visual discrimination
- Awareness of the meaning of zero
- Skill in listening for initial sounds
- Awareness of the use of letters and sounds
- Confidence

Age 4 - Activity 20 – Labeling

You will need:
- Sharpie
- Index cards or small pieces of paper for labeling
- Masking tape

Create labels for objects in the home:
1. Print in lower case letters the names of a few familiar household items on the cards like *bed*, *desk*, *television*, *sofa*, *stove*, *table*, etc.
2. Tape the label cards on the items around your home with your child's help.

Letter recognition in words: pre-reading!
- Read one of the words to the child and ask him or her to show you where to put the label on that object with tape.
- Ask the child to tell you the letters in the word.
- Point to the left of the word so that the child will recall the letters in the proper order.
- Follow the same procedure for a few other objects.

When the child can recall the letters on the labels with confidence, add one or two more words. A new word can be added each day if the child continues to be interested.

Words in our world: The child may attempt to read some of the labels, but it is more important to emphasize the letters and the beginning sounds at this age. Encourage the child to recall letters in books, labels on foods, magazines, license plates, buildings, the newspaper, etc.

Book ideas:
- *Richard Scarry's Best Word Book Ever (Giant Golden Book)* by Richard Scarry

This activity develops:
- More awareness of letters and words
- Skill in listening for sounds and identifying initial sounds
- Skill in recalling letters in words
- Skill in associating words and objects
- Confidence

Age 4 - Activity 21 – Ball Activities

You will need:
- Inflated rubber ball that bounces and can be easily handled by the child
- Tape or chalk

Bounce it!
Mark a place with tape or chalk on the floor or sidewalk. Tell the child to drop the ball on that mark and watch the ball and catch it with two hands when it bounces back up. Since the child can hear the bounce and the counting, this will help him or her to understand the use of counting.

Toss it!
Show first and then allow the child to toss the ball up gently and instruct him or her to keep his or her eyes on the ball and be ready to catch it when it comes down. Counting can also be done each time the child catches the ball.

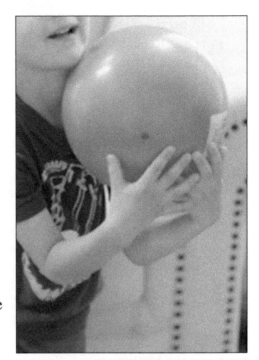

Roll it!
Roll the ball back and forth with your child in either a standing or sitting position. The child may also enjoy rolling a ball to a wall with force so that it will roll back for your child to catch.

> A child of this age should develop coordination in basic gross motor activities (large muscle skills)!

Book ideas:
- *Stop That Ball! (Beginner Books)* by Mike McClintock

This activity develops:
- Better gross motor coordination
- Skill in keeping the eyes on a moving target
- Skill in the timing of when to catch the ball
- Skill in counting

Age 4 - Activity 22 – Rope Jumping

You will need:
- Old clothesline (rope) or a regular jump rope
- Hoola hoop

> To start, tell the child to jump over the rope while it is laying on the floor.

Directions:
- Tape or tie one end of the rope to a chair, table leg or something else, so that the end of the rope is approximately four inches from the floor.
- Hold the other end of the rope at a four-inch level so that it is parallel to the floor.
- Tell the child to jump over the raised rope. Allow the child to jump back and forth at this level until he or she is confident in jumping.

> Encourage the child to practice this until he or she loses interest or appears tired. This activity should be repeated often until the child is secure in jumping over a rope in motion.

Increase the challenge:
- The height of the rope can be gradually increased. It can be secured with a stack of books or something else heavy.
- Continue to increase the height gradually until it is as high as the child can jump over comfortably.

Swing the rope:
- Choose a comfortable height for the child to jump over while one end of the rope is secured.
- Slowly swing the rope back and forth for the child to watch so that he or she can jump over the rope successfully.

Jump rope independently: Choose a jump rope that is the proper length for the child and show him or her how to hold the jump rope with both hands.

> Most children enjoy jumping rope independently at this age, but it is also perfectly normal that some children may not develop this skill until they are in school.

- Instruct the child to place the rope behind him or her and move the rope slowly over his or her head, allowing the middle of the rope to fall and touch the floor or ground.
- At that point, instruct the child to jump over the middle of the rope and bring the rope back up behind him or her from the beginning.

Practice makes progress: Encourage your child to start slowly, and as he or she becomes more confident, increase the movement of the rope. With practice, the child should be able to develop some skill in turning and jumping over the rope.

Jump and count: Count how many times he or she can jump without missing a jump.

Hoola hoop alternative: The child can also practice jumping with a hoola hoop by holding it with both hands, turning it like the jump rope, and jumping.

Book ideas:
- *Jumping Joy* by Shirley Ratisseau
- *Ten Little Monkeys Jumping On the Bed (Classic Books With Holes)* by Annie Kubler and Tina Freeman

This activity develops:
- More skill in jumping
- Gross motor coordination
- More awareness of the concept "over"
- Skill in watching a moving object and reacting at this precise moment
- More skill in counting
- Confidence and independence

Age 4 - Activity 23 – Feel and Tell

You will need:
- Box with a lid
- 5 different items that can fit through a small hole in the box
- 3 smooth items
- 3 rough items
- 3 soft items
- 3 hard items

Set up:
- Cut a hole in the lid of a box just large enough for the child's hand to go through.
- The items should be small enough to go through the hole in the box and suitable for the child to grasp easily. Some suggested items are: a spoon, a rock, an empty pill bottle, a small toy, and a large button.

Feel and name:
- Show the items to the child and allow him or her to feel and name the objects as you place them in the shoebox.
- Name one of the objects and tell the child to reach in the box, feel for the shape of the named object and pull it up through the hole in the shoebox.
- Replace the object and name another object for the child to retrieve. Continue with this activity until the child succeeds most of the time. Change the objects and repeat at another time.

Rough and smooth: As an extension, choose three things that are smooth and three things that are rough.
- Place these items in the shoebox and tell the child to feel in the box for something that is *smooth* or *rough*. Do this until the box is empty of all the smooth objects and then the rough.
- Then encourage the child to feel and tell you things that are smooth and rough in the house. The child will enjoy feeling pieces of furniture for smooth and rough areas. He or she will also enjoy moving throughout the house discovering and talking about the feel of various things that he or she feels.

Smooth item ideas:
- Button
- Piece of chalk
- Leaf
- Piece of cloth

Rough item ideas:
- Sandpaper
- Rock
- Tree bark
- Piece of burlap

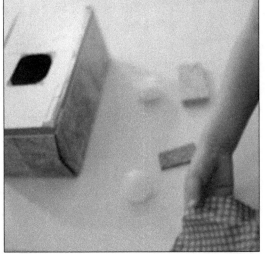

Praise the child if he or she is successful. If there is difficulty selecting the object, try to give clues as to the shape or feel it again.

Sensory words to describe:
- Soft
- Fluffy
- Scratchy
- Bumpy
- Sticky
- Lumpy

Soft item ideas:
- Cotton ball
- Piece of cloth
- Deflated balloon

Hard item ideas:
- Piece of wood
- Spoon
- Bottle lid

Soft and hard: At another time, the same procedure can be repeated with soft and hard objects. When the box is empty, the child may enjoy finding hard and soft objects within the home and telling you about them.

Book idea:
- *Wild Animals (Touch and Feel)* by DK Publishing

This activity develops:
- Further awareness of tactile sensations
- Skill in recalling the objects' names by feeling
- Skill in distinguishing rough and smooth
- Skill in distinguishing hard and soft
- Skill in decision making
- Language enrichment
- Confidence

Age 4 - Activity 24 – Healthy Foods

You will need:
- 5 paper plates
- Magazines with pictures of food or photos of various foods printed off from the internet

Set up: Label the 5 plates with the names of the 5 food groups from the USDA's My Plate:
1. Fruits
2. Vegetables
3. Grains
4. Protein
5. Dairy

Select foods for each group:
- Help the child to select and cut out pictures from a magazine or internet of the five food groups.
- Tell the child to glue the bread and cereal on one plate, the meat picture on the protein plate, the milk and cheese on the dairy plate, the fruit on the fruit plate, and the vegetable on the vegetable plate.
- The child can go looking for other pictures of food and sort what he or she finds from magazines or printed pictures from the internet into the correct food groups from My Plate.

Eating healthy: This activity is designed to identify the basic kinds of foods for the child. Children of this age should be made aware that good eating habits are essential.

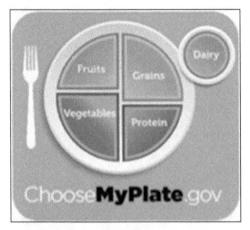

Design a menu: At another time, the child can select (with your guidance) his or her own menu. He or she can choose a picture of a food from each of the five food groups and cut them out. He or she should be encouraged to choose pictures that resemble a regular serving of a food.
- A paper plate can then be divided by using a sharpie to mark off the four sections on *My Plate* and a smaller circle can be added to the upper right hand corner to represent the fifth group.
- The child can then lay the chosen foods in the four sections of the plate.

At mealtime: The child should be able to identify the foods on his or her plate and tell which of the five food groups from My Plate it belongs. Hopefully this will encourage your child to be interested in eating a variety of healthy foods.

ChooseMyPlate.gov: You can find a wealth of information about eating healthy and talking about nutritious food choices with your child on the USDA's website. *MyPlate Kids' Place* (http://www. choosemyplate.gov/kids/index.html) features a section devoted to educating kids and has several activities to support your ongoing discussions with your child about making healthy food choices.

Book ideas:
- *Good Enough to Eat: A Kid's Guide to Food and Nutrition* by Lizzy Rockwell
- *Eat Healthy, Feel Great* by William Sears, Martha Sears, Christie Watts Kelly and Renee Andriani

---

This activity develops:
- Awareness of different food groups
- Awareness that proper foods are necessary for good health
- Language enrichment in identifying foods
- Skill in classifying or grouping foods
- Confidence
- An interest in making food selections
- Fine motor coordination in cutting and gluing

Age 4 - Activity 25 – Jumping A Distance

You will need:
- Two ropes or two pieces of yarn
- Strips of paper to tear

Set up: Two ropes parallel to each other and very close together.

Pretend the space between is a river: Instruct the child to jump over the very narrow river and to be careful not to get wet!

Gradually move ropes farther apart to widen the "river": Create three different "rivers" of varying width: the first, quite narrow; the second, further apart; and the last, the widest of all. If the child is unable to jump successfully over the wider river, allow him or her to try again or move the rope closer together.

Encourage discussion using new vocabulary: Review the words *narrow*, *wider*, and *widest* with your child. Talk about which of the three rivers was easiest and the most challenging to jump over, and why that was.

"Pick Up" game: Tear a sheet of paper into three strips of three different widths. Instruct the child to pick up one of the three that you name. Call the three strips:
- The narrow one
- The wider one
- The widest one

Book ideas:
- *Billy and the Forest Fire (Billy and Blaze Series)* by C. W. Anderson
- *Jump!* by Scott M. Fischer
- *Where The River Begins* by Thomas Locker

This activity develops:
- Gross motor coordination
- Skill in jumping a given distance
- Skill in distinguishing *narrow, wider*, and *widest*
- Skill in following directions
- Confidence

Age 4 - Activity 26 – Number Stairs and Counting

You will need:
- 55 small similar items such as (buttons, bottle caps, beans, small pebbles, etc.)
- Large grid paper (optional)
- Large index cards or small paper plates

Making stairs: Instruct the child to place one button on a flat work area (table or floor). Then have him or her place two buttons in a row under the one button. After that, add three buttons under the row of two and so on to create a staircase until he or she gets to the last row of ten buttons.

Counting stairs: Count the buttons, on the diagonal, with the child as he or she moves his or her index finger down the "stairs" and then up the "stairs." The child may also enjoy counting the total number of objects that were used.

1-10 game: Write the numbers 1 through 10 on individual index cards or small paper plates. Then have the child count that many buttons out and put them on the plate with the corresponding number. Encourage your child to count aloud with you so he or she gains familiarity with counting to ten independently and corresponding the correct number of objects with the numeral.

Reminder about counting objects! Do not get discouraged if your child struggles with this concept for some time. Start with only three objects and have your child master counting up to three with confidence. Then add on to five, and then gradually to ten so that your child is not overwhelmed.

Book ideas:
- *Make Way For Ducklings* by Robert McCloskey
- *The M&M's Brand Chocolate Candies Counting Book* by Barbara Barbieri McGrath

---

This activity develops:
- More awareness of counting consecutively
- More awareness of one more as numbers increase
- Skill in placing numbers in numerical order
- Skill in counting objects to match the correct number
- Confidence and independence in mastering a skill

Age 4 - Activity 27 – The Clock

You will need:
- Penny for tracing
- Large paper plate
- Sharpie
- Cardboard or manila folder
- Brass paper fastener
- Paper plates
- Masking tape

Set up:
1. Use the penny to trace twelve small circles around the inside edge of the paper plate.
2. You can make the circles evenly spread out if you begin with the 12 and 6, then the 3 and 9, and finally fill in the rest.
3. Label the circles 1 to 12 for the numbers on a clock.
4. Draw and cut out two clock hands from the cardboard or manila folder (one longer than the other).
5. Fasten the hands with a brass paper fastener to the center.

Two kinds of clocks: Have a conversation with your child about how there are two kinds of clocks: an analog clock and a digital clock. Show the child the difference between these clocks.

Hours on a clock: Discuss with your child that the shorter hand points to the hours on a clock. Count the hours on the clock together.
- Which hand is longer?

Discuss with your child that it takes one hour of time for the big hand to move all the way around and back to the same place.

Model for your child how to point the hour hand of the clock towards the number of the hour in the day to represent the time. For instance, instruct your child to show you 1 o'clock with the clock. If he or she does not understand, model it for him or her again and then give your child a try! (Keep the longer/minute hand on the 12 until your child has the idea of an hour, before introducing him or her to the minute hand).

Keep in mind: A child at age four may be able to count to sixty, but he or she probably will not understand number concepts that high. The child can understand the concept of hours, but minutes and seconds may be overwhelming for most children this age. Once the child is confident in identifying hourly time, minutes can be explained by watching a second hand go all the way around once on the face of a clock or watch. It is not necessary to explain morning and afternoon and a twenty-four-hour day until the child has had much practice in moving the clock hands and recalling the correct hour.

Clock on the floor activity: Mark off 12 spaces with masking tape on the floor in a large circle on the carpet. Allow the child to help you count out twelve paper plates or sheets of paper. Encourage the child to tell you what number to write on each plate, which should have the numbers 1 to 12 written on them.

Plates for hours on a clock: Ask the child to help you place the paper plates in the correct order on the masking tape pieces around the circle to create a clock. These pieces may then be secured with masking tape.

"Be the hour hand": Allow the child to walk around clockwise using the paper plates as stepping-stones. The child should be encouraged to say the correct number as he or she steps on each numbered plate. The child can then lie down on the floor and point his or her "hands" toward the hour that he or she wants to represent on the clock!

Book ideas:
- *Maisy's First Clock: A Maisy Fun-to-Learn Book* by Lucy Cousins
- *Clocks and More Clocks* by Pat Hutchins
- *Telling Time With Big Mama Cat* by Dan Harper
- *Tell the Time with Thomas (Thomas & Friends)* by Christopher Awdry

This activity develops:
- More awareness of the numbers 1-12
- Awareness of a clock
- Awareness of time and hour
- Awareness of the spatial positions of the numbers on a clock
- More awareness of the concepts, big and little and long and short
- Awareness of clockwise

Age 4 - Activity 28 – Patterns

You will need:
Objects to create patterns like: Buttons, clothespins, toothpicks, keys, colored strips, letters on index cards, numbers on index cards, forks, spoons, etc.

What is a pattern? A pattern is a way of doing something and repeating it or doing it again.

Model a pattern: Show the child a pattern and ask what comes next with the pattern as it is extended or continued with some of the objects listed above.

Pattern awareness: Make the child aware of the many patterns in the home on dishes, floor tiles, carpets, furniture, etc.

Pattern ideas:
1. Big button, little button, big button, little button, what comes next?
2. Straight clothespin, sideways clothespin, straight, sideways . . .
3. One toothpick straight up, two toothpicks parallel on their sides . . .
4. Red colored strip, blue, red, blue . . .
5. Numbers 1, 2, 3, repeat 1, 2, 3 . . .
6. Spoon, fork, spoon, fork . . .

Talk out the pattern: Once a pattern has been placed out, "read" the pattern together with your child. For example: "red, blue, red, blue, red. . ."

Clap out a patterned rhythm: Clapping out rhythms or tapping the feet or a combination of these, in addition to slapping the thighs or touching the head, can be developed into patterns. Your child can be encouraged to repeat what you do and continue with it.

Book ideas:
- *Teddy Bear Patterns (McGrath Math)* by Barbara Barbieri McGrath
- *Pattern Bugs* by Trudy Harris
- *Phases of the Moon (Patterns in Nature)* by Gillia M. Olson

This activity develops:
- Awareness of patterns
- Skill in reading patterns
- Predicting or determining what comes next in a pattern

Age 4 - Activity 29 – My Name

You will need:
- Index cards and sharpie
- Shaving cream
- Homemade play-dough
- Cooked spaghetti

Letters in a name: Print the child's first name on an index card and ask him or her what letters are in his or her name.

Name in shaving cream: On a flat surface, have the child recall the letters in his or her name as you first model and then have your child make each letter in the shaving cream. The great thing about shaving cream is that you can smooth it over to begin again easily or whenever mistakes are made. When using paper and pencil, it is difficult to make mistakes disappear completely.

Beginner writing ideas: The child may enjoy attempting to learn to print all of the letters in the alphabet. The letter puppets may once again be used as guides to print in the shaving cream, print in play dough, or with spaghetti.

Writing takes practice: If the child is eager to write, you can make dots in the shape of each letter on a sheet of paper and encourage your child to connect the dots with a crayon to form the letter. The child may also enjoy printing with chalk on a chalkboard or on the sidewalk outside.

Learning to keep trying: Stay positive and encourage your child to keep trying his or her best. This is a wonderful opportunity to read the *Little Engine That Could* with your child and to talk about how—like the Little Engine—he or she needs to "think I can—think I can—think I can!"

Book ideas:
- *The Little Engine That Could* by Watty Piper
- *Beautiful Oops!* by Barney Saltzberg

> This activity develops:
> - Gross fine coordination and confidence
> - Awareness to "keep trying"
> - Awareness that letters form words

Age 4 - Activity 30 – *Bear Loves Weather*

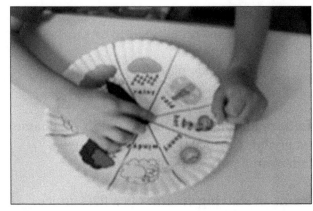

Before reading: What is the weather like outside? Is it hot or cold? Windy or rainy? Explain to your child that this is weather.

Read aloud: *Bear Loves Weather* by Janelle Cherrington

Make a weather wheel: On a large paper plate or circular cardboard, divide the circle into eight parts and draw or find pictures on the internet for each of the eight types of weather and label each on the wheel: *rainy*, *cold*, *hot*, *snowy*, *cloudy*, *windy*, *sunny*, and *stormy*. Have your child help you cut out the pictures from the internet and glue them in each section. Then cut out a cardboard arrow and fasten it in the center of the circle to point to the particular weather of the day.

> **Idea:** You may want to use cotton balls on the cloudy section of the weather wheel!

Daily weather wheel talk: Ask the child to look or stand outside to determine what the weather is like for that particular day and move the arrow on the Weather Wheel accordingly. Make this a daily practice so that your child gets in the habit of evaluating the weather outside each day and how this affects what we choose to wear.

Dressing Weather Bear: Find a simple Weather Bear on the internet to download, print, and cut out for your child to dress. Ask your child: *how should you dress Weather Bear so he is ready for the weather outside?* Encourage your child to pick out the clothing items that are appropriate and lay them on Weather Bear like a paper doll.

Dressing for the weather: Encourage your child to lay out his or her clothes so that he or she can begin to dress himself or herself independently each day.

> This activity develops:
> - Awareness of the weather and proper clothing to wear
> - Skill in making a decision
> - Listening and associating skills

Age 4 - Activity 31 – *If You Give A Mouse A Cookie*

Simple predicting: Let your child look at the picture on the front cover of the book and ask the questions:

- What do you think this book will be about?
- What makes you say that?

Read aloud: *If You Give A Mouse A Cookie* by Laura Numeroff

Finish the sentence: Encourage the child to generate the word that would come next at the end of the sentence by using the pictures in the story as clues. If the child needs a prompt, point to the picture of the word in the story and give your child a few seconds to think of the word.

- When you give him the milk, he'll probably ask you for a _____.
- He'll ask for paper and crayons. He'll draw a _____.
- He'll want to sign his name with a _____.
- And chances are if he asks for a glass of milk, he's going to want a _____.

> **Reminder:** If your child has difficulty coming up with a "guess" that makes sense, point to the pictures in the book: *what do you see?*

Ask cause and effect questions: Instruct your child to answer questions about the story during or after reading the book that answer the question why:

- Why did the mouse ask for milk?
- Why did the mouse start sweeping?
- Why did the mouse want to take a nap?
- Why did the mouse need a pen?

Act-it-out: Have your child act out a page from the story without using words and have you guess which part of the story he or she is acting out. Take turns playing "charades" using the parts of the story as prompts.

Bake cookies with your child: Invite your child to help you make chocolate chip cookies together in the kitchen. Children love to help pour ingredients into the bowl and stir. The

Circular Story: *If You Give A Mouse a Cookie* is a circular story, ending where the story began. What other things go around in a circle?

preparation process will take longer, but involving your child in the baking experience will be worth it. You can even sit down to eat the cookies together with a glass of milk and read the story all over again!

This activity develops
- Growth in oral language
- Listen to a variety of literary forms
- Participate in choral speaking and reciting stories with repeated patterns
- Participate in creative dramatics
- Use number words
- Awareness of cause and effect

Age 4 - Activity 32 – *The Little Red Hen*

Parts of a book: Ask your child some basic questions about books to guide him or her to understanding the parts of a book.
- How should I hold the book so I can read it?
- Where is the front cover of the book?
- Where is the back cover of the book?
- Where is the title of the book?

Read aloud: *The Little Red Hen* by Diane Muldrow

Discuss the characters and their feelings:
- What kind of words could we use to describe (tell us about) the Little Red Hen?
- How would you describe the goose, the cat, the dog, and the pig?
- How do you think the Little Red Hen felt about doing all of the work without any help from her friends?
- How do you think the Little Red Hen felt when all the animals wanted to eat the bread she had made at the end of the story?

What we can learn from this story:
- Why do you think the Little Red Hen did not let her friends eat the bread she had made?
- What lesson did the animals learn in the story?
- Do you think the animals will help her when she asks them next time?
- Do you think the story would have been different if the friends had helped her when she had asked them?

Keep in mind: Sometimes children may not immediately understand the answers to these questions as they are "higher level thinking questions." It is important to give the child "wait time" to think. However, if he or she cannot generate an answer yet on his or her own, model an answer, and then return to the question again later for further discussion. This will build your child's confidence.

Reminder: While you read, encourage your child to help you turn the pages and to point to where you should start reading on the next page to reinforce that reading is from left to right and from top to bottom on a printed page. These are skills that kindergarten teachers are looking for during pre-assessment!

Sequence the story: Have your child draw pictures on index cards of:

1. The hen **planting** the grain of wheat.
1. The hen **reaping** the wheat.
1. The hen **carrying** the wheat to the mill.
1. The hen **making** the dough.
2. The hen **baking** the bread.

> **Folk tale:** *The Little Red Hen* is a folk tale, a story that has been passed down from one storyteller to the next over many years and teaches a lesson.

Ask your child to lay the story cards in order of what happened first, second, third, fourth, and fifth. Encourage your child to retell the story to you using the story cards. If your child has difficulty, point to the picture your child has drawn or the matching illustration from the pages of the book and ask: what is happening in this picture?

Add on: Ask your child what he or she should draw a picture of on the last index card if another one was added to the story sequence.

Bake bread together: Encourage your child to help you in the kitchen to make homemade bread just like the Little Red Hen!

This activity develops:
- Holding print materials in the correct position.
- Identifying the front cover, back cover, and title page of a book
- Following words from left to right and from top to bottom on a printed page
- Describing a character from a story
- Participating in discussions about books
- Retelling familiar parts of the story and sequencing

Age 4 - Activity 33 – *Curious George*

More about book parts: Talk to your child about the title of a book and where it is located on the front cover. Point out to your child that often times, books have a title page too. Show your child the name of the author on the title page.

Read aloud: *Curious George* by H.A. Rey

Talk about what words and phrases mean:
- What does the word *curious* mean?
- How is George curious in the story?
- Where is Africa? What is it like there?
- What do you think "Man overboard!" means? What makes you think this?
- On page 30, it says *George was fascinated.* What does the word *fascinated* mean?
- On page 40, it says that *the bed tipped up, the watchman fell over, and quick as lightning, George ran out through the open door*. What does "quick as lightning" mean?

Map activity: The book mentions that George was found in Africa. Show your child a map of the world or a globe. Discuss with your child where Africa is located on a map in relationship to where you live.

Yellow hat letter match: Use the yellow hats from Activity 1 in the Age 4 section to match uppercase and lowercase letters of the alphabet.

Reminder: *Curious George* is a lengthier picture book. So if your child has difficulty staying still or paying attention for more than a few minutes, you may want to break the book into several sittings. Read the first half in one sitting and the second half in another sitting. This way, your child is still interested in the story!

Add on to the activity by adding more upper and lower case letters Ii-Zz. Your child can match the upper and lowercase of the same letter together to form matches. You can also use these yellow hats as an opportunity to practice letter recognition, randomly selecting letters and asking your child the name of the letter and the sound that it makes.

Banana pudding: Encourage your child to help you in the kitchen to make banana pudding made from bananas that Curious George loves to snack on!

Letter Recognition: Letter recognition in random order of upper and lowercase letters is a skill that kindergarten teachers are looking to see during pre-assessment.

This activity develops:
- Identifying the title, title page, and author of a book
- Building stamina to listen and pay attention for a longer amount of time
- Identifying what words and phrases mean
- Participating in discussions about books
- Letter recognition of upper and lower case letters
- Identifying locations on a map

Age 4 - Activity 34 – *The Story of Ferdinand*

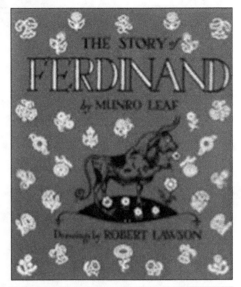

Author and illustrator: Discuss with your child how an *author* writes the words in the story, and the *illustrator* draws the pictures that go along with the words. Point out to your child the two different names on the front cover of this book that give mention of the author and illustrator.

Read aloud: *The Story of Ferdinand* by Munro Leaf

If your child has older siblings, this is a wonderful opportunity for them to read aloud to your child as well!

Reminder: Continue to have your child show you where the words are on each page and where you should begin reading. You may want to use your finger as you read aloud so that the child can connect the written word on the page with the audible word you are saying.

Compare and contrast:
- What does Ferdinand like to do during the day?
- How is that different from what the other little bulls liked to do?
- What did all the bulls want to grow up and do?
- Did Ferdinand want to do that too?
- How were the bullfighters the same?
- How were the bullfighters different?

Sound alike game: Print out several pictures of the following items from the internet or cut them out of a magazine and glue them on index cards.

bull	*flowers*	*tree*	*bell*	*hats*	*bumblebee*	*hands*
hair	*sword*	*cape*	*cart*	*turtle*	*feathers*	*sink*

Start with only a few pictures of similar beginning sounds like: *bull*, *bumblebee*, *bell*, *tree*, and *turtle*.

Instruct your child to listen to the beginning sound of the word and find the picture of the word that also begins with the same sound. Take the time to emphasize the beginning sounds of matching words.

Model how to match the beginning sounds together and point out the matching cards to your child. Then you can add on to the group of pictures to practice listening for the similar beginning sounds.

Map activity: The book mentions that Ferdinand lived in Spain. Show your child a map of the world or a globe. Discuss with your child where Spain is located on a map in relationship to where you live. Review with your child where Africa is located from the previous activity.

Phonemic awareness is the ability to hear, identify, and work with individual sounds called phonemes in the words that we speak. Building your child's phonemic awareness will help him or her when learning to read and learning to spell.

This activity develops:
- Identifying the author and illustrator of a book
- Building stamina to listen and pay attention for a longer amount of time
- Comparing and contrasting characters in a story
- Participating in discussions about books
- Phonemic awareness with beginning sound recognition and matching
- Identifying locations on a map

Age 4 - Activity 35 – *Are You My Mother?*

Before reading: Read the title of the book to your child and show him or her the book's front cover. Ask him or her to tell you what he or she thinks the story will be about and what makes him or her think so.

Read aloud: *Are You My Mother?* by P.D. Eastman

How many times is the question asked? While reading the story, invite your child to count how many times the bird asks the question: "Are you my mother?"

Keep a tally chart: On a piece of paper, have your child mark a tally with a crayon each time he or she hears the baby bird ask the question while you are reading aloud.

Count the tally marks: Count the tally marks together and write the grand total number on the piece of paper once the book is completely read.

Living and non-living things T-chart: Discuss with your child the difference between the living and nonliving things that the bird asked in the story. Go back through the pages of the book and ask your child to tell you which things are living and which were not. As you and your child discuss, make a T-chart with your child, sorting which things in the story are living and which are nonliving. Leave room above or under each word in the chart for your child to draw a corresponding picture. Actively engage your child in the process of creating this chart too.

> **Thinking while reading:** Having a purpose for reading enables your child to better engage his or her thinking skills while he or she is listening to the story. This will prepare your child to read for a purpose in the future.

Which thing could ONLY be the baby bird's mother? Reiterate that only the bird could be the baby bird's mother because they are the *same* animal. They also look alike.

Draw a picture of your family: Instruct your child to take the opportunity to draw the members of his or her family. You can help him or her label the family portrait with names. Encourage your child to write his or her name next to where he or she has drawn himself or herself.

Learning about the life of a bird: Use this as an opportunity to learn about the life of real birds from a nonfiction text like: *About Birds: A Guide for Children, 2nd edition* by Cathryn Sill.

Reminder: Kindergarten teachers are looking for your child to be able to draw a simple self-portrait of themselves independently during pre-assessment.

Telling the difference between nonfiction and fiction:
- How were the two books different?
- Which book was about real birds?
- Which book was about imaginary birds?
- How do you know?

This activity develops:
- Reading with a purpose
- Keeping a tally chart
- Identifying the difference between living and nonliving things
- Organizing information in a chart
- Participating in discussions about books
- Drawing a picture to match a word
- Awareness of fiction and nonfiction books

Age 4 - Activity 36 – *The Colorful Mouse*

Before reading: Encourage your child to listen for words that rhyme in the story.

Read aloud: *The Colorful Mouse: A Story About Colors* by Julie Durrell

While reading: Ask your child to point to the colored items read about in the story like:

- The grey sky
- The green umbrella
- The purple socks
- The brown sweater
- The red vest
- The royal blue pants
- The pink raincoat
- The yellow boots
- The orange hat

Colors of the rainbow: At the end of the book, the colorful mouse asks the reader to name the colors of the rainbow. Instruct your child to point to the color on the rainbow while he or she names it.

Count the colors of the rainbow: In addition, your child can count the colors of the rainbow on the last page of the book and assist you in gathering those colors together to make his or her own rainbow out of construction paper.

Make a colorful rainbow: Use a coffee can lid to trace a half circle out of each color for your child: red, orange, yellow, green, blue, purple, pink. Your child can help you cut out the half circles with scissors. Then line them up underneath one another to create a construction paper rainbow. Finally glue the rainbow pieces on top of each other onto a light blue or white piece of paper.

Reminder: If your child has trouble generating the color names on his or her own, give your child three colors to choose from, so that he or she is progressing towards naming the colors.

Reviewing colors: Go back through the pages of the book and ask your child to name the color of the items in the pictures. For instance, *what color are the mouse's socks*? Point to the socks on the page and wait for your child to think of the color name.

Rhyming words: What rhyming words did you find while reading the story?

Reminder: If your child has difficulty recognizing rhyming words, point them out to him or her by saying, "Pouring and boring are rhyming words."

You can make a list of rhyming words with your child from the story together and then write the words on index cards.

Rhyming words match: Your child can help you draw reference pictures to go along with the rhyming words that you wrote down on the index cards that may include:

- *Pouring, boring*
- *Today, anyway*
- *Wonder, thunder*
- *Socks, box*

- *Old, cold*
- *Vest, chest*
- *Blue, too*
- *Forget, wet*
- *Stay, play*

- *Warm, storm*
- *Door, anymore*
- *Why, sky*

Ask your child to match the word/picture cards that rhyme together when you read them aloud. Start with only three words and ask: "Which two words rhyme? Old and cold or old and vest?" This will help train your child to listen and compare the ending sounds of only a few words at a time.

This activity develops:
- Reading with a purpose
- Identifying colors
- Generating color names
- Cutting and gluing
- Following directions
- Drawing a picture to match a word
- Counting review
- Identifying rhyming words by listening

Age 4 - Activity 37 – *Mike Mulligan and His Steam Shovel*

Before reading: Make sure your child knows what a steam shovel is and what it is used for.

Read aloud: *Mike Mulligan and His Steam Shovel* by Viginia Lee Burton

Discuss the problem in the story: Ask your child what problems Mike and Mary Anne had at the beginning of the story. If your child does not recognize the problem, turn to page 14 and 15 to show your child the pictures that depict the problem. Allow your child to talk about what he or she sees in the pictures.

Solution: Discuss the idea that the little boy in the story had to help Mike and Mary Anne at the end of the book when they are stuck in the hole. Are there any other solutions to the problem that you can think of?

Explain to your child that a solution is a way that a problem can be fixed.

What is Popperville like? Talk with your child about the *setting* of the story. Tape several pieces of blank white paper together to create a small backdrop for your child to paint or draw the scenery of the town that includes the general store, church, schoolhouse, and town hall.

Shoveling: Encourage your child to "reenact" the story of *Mike Mulligan and His Steam Shovel* during his or her independent play with a stick, spoon, or small toy shovel in the sandbox.

This activity develops:
- Awareness of problems and solutions
- Awareness of setting
- Independent play

Age 4 - Activity 38 – *Corduroy*

Read aloud: *Corduroy* by Don Freeman

Comprehension questions: While reading the book, pause to ask questions so that your child is encouraged to think while listening. Here are a few:
1. Where does Corduroy live at the beginning of the story?
2. What is a reason why the little girl's mother tells her not to buy Corduroy?
3. Why does Corduroy go exploring that evening?
4. Who comes to buy Corduroy in the morning?
5. What has Lisa done so that she can buy Corduroy?

Hide and seek with buttons: Hide buttons around the room and have your child search for the hidden buttons. As he or she collects the buttons, count them to see how many he or she has found and how many are still missing and need to be found!

Counting money: Have your child sort a small pile of nickels, dimes, and pennies into three groups. If your child has difficulty, show him or her the size differences and the various pictures inscribed on the coins to help him or her distinguish them.

Money talk: This is a wonderful opportunity to teach your child what to do with his or her money. Introduce your child to the three ways money can be used: to spend, to save, and to give (charitable giving).

Just like Lisa saved her money in her piggy bank to buy Corduroy, your child can begin saving his or her coins to do something similar. Talk to your child about the importance of saving his or her money over a period of time to buy something that costs more money. Share with your child about the importance of giving to others in need as well.

If your child is confident counting up to twenty, you may want to introduce counting by 5s or 10s with your child with the coins.

Saving, spending, and giving jars: Gather three jars or cans to devote them toward teaching your child about money management. Label each one with a word and a picture: *spending* (money), *saving* (piggy bank), and *giving* (people).

This may be an effective opportunity to begin a simple allowance with your child. Start small and with coins he or she is familiar with; for instance, ten pennies a week.

Money management: Show your child how to put a few coins in each jar after he or she receives them. Then follow through by enabling your child to "spend" his or her coins on something small, to "save" his or her coins over several weeks to buy something of more value, and "to give" his or her coins to a meaningful charity. Over time, you may want to increase your child's allowance earnings or "pay" him or her for completing simple chores around the home to help out.

Keep in mind that learning to manage money is an ongoing process and giving your child responsibility will increase his or her decision-making in the future!

This activity develops:
- Awareness of problems and solutions
- Counting practice
- Awareness of money's value
- Awareness of the ways money is used
- Language enrichment
- Basic money management skills

Age 4 - Activity 39 – *The Little House*

Before reading: Ask your child about what change she or she notices in each picture of the book. What is different around the little house on this page?

Read aloud: *The Little House* by Virginia Lee Burton

After reading: Go back to the pages in the beginning of the story and point out each season that is represented.

- Example: What tells us in this picture that it is winter?
- If your child does not recognize particular seasonal details in the picture, point them out to him or her to model and then try again.

Reminder: Give your child "wait time," to point out what he or she notices about the changes on the next page.

Make a season wheel: Use two paper plates and a metal paper fastener. Divide the paper plate into four sections with a sharpie. You can use the pages from *The Little House* or encourage your child to help you draw a tree/landscape that represents a season in each of the four sections of the paper plate.

Label each picture with the season's name. Then cut out one of the sections on the second paper plate and fasten this plate on top in the center with the metal fastener. Turn the wheel to show one season at a time, and ask your child to tell you what season is represented by the picture.

Four seasons sort: In preparation for this activity, collect pictures that represent the different seasons like: playing at the beach, building a snowman, planting flowers, etc. Glue these on index cards along with the names of each season. Have your child look at the picture and determine which season the picture goes with.

Idea: You can also cut out simple clipart from the internet for each season and glue it in each of the four sections on the paper plate.

More books about the seasons:
- *A Book About the Four Seasons Caps, Hats, Socks, and Mittens* by Louise W. Borden
- *Four Seasons Make a Year* by Anne Rockwell and Megan Halsey
- *The Apple Pie Tree* by Zoe Hall and Shari Halpern
- *Watching the Seasons* by Edana Eckart

> This activity develops:
> - Analyzing pictures for details
> - Drawing conclusions
> - Awareness of the four seasons and seasonal change
> - Sorting
> - Language enrichment

Age 4 - Activity 40 – *City Mouse, Country Mouse*

Before reading: Talk to your child about the differences between the city and the country. Discuss with your child about where he or she lives (city, country, or in-between). You can introduce the word *suburb* to your child if he or she is curious about what is in-between.

Read aloud: *City Mouse, Country Mouse* by John Wallner

After reading: Ask your child questions about the story and go back to the pages that may prompt your child to remember or respond correctly:

1. How was the food at the city mouse's house different from the food at the country mouse's house?
2. How do you think the country mouse felt at the city mouse's home?
3. Which home did the country mouse like better? Why?

Reminder: Give your child "wait time," to answer the questions to think about the story. Do not just immediately respond for your child.

City, country sort: Find pictures on the internet that you may find in the city or the country or in-between (suburban). Pictures could include:

City Pictures	Country Pictures
car and taxi	tractor
train and subway	barn
bus	fence
tall buildings	cow
street lights	forest
fountain	small stream

Have your child color or draw a picture of the city mouse and the country mouse. Assist your child in cutting out the mice and gluing them on separate paper plates. Then label each plate *country* or *city*. Have your child sort the pictures by recognizing whether the picture belongs in the city or the country paper plates.

Idea: You can easily find a mouse for your child to color by googling "city mouse" or "country mouse" and "coloring page."

This activity develops:
- Learning the differences between the city and the country
- Analyzing pictures for details
- Drawing conclusions
- Sorting
- Language enrichment
- Eye hand coordination with coloring, cutting, and gluing

Age 4 - Activity 41 – *Richard Scarry's Please and Thank You Book*

Before reading: Ask your child what it means to have manners and to be polite. Discuss with your child that having manners shows others respect.

Read aloud: *Richard Scarry's Please and Thank You Book*

After reading: The following questions go along with the mini stories below. These questions will prompt positive discussion with your child about having manners in real life scenarios.

Keep in mind: This book has multiple, short stories about manners throughout. So you may want to read a few and then revisit the book at another setting.

The Busy Day
1. Who helped Mommy clear the table?
2. How did the children greet their teacher?
3. What did the children do while playing on the slide at recess?

Pig Will and Pig Won't
1. Why did Pig Won't spend an afternoon very bored?
2. What did Pig Will do at the boatyard?
3. What did Pig Won't begin to understand at the end of the story?

A Visit with Tillie
1. What did Huckle do when he arrived at Tillie's house?
2. What was the first thing Harry Hyena did at Tillie's house? Should he have done this?
3. How should you eat at the table?

Sergeant Murphy's Safety Rules
1. What should you always do in the car?
2. *Where* should you not play? Why?
3. Where should you not leave your toys? Why?

Dolly's Birthday Party
1. What should Dolly's brother have done while she was opening her gifts?
2. What did Dolly do after opening her gifts?
3. What did Lowly remember to say to Dolly and her mother when he left?

Lowly Worm's Horrid Pests
1. What should Gobbling Pest do instead?
2. What should Interrupting Pest do instead?
3. What should Whining Pest do instead?

Good Friends and Neighbors
1. What do you notice about Pig Will and Pig Me Too as they are helping Grandma?
2. What should you do when you sneeze or cough?
3. What does Lowly say when someone gives him something?

Reminder: Asking your child the follow-up question why enables him or her to think about the consequences of these safety rules and gives reasons that make sense rather than only do and don't.

Idea: Point to the particular pest on the page in the book about who you are asking the question about so that your child can remember how this pest acted and what would have been a better response/behavior?

Making good manners a habit: The key to making good manners a habit in your home is to reinforce these skills consistently. Not only are please and thank you good manners to expect your child to say, but also rules of polite communication.

1. **Eye contact:** Look in a person's eyes when they are speaking to you.
   Idea: Encourage your child to look for what color the person's eyes are.

2. **Answer** if you are asked a question.
   Idea: Prompt your child to speak when he or she is asked a question. Remind your child that it is ok to say, "I don't know."

3. **Don't interrupt:** Wait until the other person is finished speaking to answer or to talk.
   Idea: Suggest to your child to count to five before speaking to encourage patience.

Recommended books about manners:
- *Excuse Me! A Little Book of Manners* by Karen Katz
- *Clifford's Manners* by Norman Bridwell

This activity develops:
- Listening and answering questions
- Awareness of manners and the reasons for rules
- Awareness of people's negative and positive responses and behaviors to various situations

Age 4 - Activity 42 – *Madeline*

Where is France? Talk to your child about the country of France and where it is located on a map of the world or a globe in relation to where your child lives.

Read aloud: *Madeline* by Ludwig Bemelmans

Which rhyming word does not belong? Have your child identify which word does not belong from the group of three:

- *Vines, lines, **bread***
- *Bad, **bed**, sad*
- *Nine, shine, **again***
- ***Door**, mice, ice*
- *Night, right, **bed***
- ***Rabbit**, light, night*
- *Face, case, **light***

Toilet paper roll people: Print out simple Madeline pictures by googling "Madeline to color" for your child to color and cut out. Wrap the cut-out paper doll around a used toilet paper roll to create a small 3D doll for your child to "act out" parts of the story on his or her own. You may wish to make a second doll or a Miss Clavel to add to your child's play.

Keep in mind: Classic picture books are read aloud online on YouTube with their pictures shown in the video. You may wish to take advantage of this and have your child watch the video online.

Where is your appendix? After reading *Madeline*, your child may be curious about his or her appendix. Explain to your child that it is found inside the body on the right-hand side near the bottom of his or her tummy. Kidshealth.org is an informative website that may assist in answering your child's questions about an appendicitis.

This activity develops:
- Identifying rhyming words
- Dramatic play
- Awareness of an appendix

Age 4 - Activity 43 – *Blueberries For Sal*

Before reading: Review with your child the front cover of a book, the title, and the author's name. While reading the book to your child, encourage him or her to show you where you should start reading after turning a page.

> **Keep in mind:** Kindergarten teachers are looking to see whether your child has pre-reading readiness skills, so reviewing these with your child each time you read a new book is a great way to build his or her confidence!

Picture walk: Have your child look through the pictures before you begin reading and make predictions about what he or she thinks will happen in the story based on the order of the pictures.

Read aloud: *Blueberries For Sal* by Robert McCloskey

One-to-one correspondence: Allow your child to count blueberries from a container. You may want to use an old egg carton with numbers written in it for your child to review one-to-one number correspondence by counting and placing that many blueberries into each part of the carton. You may want to review numbers between twelve and twenty with your child if he or she has mastered 1-12.

Counting backwards: You may want to introduce your child to counting backwards from 10 to 1. Use piles of blueberries of that number and small index cards with corresponding numbers on them to assist with learning how to do this activity. Always model for your child first, so he or she knows what to do and then guide your child as he or she attempts on his or her own.

Blueberry alphabet Bingo: Print out a simple alphabet bingo board by googling for it on the internet. Show your child how to play the bingo game by covering up the space with a blueberry! If the child gets five blueberries in a row, he or she has won! You may want to play with your child at first or introduce the game to a sibling or friend to play along.

Reminder: You can either call out the letter name during the BINGO game or the letter sound to encourage your child to recognize both the letter names as well as the sounds the letters make!

Blueberry cork or potato stamps: You can make a simple stamping project for your child, by dipping the end of a cork into blue paint or cutting the end of a potato off and using that as a stamp for your child to create a blueberry patch on paper. Once the paint is dry, you can even help your child glue popsicle sticks over the blueberry patch to make a simple fence.

This activity develops:
- Practice with one-to-one correspondence with counting
- Practice counting between 12 and 20
- Practice counting backwards from 10 to 1
- Letter name recognition
- Letter sound recognition
- Eye hand coordination through the stamping activity

Age 4 - Activity 44 – *The Tale of Peter Rabbit*

Before reading: Ask your child some questions before you start reading, making connections to what he or she already knows:
1. What does a garden look like?
2. Why would a rabbit visit a garden?
3. How do you know a story is make believe?

Read aloud: *The Tale of Peter Rabbit* by Beatrix Potter

After reading: Ask your child some questions about the story and encourage your child to turn back to the pages with the pictures that match the answers he or she may give in response.
1. How was Peter different from his siblings?
2. Why do you think Peter disobeyed his mother?
3. How do you know Peter regretted his decision to visit Mr. McGregor's garden?
4. If this was the second pair he had, what do you think happened to the first pair of shoes and jacket Peter owned?
5. What lessons did Peter learn from his day in Mr. McGregor's garden?
6. How would you change the story?

Keep in mind: Beatrix Potter intended her books to be printed in a small size so that children would have to sit on their parent's laps as they listened to the story as it was read aloud to them so that they could see the pictures and be close to their mother or father.

Grow a bean plant: Talk to your child about growing plants just like Mr. McGregor grew plants in his garden.
1. Put some water in a small jar and then pour it out to make it wet inside.
2. Roll up a napkin or paper towel in the wet jar and press it up against the side of the glass.
3. Then place your bean between the glass and the paper towel so that you can see it from the outside.
4. Keep the jar near a window so that it will get light each day.
5. Use a spray bottle to lightly spray the jar to keep the paper towel moist for the bean to grow.
6. After a few days, the bean should begin to sprout roots and then a stem with leaves!

Keep a plant journal: You may want to make a simple plant journal for your child to record the plant's growth progress over the next few days. You can make this by folding several pieces of paper together to make a little booklet and labeling each page with the day of its growth.

The day you "plant" the seed will be Day1. Your child can draw a simple picture on the labeled page of what the plant looks like and how it changes over time.

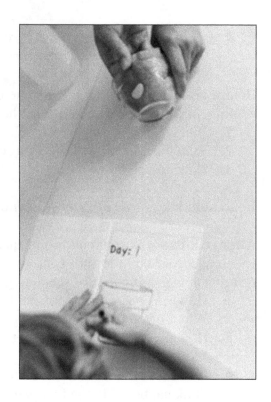

This activity develops:
- Awareness of making connections to a story
- Awareness of a character's consequences from his actions
- Answering comprehension questions about a story
- Practice suggesting an alternative ending
- Awareness of plant growth
- Practice recording data about a plant's growth with changes over time

Age 4 - Activity 45 – *Billy and Blaze: A Boy and His Pony*

Read aloud: *Billy and Blaze: A Boy and His Pony* by C.W. Anderson

Context clues: On several pages throughout the book, there are unfamiliar words that your child may have never heard of before.

Use these question prompts to help your child make reasonable guesses to what these words mean based on the clues in the text or the pictures in the story.

> **Keep in mind:** Your child may have difficulty accurately guessing what these words mean. So use the pictures and word clues to help your child by modeling first and then having your child repeat back how he or she knows the correct answer!

p. 2 What do you think the word *prancing* means?
"He used to pretend that it was a prancing pony."
Do you think *prancing* means to walk quickly in a happy way or to lay around and eat grass?

p. 6 What do you think the word *bay* means?
"And there stood a beautiful bay pony with four white feet."
Do you think *bay* means a spotted pony or a reddish brown pony?

p. 16 What do you think the word *galloping* means?
"It was not long before Blaze would come galloping whenever Billy called."
Do you think *galloping* means running quickly or walking slowly?

p. 22 What do you think the word *gripped* means?
"He leaned forward and gripped with his knees and over they sailed."
Do you think *gripped* means to let go or to hold onto tightly?

Galloping: Review Gallop Fun from Age 3 Activity 26.

p. 24 What do you think the word *howling* means?
"They heard a dog howling as if in pain."
Do you think it means a long, sad sound or a funny laugh?

p. 26 What do you think the word *limped* means?
"And then he limped along home with Billy and Blaze."
Do you think **limped** means to run fast or to walk slowly with difficulty?

p. 28 What do you think the word *bandaged* means?
"When they got home Billy bandaged the dog's foot."
Do you think **bandaged** means to take care of a hurt place with a bandage or to trip over because it's in the way?

p. 32 What do you think the word *stable* means?
"He went down to the stable to see Blaze very often."
"Do you think **stable** means the barn or the store?

p. 36 What do you think the word *fine* means?
"When Billy got to the show with Blaze and Rex and saw how many fine ponies were there."
Do you think **fine** means very sick or very nice?

p. 42-43 What do you think the word *bridle* means?
"Then the judge pinned a blue ribbon on Blaze's bridle."
Do you think **bridle** means the reigns around a horse's head or the horse's saddle strap?

Taking care of a pet: Billy takes good care of his pets, Blaze and Rex. Discuss with your child what responsibilities are involved with taking care of animals. Talk to your child about what responsibilities he or she has at home to help out.

> This activity develops:
> * Awareness of unfamiliar vocabulary in books
> * Awareness of using pictures and context clues to help make reasonable guesses to word meanings
> * Language development
> * Awareness of pet care and responsibility

Age 4 - Activity 46 – *The Giving Tree*

Cover quest: What do you think the story will be about by looking at the cover? What makes you think that?

Pre-reading picture walk: Browse the pages of the book with your child to look at the pictures throughout. Ask your child to point out what he or she notices about the main character.

Read aloud: *The Giving Tree* by Shel Silverstein

After reading: Discuss the story with your child using these questions:
- Why do you think the author named this book *The Giving Tree*?
- How did the boy treat the tree?
- How did the tree treat the boy?
- How do you think the tree felt?
- How do you think the boy felt at the end of the book?

Keep in mind: By discussing this book with your child, he or she will begin to think about thankfulness, giving, and how we should treat others. This book has a powerful message that can inspire you and your child to show love and kindness to others.

Phonemic awareness game: Use index cards to write words that have similar, beginning sounds on them from the book. Print out simple clipart pictures from the internet to glue them on each index card to represent the word written on it. Have your child make matches out of the index cards whose beginning sounds are the same. Read the words aloud to your child so that he or she gains familiarity with what words the pictures represent on the cards.

tree, trunk	*house, happy*
sail, said	*boy, boat*
money, make	*sit, sorry*
after, apple	

Make a family tree: Hang chart paper on a blank space on a wall or door. Use a brown marker to draw a tree trunk with your child's name on it. There should be 6 branches for the key family members: mother, maternal grandmother, maternal grandfather, father, paternal grandmother, and paternal grandfather.

The child's leaf (made with green construction paper or a green marker) is already on the trunk, and your child should glue leaves for their brothers and sisters in this same trunk area.

Talk with your child about how his or her family is like a tree with many branches. Show him or her how he or she is related to a mother and father, drawn on branches coming out of the tree trunk. From there, discuss with your child about grandparents, aunts, uncles, and possibly cousins to fill in the family tree with leaves of names along the drawn branches on the chart paper.

This activity develops:
- Awareness of using pictures to predict a story
- Awareness of a character's consequences from his actions
- Awareness of feelings and how to treat others
- Phonemic awareness
- Awareness of family and extended family

Age 4 - Activity 47 – *Make Way For Ducklings*

Read aloud: *Make Way For Ducklings* by Robert McCloskey

Beginning phonics activity: Write the letters "ack" on an index card in red.

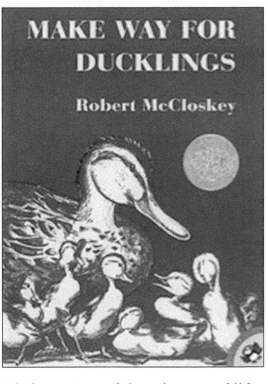

On other index cards, write the letters: "b," "j," "l," "m," "n," "p," "qu," "r," "s," and "t" in blue.

1. Show your child the index card with the blue "ack" on it and sound out "ack" together just like in the book. Tell your child that these letters make the sound "ack."
2. Explain to your child that by putting the cards with letters in front of the "ack" card, he or she can make words.
3. Add the letters in front one at a time. Have your child make the first letter sound and then add on "ack" to the end to create the word.
4. Example: "s" + "ack" is "sack"
5. If at first your child does not understand, model the whole process and then give your child another try! You may want to color code the index cards. All front letter sounds can be written in blue and the ending "ack" sound can be written in red.

Grouping activity with ducklings and peanuts: Cut out eight yellow ducklings from a simple template you can google online. Give your child simple grouping problems he or she can work out with the duckling cut-outs and a handful of peanuts. Grouping problems can include ones like the following:

1. Mrs. Mallard wants to give each duckling 2 peanuts, how many does she need in all?
2. Mrs. Mallard wants to give each duckling 3 peanuts, how many does she need in all?
3. If there are 20 peanuts, how many will each of the ducklings get? Will there be any leftover?
4. Each duckling has one peanut. Two peanuts go missing. How many peanuts are left?

Keep in mind: Stay positive as sounding out words and sounds is a process and will take time.

This activity develops:
- Letter sound recognition
- Phonemic awareness and basic phonics
- Grouping practice
- Counting with one-to-one correspondence
- Simple adding and subtracting

Age 4 - Activity 48 – *The Story About Ping*

Where is China? Since the setting of the story is in China, help your child locate China on a map of the world or a globe in relation to where your child lives. You may want to point out to your child where the Yangtze River is in China as well.

Read aloud: *The Story About Ping* by Marjorie Flack and Kurt Wiese

Making number rods: *Ping* is a great book to learn larger numbers as he has a large family. Start with what your child knows by having him or her glue 10 small pom-pom balls, googly eyes, or even colored paper circles to a strip of cardboard to make a number rod. After he or she has completed the first number rod, have him or her create three more.

Base 10 activity: Ping has forty-two cousins, so use the number rods to represent 10 with your child and the individual pom-poms as ones. Introduce your child to count by tens with the number rods up to forty. Show your child how each number rod is ten googly-eyes. Teach your child how to count up to forty by counting the individual googly-eyes on all four rods.

Keep in mind: Your child may be content counting out tens to make the number rods. Don't push your child to count by tens if he or she is not ready.

Picture-sound search: Continue to review letter names and sounds so that your child can pick out what words begin with what letter based on their sounds. Choose a page from the story and ask your child to show you something in the picture that begins with a particular sound.

Here are a few examples:
*   p. 4-5 What makes the same sound as *heart* in the picture? Answer: hat
*   p. 10-11 What makes the same sound as *bathtub* in the picture? Answer: boats

- p. 14 What makes the same sound as *fan* in the picture? Answer: fish

Feed and count ducks: Use this as an opportunity to take your child to a local pond or lake to feed some ducks like Ping and the Mallards from *Make Way For Ducklings*. Bring along some bread pieces or some frozen peas to feed the ducks. While you are feeding the ducks, encourage your child to count how many he or she sees.

This activity develops:
- Map skills
- Counting to ten
- Recognizing ten in a set
- Counting by tens and basic base 10
- Phonemic awareness

Age 4 - Activity 49 – *Ox Cart Man*

Picture walk: Before reading the book aloud, have your child take a picture walk through the pages and notice what is going on. Ask your child to tell you about the events taking place in the pictures.

Read aloud: *Ox-Cart Man* by Donald Hall

Review the seasons: Review with your child the four seasons and use your season wheel from the *Little House* lesson to jog your child's memory. Discuss with your child what the family in the *Ox-Cart Man* did in each season.

Talk about wants and needs: The Ox-Cart Man buys several items at Portsmouth Market. Talk with your child about the difference between wants and needs.

- What does the Ox-Cart man buy that is a need for the family?
- What does he buy that is a want?

Keep in mind: This is also a wonderful book to review the city and the country. You can incorporate the city and country sort from the previous activity with the *City Mouse and Country* Mouse as well.

Apply buying wants and needs to a shopping trip to the grocery store. Ask your child about the items that you are purchasing and which ones are *wants* and which ones are *needs*.

Taking responsibility: The children in the story help their parents with household chores to help their family. Discuss with your child what responsibilities/chores/jobs he or she does or can do around the house to help your family out. Children should be picking up their own toys at this age.

Job chart: You may even want to make your child a job chart and fill it with stickers each time he or she accomplishes a helpful task for the family.

Packing for a trip: Just like the Ox-Cart Man packs up for his trip to Portsmouth Market, your child can practice packing for a trip too. He or she can fill a suitcase or over-night bag with clothes and items that he or she will need to spend the night away from home.

What to take? Guide your child about the appropriate clothing he or she will need to remember when packing and for how many days and nights the child should plan for when filling the suitcase. Discuss what he or she can leave at home and is unnecessary to bring along.

This activity develops:
- Analyzing pictures and making accurate predictions
- Review of seasons and the differences between the *city* and the *country*
- Differences between *wants* and *needs*
- Responsibility and independence
- Confidence and planning

Age 4 - Activity 50 – *Alexander and the Terrible, Horrible, No Good, Very Bad Day*

Read aloud: *Alexander and the Terrible, Horrible, No Good, Very Bad Day* by Judith Viorst

Where is Australia? Alexander wants to move to Australia, show your child where this continent is on a world map or globe in relation to where he or she lives.

Expressing feelings: Talk to your child about how having a bad day is something everyone experiences sometimes. Discuss how facial expressions show emotion. Use a mirror with your child to make faces that express feelings such as: sad, happy, grumpy, excited, tired, scared, surprised, etc.

Keep in mind: This book repeats the title's line multiple times, encourage your child to read this repeated line along with you by prompting him or her as you read aloud.

Problem solving in real life: Discuss with your child about how to solve problems that he or she may have in his or her own life. Discuss how preventing problems from happening will cause less frustration in the future. Also, talk about appropriate responses when bad things happen. Provide some strategies that may help:
- Be preventative! Plan ahead to avoid problems.
- Use words rather than physical means to express anger!
- Say, "I'm mad" and explain why.
- Ask an adult to help in certain situations.

Help Alexander problem solve: Prompt your child to help solve some of Alexander's problems that he has in the story.
- What could Alexander have done differently, so he wouldn't have tripped on his skateboard?
- What could have made Alexander feel better at breakfast?
- What could have been done or said to make Alexander feel better during the ride to school?
- What else could Alexander have done when his friend, Paul, told Alexander that he was only his third best friend?
- What could have been done so that Alexander might not have gotten into so much trouble at his father's office?

Being thankful: Instead of focusing so much on the negative feelings that make people feel angry or frustrated, look at the bright side by focusing on the things that are going well.

Gratitude journal: One way to do this is to create a Gratitude Journal. Staple a few pages of folded white printer paper together to create a small booklet for your child. Inside, have your child draw people, things, situations, and events that he or she is thankful for. You can label with a word or phrase to go along with each page of your child's journal.

This activity develops:
- Map Skills
- Repeating patterned phrases
- Self-awareness through expressing feelings
- Problem solving
- Independence and confidence

Age 4 - Activity 51 – *Wemberly Worried*

Before reading: Ask your child about the front cover.
- Which one do you think is Wemberly?
- How do you think that character feels?
- What makes you think that?
- Have you ever looked that way?

Read aloud: *Wemberly Worried* by Kevin Henkes

After reading: Ask your child some questions about the story:
1. What caused Wemberly's worries about school to go away?
2. What helps your worries to go away?
3. Do you think that Wemberly will continue to worry?
4. What might she worry about now that she has completed her first day of school?

Keep in mind: Worrying is universal, and comforting your child by talking about what is worrying him or her and the truth behind the worries will help disperse some anxiety.

Big worries and little worries chart: Use a white board or a big piece of paper and write *Big Worries* at the top and *Little Worries* on the bottom. Ask your child to talk to you about the worries he or she has and to identify whether they are big worries or little worries. As your child dictates to you, write some of the key words on the top or bottom where the worry belongs or have your child draw a picture to represent it instead.

Just might happen or not likely: Once you and your child have discussed some of their worries, take time to sort them between "Just Might Happen" or "Not Likely," and highlight the worries from the Big and Little chart that "Just Might Happen," so that you and your child can talk through strategies to alleviate anxiety.

Talk through your worries: Many of your child's worries may revolve around going to school for the first time. Here are a few common worries children may have and some strategies that you can talk through with them:

Worry: I forget my lunch.
Strategy: If this happens, make a plan with your child about putting money in a lunch account at school so that he or she can buy lunch in the cafeteria if the lunchbox is left at home.

Worry: I won't have any friends.
Strategies: Remind your child that there will be other children in the class who do not know anybody either and that these children are worrying about the same thing!

- **Be friendly:** Encourage your child to say "hi" to at least three children they do not know on the first day of school. Being friendly and smiling makes other children feel welcome to become a friend. Ask your child to remember at least three names of the children in the class.
- **Compliments and kindness:** Brainstorm with your child ahead of time about ways they can compliment other students in their class like, "Nice shot!" or "Your sweater is pretty." Practicing these at home will help your child develop confidence on his or her own in the given situation. Remind your child that kindness is contagious. Talk with your child about ways that he or she can show kindness to others like helping someone pick up something that has spilled or dropped, saving a seat for them at lunch, or helping someone else carry something.

Worry: I won't know the answers.
Strategy: Remind your child that the truth is: he or she is not supposed to know all the answers and that is the whole reason to go to school—to learn. Prompt your child to ask questions when he or she does not understand. Encourage your child that the teacher is there to help him or her learn the answers and to understand.

Worry: I am going to miss my mom and/or dad.
Strategy: Remind your child that you cannot go to school with your child and that is something he or she needs to be brave about and do himself or herself at this stage of life.

- The best way to overcome this worry is to practice separation on a consistent basis by leaving your child with a caregiver for brief periods and short distances at first and gradually making the length longer to help your child ease into this pattern.
- Another strategy is to have a "goodbye ritual" which can be reassuring for your child when you part with them. It can be as simple as a special wave through the window or a goodbye hug.
- Providing a consistent pattern for each day will also ease your child into the predictability of going to school and being separated from you for a few hours.

This activity develops:
- Predicting skills
- Discussing feelings of worry
- Sorting between big and little and "just might happen" and "not likely"
- Problem solving
- Independence
- Anticipation for attending school

Age 4 - Activity 52 – *Look Out Kindergarten, Here I Come!*

Before reading: Ask your child to identify the front cover, the title, and the author. Encourage your child to help you turn the pages and show you where to begin reading on each page.

Read aloud: *Look Out Kindergarten, Here I Come!* by Nancy Carlson

After reading: Ask your child some questions about the story:
1. What has Henry learned already to be ready for kindergarten?
2. Why did Henry want to go home?
3. Why did he decide to stay?
4. Will Henry like being a kindergartener? Why or why not?

Sequencing activity: Create a few cards with pictures from the story on them. Have your child put them in order from what happens first, second, third, fourth, and so on. Go back to the pages of the book to help your child if he or she has difficulty.
1. Henry brushing his teeth.
2. Henry eating his breakfast.
3. Henry counting the flowers on his walk to school.
4. Henry being afraid to go to kindergarten.
5. Henry looking around the kindergarten classroom.
6. Henry deciding to stay for the day.

Sequencing: This skill is so important for a child to practice before kindergarten. Putting things in order from first to last is a skill that you can reinforce each time you read your child a story or do household tasks that he or she can help you with.

Practice getting ready for school: To take some anxiety out of going to school for the first time, practice the morning routine with your child. This can include how to get dressed in the morning, eating breakfast, putting on his or her shoes, and getting packed for the day just like Henry.

Take a tour of the school: It is a wonderful idea to take your child to the local elementary school that he or she will be attending for kindergarten ahead of time. This will calm your child's nerves about where he or she will be going at the beginning of the school year.

Meet the kindergarten teacher: You may want to call the school ahead of time to see if they can give you a tour with your child so that he or she can gain familiarity of the classrooms, hallways, bathrooms, cafeteria, schoolyard, gym, office, etc. There may even be a particular "Open House Day" at your school for this very thing. You may check to see if your child's future kindergarten teacher is available to meet so that your child has a familiar face to look for on the first day of school.

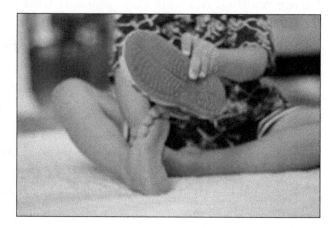

Keep in mind: You can get even more activities and lesson ideas for any of the picture books I have recommended as activity starters by simply googling the title of the book along with the words "preschool" and "lesson" or "activity." Many kindergarten and preschool teachers as well as creative moms have blogs online and are more than willing to share ideas that are working for them that correspond with these books.

This activity develops:
- Literacy and listening skills
- Reasoning skills while answering the questions
- Problem solving
- Independence
- Sequencing skills
- Confidence
- Anticipation for attending school